EMBRACING THE POWER
OF HUMANISM

EMBRACING THE POWER OF HUMANISM

PAUL KURTZ

ROWMAN & LITTLEFIELD PUBLISHERS, INC.
Lanham • Boulder • New York • Oxford

ROWMAN & LITTLEFIELD PUBLISHERS, INC.

Published in the United States of America
by Rowman & Littlefield Publishers, Inc.
4720 Boston Way, Lanham, Maryland 20706
http://www.rowmanlittlefield.com

12 Hid's Copse Road
Comnor Hill, Oxford OX2 9JJ, England

British Library Cataloguing in Publication Information Available

Library of Congress Cataloging-in-Publication Data

Kurtz, Paul, 1925–
    Embracing the power of humanism / Paul Kurtz.
        p.   cm.
    Includes bibliographical references and index.
    ISBN 0-8476-9966-8 (hardcover : alk. paper)
        1. Humanistic ethics.   I. Title.
    BJ1360.K787   2000
    171'.2—dc21   99-059830

Printed in the United States of America

♾™ The paper used in this publication meets the minimum requirements of
American National Standard for Information Sciences—Permanence of Paper for
Printed Library Materials, ANSI/NISO Z39.48-1992.

CONTENTS

PREFACE

You have only one life to live, and it's yours alone. No one can live it for you: it's your lungs that fill with air, your heart and pulse that beat, your blood that flows through your arteries and veins, and you who walk around, work, eat, make love, and do whatever you decide in order to express your interests and wants, your creative capacities and needs. It is *you* who are the center of your life world, of consciousness and attention, of dreams and reveries, of plans and projects; it is your action undertaken to fulfill them. Thus you are free! This freedom is not unlimited, for your choices operate within the boundaries present in the natural and social environment in which you live. Nevertheless, your choices are yours: you are responsible for your own destiny.

Can you accept this freedom? Or is it a burden too heavy to endure? For many people freedom is frightening, and it is forfeited to others in their midst: parents or grandparents, sisters or brothers, friends or relatives, teachers or farmers, physicians or policemen. It is penned in by the laws and customs of the larger community in which you live.

And it is forfeited to "the gods on high," who have been contrived by human ingenuity to limit individual choices and regulate conduct, and to provide an answer to the riddle: What is the meaning of life? The ancient parables and tales spun out long ago by human imagination are still retold to countless generations. The moral faiths of premodern, preurban men and women, living millennia or centuries ago, still determine *how* we should live and *why*. These ancient formulas structure our realities, our hopes, and our expectations.

The power implicit in freedom and self-determination is always there for you to untap, to express in your own terms. But social habits and norms thwart personal freedom and dictate how and why you should behave. After all, you have to make a living, and you depend on those around you to provide security and the goods and services necessary to survive and prosper. Society fears that a free person, fully conscious of one's own powers—of autonomy and of becoming what one wants—will be harmful to the social order. So this power is everywhere constrained, especially by the purveyors of the sacred myths, who tell you what "thou shalt" and "shalt not do"—or else. Or else what? Be punished by the greater power that exists, even though it is hidden? As if He, She, or It gives a damn, or even exists!

What if you are able to recognize your own powers, untap the hidden talents and capacities within—and thus be liberated from the blind hold of the sacred deities. What then? Will you become a wild beast, prey to every lust and passion and insensitive to the needs and interests of others? Or can you be temperate and show self-restraint, empathize with other persons, and express sympathy and fairness to them?

That is the theme of this book: How can the free, autonomous, self-reliant, and rational person find life meaningful, exciting, and vibrant, and yet learn to harmonize one's dreams and values with others in moral communities? How can the free person become the responsible person, aware of the needs, interests, suffering, pain, and demands of others?

The model of the good life presented herein is that of the Promethean spirit: audacious, self-affirming, accepting of one's own freedom, and willing to take risks to attain one's goals, yet finding life full of significance and richness and being deeply concerned with the common moral decencies and the pagan virtues of nobility and excellence. This book, then, is about normative ethics. It does not deal essentially with metaethical questions, abstract philosophical analyses per se, but with the concrete, practical implications of rational freedom for the moral life.

The idea for this volume was first suggested to me by Brandon Stickney, who, reading from various books that I have written over the years, thought that I should collect in one place my views of humanist ethics as they pertain to the autonomous person. In cooperation with Ranjit Sandhu, my colleague and associate on so many research projects, he compiled various excerpts from my writings, including *Decision and the Condition of Man*, *The Fullness of Life*, *Exuberance*, *Forbidden Fruit*, *The New Skepticism*, *The Transcendental Temptation*, *Living without Religion*, *The Courage to Become*, and various articles. I have since gone over this collection, added some sections and deleted others, and attempted to integrate the entire volume. Brandon Stickney has drawn a brief biographical sketch, which follows.

It is the theme of this volume that embracing humanism intellectually and emotionally can liberate you from the regnant spiritual theologies of the day, mythologies that bind you and put you out of cognitive touch with the real world. By embracing the power of humanism, I submit, you can lead an enriched life that is filled with joyful exuberance yet is intrinsically meaningful and is developed within shared moral communities.

BIOGRAPHICAL INTRODUCTION

As they sit in the university classroom, students must wonder what it would have been like to walk with Socrates as he questioned the good life, or to dine with Voltaire as he exposed the foibles of humanity, or to talk to David Hume as he pondered the nature of human knowledge and the persistence of human follies. I have had the good fortune to have that experience with today's best-known and most energetic secular humanist—Dr. Paul Kurtz. A hundred years from now, students seeking a new personal and worldly freedom may wonder what it was like to walk with Dr. Kurtz as he questioned the religious and paranormal currents that threatened to divide America and as he knew (and offered to the thousands intelligent enough to listen objectively) that peace of mind is found within each person, not through the mystical or spiritual forces so widely accepted by society. It is humanism, he explained, that leads to the purest forms of happiness, truth, love, and independence. Dr. Kurtz's powerful legacy, which began when he was a student of Sidney Hook, one of America's most influential social philosophers, stands as a prime example of understanding personal liberty and responsibility within a democratic society.

In autobiographical notes he shared with me in November 1998, Dr. Kurtz explained that his "path to humanism" began when he was just twelve years old and he started to question the Old Testament's story of creation. "How could the world have been created in six days, I asked, when the fossil record as uncovered by anthropologists, paleontologists, and other scientists show long stages of evolutionary change from which the human species eventually emerged?" The mold was set. This young man, who would one day launch his educational career at Columbia University, was setting himself apart from the beliefs that motivated most others, the beliefs that doomed "the masses" to being controlled and to living the status quo. It would be just a few short years before he learned that the words of freedom from religious, political, and cultural chains must be spread.

The son of a New Jersey businessman, Dr. Kurtz was born in 1925 and was raised in Newark, where he became interested in religion, politics, and the arts at an early age. His parents and teachers, recognizing him as a brilliant boy and an energetic student, encouraged his interest in political issues and participation in debates and plays in high school. Dr. Kurtz's father, Martin, took great interest in seeing his son become so involved because his side of the family, originating from Russia, held very strong beliefs on both sides of communism. Yet it was the Great Depression, followed by the ravages of World War II, that moved the young Kurtz toward an understanding of world politics and economics. "I was attracted by [the] vision of a possible utopia in which injustice and oppression would disappear," he said, describing an enthusiasm for the literature of the left wing. When the war broke, Kurtz was just fourteen and was "deeply shocked by the brutality of fascism and Nazism."

After graduation from high school, Kurtz enrolled at Washington Square College at New York University and was elected freshman class president and the head of a student group, American Youth for Democracy. These outspoken undergraduates participated in demonstrations that were precipitant of the student protests that would follow three decades later in universities across the United States. Dr. Kurtz explained, "We were disturbed at the victories of the Nazis in Europe and attended rally after rally in favor of a second front. Eleanor Roosevelt delivered an outdoor talk at a rally, and we raised a loud chorus in favor of the second front. She was evidently flustered at our demands and asked for us to be patient, for she was sure it would eventually occur." This was a time of domestic uprising when students were destroying school newspapers that didn't reflect their views ("I was appalled by that," Kurtz related); the son of Paul Robeson attended a dance and flaunted convention by dancing with a white woman; Marxist philosophy was a strong undercurrent; and liberals like Max Lerner were writing to challenge the radical right and expose the atrocities of ethnic cleansing.

Kurtz was overwhelmed by the call to fight the fascists, and he enlisted in the Army six months before his eighteenth birthday, meeting with America's own version of racial division: segregation. "This was my first trip to the South. I was sent to Fort Stewart, near Savannah, Georgia. The moral blot of racism deeply offended me. One time I decided to move to the back of the bus to sit with black people, but the bus driver became so enraged at the 'damn Yankee' that I had to move back up front."

In 1944, Kurtz's antiaircraft unit was rushed from England to the Battle of the Bulge, charged with stopping Von Runstadt's tanks and the Luftwaffe. For the great teacher and philosopher Kurtz would one day become, it seemed that these experiences *must* occur, that he had to witness man at his most evil to understand the real meaning to humanity's existence. "I was on the front lines for the rest of the war," Dr. Kurtz recalled, "in units liberating France, Belgium, Holland, and Czechoslovakia, where I remained for several weeks after VE day.

"I entered both Buchenwald and Dachau shortly after they were liberated, and I met the survivors of Nazi brutality and their SS captors. Antisemitic hatred mystified me, as did Germany itself, which I considered a mystery wrapped in an enigma. How could such a cultured nation sink into barbarism?"

Hitler's control over much of Europe included the enslavement of foreign laborers. He encountered many on the farms and in the factories of liberated portions of Germany. Citizens from Russia were displaced by the Nazis, but they declined to return to their native country. "Soviet prisoners related to me tales of horror and hardship they had endured under Stalin. This led me to question my earlier idealistic commitment to Marxism," Dr. Kurtz recalled.

Kurtz's military service afforded him the opportunity to attend Shrivenham University in England, where he learned more about that nation's tolerance for all forms of expression and speech. "Even at the height of the war the pacifists, communists, fascists, and atheists were given an opportunity to hold forth on soapboxes, and the British politely listened and often applauded." Kurtz wrote letters home to his parents every day, penned many early essays, attended lectures, and sought out the most influential thinkers in England at the time, with copies of the works of Socrates and *The Republic* by Plato in hand.

Plato's writings influenced Kurtz greatly and gently shoved him in the direction of philosophy, filling him with the deeper messages of the good life, a *firsthand* global historical perspective, and a feeling of necessity with regard to understanding and tolerance. The war ended and Kurtz returned to the United States, enrolling at New York University and focusing his energies on intellectual inquiry. He shed his desire, for a time, for political action. Yet his interest remained, and he ambitiously took on a triple major: philosophy, political science, and economic theory. He sought unification in the overlapping of the different schools and ideas, finding himself on a level that would open his mind to the man who would become his mentor, Sidney Hook.

In the summer of 1946, when the Cold War seeped across the West, Kurtz was "pouring over Aristotelian texts" and living in a hot garret on East Fourth Street. This was the section of Greenwich Village where Edgar Allan Poe wrote *The Raven*; where Edna St. Vincent Millay wrote the influential *Renaissance*; where Eugene O'Neill drank and pondered the love affairs of his distant American South, and where the great moralist of fiction, O. Henry, had lived. Kurtz felt much at home. He was developing his own unique theories in philosophy and was often more comfortable with the dissenting opinion.

"A. J. Ayer was a famous logical positivist who was a visiting professor at NYU," Dr. Kurtz said. "At that time, I was influenced by everything he said, except I did not accept his critique of normative philosophy, for I thought it was possible to use reason to some extent in objectively evaluating ethical and political issues. I remember having a long discussion with Ayer on a bench in Washington Square Park—what an impertinent undergraduate!"

It was at NYU that Kurtz had his "most important intellectual experience": taking a course from Sidney Hook. A whirlwind of imagination and positivity, the bespectacled Hook was a student of John Dewey's pragmatism and a leading thinker of the twentieth century who stressed that philosophy must be applied to practical concerns and current issues.

Like Kurtz, Hook had once embraced Marxism and later rejected its totalitarian and revolutionary manifestations. Kurtz sought out Hook at NYU because of Hook's connection to Dewey. "He was NYU's most famous and notorious professor and he aroused my fierce intellectual interests. I took only one course from him and that was the Philosophy of Democracy," Dr. Kurtz recalled, a smile coming to his face at the mere mention of Hook's brilliance. "Hook had been the first Communist professor in America and had written provocative articles and books defending revolutionary Marxism. He attempted to reinterpret Marx in light of pragmatism. The key economic interpretation of history thus became a method of investigation and a guide for practical action; it was not to be taken as dogma. Hook broke with the Communist Party early. Coming under the influence of Trotsky, he became a persistent critic of Stalinism. At the eve of the Second World War, he argued that the key issue was not communism versus capitalism, but totalitarianism versus democracy. Hook convinced me about the merits of democracy and its viable importance."

Though Hook recognized him as a standout student, Kurtz's youthful enthusiasm and efforts to please his mentor were not altogether welcome. Kurtz spent late hours in the university library examining Hook's writings and studying far beyond the class assignments. When, in fine Socratic style, Hook hurled questions at the full classroom, seeking a spontaneous flow of inquiry and learning, Kurtz, with great respect, often unknowingly tripped him up. "I knew the responses he wanted so I blurted them out each time. This annoyed Professor Hook because Socratic method works best when there is surprise and when the solution is painstakingly developed later. And here I was answering exactly as I knew Hook had. In any case, I would follow him after the class to his office and continue the dialogue with him, and we became, from then on, fast friends."

In 1948, Kurtz completed his undergraduate studies in philosophy and decided to move to Columbia University to pursue his doctorate. Hook was disappointed at the decision, but Kurtz countered by noting it was time to get his education "straight from the horse's mouth and study with other Deweyites."

Columbia University, where Hook himself had studied, had maintained its distinction in the field of philosophy. Dr. Kurtz explained: "Dewey's influence at the university was still strong. I was immeasurably pleased by the years I spent at Columbia. In fact, I studied with many of Dewey's students—Ernest Nagel, John Herman Randall Jr., Herbert W. Schneider, Irwin Edman, Charles Frankel, Justus Buchler, and Horace W. Friess. I read virtually everything Dewey ever wrote, and I read the *Journal of Philosophy* from its inception through 1950."

A member of the Philosophy Club, Kurtz was instrumental in inviting Dewey to lecture at the distinguished Low Memorial Library. "I'm surprised," Dewey quipped at the opening of the talk, "that anyone is still interested in my philosophy."

It was an exciting time at Columbia. Kurtz often saw General Eisenhower in the halls because he had been brought to the university as part of his grooming for president. Eisenhower was cribbing jokes from Philosophy Department Chairman Irwin Edman for his speeches, witty pieces that the student body would see reprinted in the *New York Times* and attributed to the general. The department was enamored with many greats of the period, including the New York literati. Kurtz not only met Dewey but also had the rare opportunity to hear and meet Somerset Maugham, Margaret Mead, Robert Benchley, and many others. Edman, who had secured these personalities to visit the college, was quite impressed by the charismatic Kurtz, who had come into his own right of distinction in the classroom.

Dr. Kurtz remembered, "Once, after one of his classes in which I had been particularly vocal, Professor Edman called me into his office, put his hands on my shoulders at arm's length, looked into my eyes, and proclaimed, 'Paul Kurtz! You are going to be *very famous* some day!'"

The defining point of his life, as well as of his humanism, Columbia University enabled Kurtz to form a philosophical perspective that he would carry with him for the rest of his life. Studying under C. Wright Mills, Herbert Marcuse, and others, Kurtz organized his views on the nature of the universe, human life, and his ethical and social philosophy.

He formed a friendship with Albert Schanker (the future leader of the American Federation of Teachers), and their talks centered on politics and the rights of man. "By this time, I broke with any illusions about the Soviet system," Dr. Kurtz recalled, learning from world developments and through the stories told by his relatives from Russia who had experienced the poverty and the atrocities born from an all-controlling government. "How could one build a utopian society based on intolerance?" Kurtz asked. He edited *The Humanist*, which tackled such topics, for over a decade (from 1967 to 1977), and he invited Schanker to write for the popular magazine.

Kurtz's doctoral dissertation was formulated with Herbert W. Schneider, who was chief editor of the *Journal of Philosophy*. *The Problems of Value Theory*, which supported a positivist defense of science and logic and the criticism of metaphysics and theology, was quite powerful. It struck a nerve with Harvard professor Henry David Aiken, who wrote in the *Journal of Philosophy* that Kurtz did not take British analytic tradition into account. "I had become a critic of such philosophy because it focused on language rather than behavior and practice," Kurtz said in his defense.

Humanism became a way of life for Dr. Kurtz, in part because philosophers had retreated to the cave offices of their universities, refusing to comment on social issues. "Only Hook and Frankel hadn't gone into that ostrich-like hibernation. I could then see the relevance of James's remark that 'philosophy baked no bread'—nor did it, in my judgment, do anything else practical." Dr. Kurtz is unique in American philosophy, for he attempted to relate theory to building institutions and to take philosophical inquiry into the open marketplace of ideas in the broader society.

Awarded his doctorate in 1952, Dr. Kurtz accepted his first full-time position at Trinity College in Hartford, Connecticut. Philosophy Department Chairman Harry T. Costello and Dr. Kurtz formed an instant bond. "My first meeting with him was hilarious and reassuring," Dr. Kurtz recalled. "He said, 'I hate God.' We got along famously thereafter, for he knew my feelings on the matter." Dr. Kurtz remained at Trinity for several years, in addition to taking positions at Queens College of the City University of New York, Vassar College in Poughkeepsie, and Union College in Schenectady. He accepted a position as professor of philosophy at the State University of New York at Buffalo in 1965. In these exciting years, Kurtz would do the work of ten men, writing and editing more than thirty books, including the most important ones on humanism published in America in the twentieth century. His harsh yet verifiably factual criticisms of religion, miracles, and the paranormal in a nation so enamored with the same in the 1960s and 1970s earned him the title "pope of the unbelievers." His national impact was impressive because it was Kurtz who was always on the side of reason, from the local radio waves to nationally broadcast programs—including *Donahue, 20/20, Oprah, Dick Cavett, Larry King Live, Nightline*, and *Crossfire*—presenting arguments that were impossible to ignore. By refusing the trend among colleagues to hide within the cloistered university, Dr. Kurtz became one of the most influential secular humanists in America.

In 1976, Dr. Kurtz founded the Committee for the Scientific Investigation of Claims of the Paranormal, which has developed into an international movement. As a skeptic, he has emphasized the need for critical thinking and skepticism as paths of knowledge. Not simply interested in debunking mistaken beliefs, he has always sought to emphasize the positive aspects of skepticism and the power of reason and scientific method in establishing reliable knowledge.

In 1980, he founded both the Council for Democratic and Secular Humanism and *Free Inquiry* magazine, which is now the leading secular humanist magazine in the world. His task was not only to examine religious claims critically but also to provide a positive and constructive alternative—a *eupraxsophy* (good wisdom in practice)—to the reigning religious orthodoxies.

Dr. Kurtz has been deeply involved in the international humanist movement throughout his life, and he was responsible for arranging Marxist–non-Marxist humanist dialogues, dialogues between the Vatican and humanists, and dialogues between Baptists and humanists and between Mormons and humanists. He served on the Board of the International Humanist and Ethical Union for thirty years, and was copresident for eight years.

Dr. Kurtz retired from the State University of New York in 1991, after having created Prometheus Books, *Skeptical Inquirer* magazine, and *Free Inquiry* magazine, and publishing many more important articles and books. To date he has published more than six hundred articles and reviews as well as thirty-six books. In 1995 he launched the Center for Inquiry in Amherst, New York, followed by the opening of other such centers elsewhere in the world. While making his home in Amherst, New York, Dr. Kurtz has traveled around the world. His list of friends has included Isaac Asimov, Carl Sagan, B. F. Skinner, Francis Crick, E. O. Wilson, Thomas Szasz, Andrei Sakharov, Betty Freidan, Ray Bradbury, Steve Allen, Peter Ustinov, Antony Flew, Elizabeth Loftus, James Randi, Martin Gardner, Jill Tarter, John Maddox, and many other influential visionaries.

In *Exuberance: A Philosophy of Happiness*, Dr. Kurtz provides highly accessible recommendations (excerpted in this book) for living a meaningful, productive life without the stifling burden of religion. "So good, so perfect in every way, and so empowering that after you read it, you'll wish you had written it," said one reviewer of *Exuberance*. Reprinted fifteen times, *Exuberance* expresses the keys to good living and perhaps, yes *perhaps*, even the answer to the meaning of life.

Longtime friend and colleague Vern Bullough said that Dr. Kurtz "has always been involved in the battle for civil rights, civil liberties, feminism, and the cutting issues of the day. He is cheerful, *exuberant* is his term, full of energy, convinced that secular humanism is the future."

While admitting he flirted with excess in his early years, Kurtz has also been "an exercise addict" for more than a quarter century. In 1996, he suffered chest pains after a trip to Mexico City for the organization of a World Humanist Congress. He had open heart surgery to bypass a blocked artery. Again, his life view was reinforced.

"Facing the possibility of my own death enabled me to put my life in some existential perspective," he wrote when snowed in by a Buffalo blizzard in January of 1997. "I have been so busy, working on so many projects, traveling, living life exuberantly, literally bursting at the seams, that I have often not had a chance to savor the delicacies of life, and have not taken enough time to smell the daffodils. . . . In any case, my illness dramatically impressed on me the need to appreciate each moment of experience and how precious life is."

And that, for the reader, is the purpose of this book.

Part I, "The Exuberant Life," shows that the good life, as Dr. Kurtz explains, is within reach of everyone. Opening the door to the good life is easy when you understand the philosophy and eupraxsophy of humanism. Humanism is interested in fulfilling the greatest potential of persons and contributing to the enrichment of human experience. Everyone is capable of leading a joyous and creative life—this is the message that humanists bring to humanity. Humanism is a philosophy that equates the best living with an expression of our highest talents.

The most important point to understand before reading this book is that self-determination is the key to good living—realizing that you are solely responsible for your own life. "Look at life," Dr. Kurtz says, "as a work of art, or as a career, and through self-motivation you will succeed."

In this first part you will also come to understand that uncertainty and change are part of the journey in life. But many people have "been trained since birth to carry a sense of guilt and self-doubt along with them," which ultimately defeats them in the things they try to accomplish. They have been taught by superstition that their inner power comes from supernatural sources other than themselves, and if they betray these forces, the power will be taken away. Humanism can help you get that guilt and self-doubt off your back and help you tap into that built-in power and confidence.

In part II, "Independence," Dr. Kurtz explains that humanists believe in the power of free individuals to realize their goals and to find the courage to become what they wish. Free, autonomous persons willing to express their goals is the ideal.

Part III, "Altruism," reveals that humanists believe love and friendship are among the highest of virtues a human being can express. Humanists realize that each person has this inner power and dignity. In relationships with others, empathy and caring are essential to ensure that others may also live the good life.

Part IV explores "Humanism," defined as a eupraxsophy. Belief in the self, the individual, usurps religious doctrine and even the existence of a supreme being. Humanists do not accept religions that demean the power of the self or denigrate human capacities. Humanists are skeptical of supernatural claims, noting that because there is no scientific proof of such otherworldly power, this is instead wishful thinking.

Socrates and Epicurus paved the way for free thought in ancient times, and their teachings formed the foundation of what humanists believe today. Well-known humanists are easily recognized: Mark Twain, Elizabeth Cady Stanton, Robert Ingersoll, Clarence Darrow, Margaret Sanger, John Dewey, Bertrand Russell, Isaac Asimov, and Carl Sagan.

Part V sums up Dr. Kurtz's views of "Ethical Truth" and the relation between skepticism and truth in the moral life.

Humanists also strongly believe in democracy, the separation of church and state, the peaceful negotiation and resolution of conflicts, and human freedom and human rights. Much of this is spelled out in *Humanist Manifesto II* (1973) and *A Secular Humanist Declaration* (1980), which Dr. Kurtz drafted, and *Humanist Manifesto 2000* (1999), the latest statement of Planetary Humanism.

Dr. Kurtz has always sought to relate humanism to the individual. He has emphasized his key point: in embracing humanism, you can fully realize the purest form of freedom, and power, during your lifetime. Dr. Kurtz has reiterated this point in his books *Decision and the Condition of Man* (1966), *The Fullness of*

Life (1973), *Forbidden Fruit* (1988), *Eupraxophy* (1989), and *The Courage to Become* (1997). Selections from these writings primarily make up this collection.

In the time I have known Dr. Paul Kurtz, I have been fascinated with his lust for life and his ability to pass great truth on to others. The philosophers of the bygone age challenged established beliefs and myths while calling on their students to think for themselves. Dr. Kurtz is today's *superhumanist*, who, with unmatched energy, courage, and compassion, brings the words of reason to the millions so lost in today's New Age and paranormal-spiritual obsessions.

On an overcast day in early November 1998, I walked with Dr. Kurtz to the site outside the offices of his Center for Inquiry where a pine tree had been planted in memory and in celebration of his mother, Sarah, who died October 29, 1998, in Florida at the age of ninety-five. Across the street, the State University of New York at Buffalo, from which Kurtz had retired in 1991, loomed in the distance as a soft mist fell on the quiet gathering of thirty friends and relatives.

Dr. Kurtz smiled when recalling his mother's own questioning of life on her deathbed. "She was a humanist," he said, "but she still believed in God." Kurtz gently related to the gathering how Sarah had looked at him on that day and said, "I asked God, why me? Why now?" Then with a brave grin she concluded, "I guess it's just that the world's population has grown too large."

Then Kurtz's thirty-three-year-old son, Jonathan, said a few words about his grandmother, noting that the pine tree represented longevity and strength, two things she possessed and passed on to her family. "Six months ago, the family was in Florida with grandmother and she went on a two-mile walk with us. Two miles at her age! And when we were done, she said that was the greatest day of her life."

It was that emotional memorial service, for me, that made all the writings in this book ring true: to live each day of your life, each moment, to the fullest. Challenges are a part of that life, and overcoming them by using the power within makes the joys that much greater and the new challenges that much more exciting to take on. Living the good life is possible for most everyone, but first you need to understand that *you* are in control of your own destiny.

Brandon M. Stickney

PART I

THE EXUBERANT LIFE

1

WHAT IS HAPPINESS?

What is the good life? Is it achievable? People have long sought happiness, and they have explored the ends of the earth for its realization, but in different ways: the quest for the Holy Grail; a life of service; the delights of pleasure and sensual consummation, or of quiet withdrawal.

Happiness is, no doubt, available in many forms; different individuals and cultures have endowed diverse objects with value. I have emphasized the virtues of action. Perhaps not everyone will wish to be *engagé*, fully involved, creatively exercised; they may wish, instead, for repose and quiet, peace and security, a life of leisure and retreat. Yet, without overemphasizing the point, the very essence of life—human life—is creative achievement. Thus I have heralded the life of the doer, of the Leonardos of action, the life of the continuing pursuit of new goals and of the conquering of frontiers. We are defined as persons by the plans and projects that we initiate and fulfill in the world. The humanist saint is Prometheus, not Christ; the activist, not the passivist; the skeptic, not the believer; the creator, not the conniver.

As I see it, creative achievement is the very heart of the human enterprise. It typifies the human species as it has evolved, particularly over the past forty thousand to fifty thousand years: leaving the life of the hunter and the nomad, developing agriculture and rural society, inventing industry and technology, building urban societies and a world community, breaking out of the earth's gravitational field, exploring the solar system and beyond. The destiny of human beings, of each man and woman, is that we are condemned to invent what we will be—condemned if we are fearful but blessed if we welcome the great adventure. We are responsible in the last analysis, not simply for what we are, but for what we will *become*—and that is a source of either high excitement or distress.

The human species is biologically determined, in part, by its genetic inheritance, which is the result of a long process of evolution. But we are also social animals and culture builders, and it is in the creation of the arts of civilization that we truly express our potential natures. It is central to the nature

3

of the human being that we can—within limits—recreate and redefine our culture and even our biological structure. By means of technology and science we are constantly transforming our biology: by surgical operations and biogenetic engineering, we can improve our organs and functions, and by medicine and culture we even modify our sexuality. We build a world not only to nourish and protect our bodies, but also to extend and enhance our desires and ideals.

There are those, of course, who add not one whit to the fund of human knowledge or to the enterprise of life, but who feed on others; they are afraid to discover or dream. They merely go through life as passive consumers or delicate fawners. They wish to contemplate or accept the universe, not remake it according to their interests. But the key to human life is precisely its ingenuity and its inventiveness. This is the essence of human culture; the life of the doer and the maker, the dreamer and the innovator, the hero and the artist expresses the deepest thrill of human exploration: the experience of creating something new.

There are all too few individuals who have the audacity to follow their visions—in spite of the forces in the world that seek to destroy these visions—who will neither give in nor retreat, but who will seek to add something to the world. Human life is as much a part of reality as is anything else, and what we want and feel, think and imagine, create and do is as important for our destiny as other kinds of existence. We can change nature, though we are of it, and our ability to restructure nature is as natural as anything else. Nature is not sacred, nor immune to change. It is constantly being modified by blind and unconscious forces: the winds and the rain assault the terrain; plants and animals feed upon the land and upon each other. There are those who say that it is evil for humans to modify the natural ecology, as if it were some holy shrine beyond transformation. But to live is to modify nature and life in some way; we cannot avoid doing so. Everything that we do has a transforming effect. There are those who wish to flee from urban life and technology back to a rural, so-called idyllic, existence. However, they fail to appreciate the fact that the introduction of agriculture was itself a rude shock to nature, for it felled the trees and cleared the jungles, domesticated the animals, and bred new forms of plant life. To retreat to nature, even if we could, is to return to life as it was in the Neolithic age, when humans were hunters and nomads who lived in caves and trees. We cannot turn back or abandon our efforts; we can only move ahead. To build the Pantheon or the Taj Mahal is to hew rock out of the quarries and to change nature. Art adds to nature; technology is the purest art of civilized life.

Granted that our technology should not destroy the natural balance in nature, do irreparable damage to the ecology, or so pollute the atmosphere and waterways as to render life impossible. We need to modify our goals in terms of their consequences, and if the consequences are harmful, to correct our mistakes. But we have to guard against a new ecological religiosity that idealizes repose and rest, sanctifies nature as it is, and demeans human adventure and change.

The tasks that emerge in human civilization are for each individual and each society to forge his, or its, own destiny. Human life has no meaning independent of itself. There is no cosmic force or deity to give it meaning or significance. There is no ultimate destiny for the human species. Such a belief is an illusion of humankind's infancy. The meaning of life is what we choose to give it. Meaning grows out of human purposes alone. Nature provides us with an infinite range of opportunities, but it is only our vision and our action that select and realize those that we desire.

Thus the good life is achieved, invented, fashioned in an active life of enterprise and endeavor. But whether or not an individual chooses to enter into the arena depends upon the person alone. Those who do can find it energizing, exhilarating, full of triumph and satisfaction. In spite of failures, setbacks, suffering, and pain, life can be fun.

To achieve the good life is an accomplishment. It involves the development of skills, the proper attitude, and intelligence. It involves the destruction of fantasies about nature and life and the cultivation of the pagan excellencies. The first humanist virtue is the development of one's own sense of power—of the belief that we *can* do something, that we *can* succeed, that our own preparations and efforts *will* pay off. The courage to excel—the courage to become what we want, to realize what we will—is essential. It is in the process of attainment that we thrive: Sisyphus is not to be condemned; there are always new mountains to climb, new stones to heave, and they are never the same.

However, in order to have a sense of our own self-power, it is necessary to be able to live in an ambiguous world of indeterminacy and contingency. Nature is not fixed, nor is our destiny preplanned. We can build new monuments and discover new theorems; there are new worlds to be conquered and created. We must not let ourselves be mastered by events, but we must master them—as far as we can—without fear or recrimination.

If cowardice and fear are our nemeses, so are gullibility and nincompoopery, which must be controlled by the use of reason. To use reason is to demand evidence for our beliefs, and to suspend belief wherever we do not have adequate grounds for it; it requires that we not be deluded by the purveyors of false wares, but that we base our desires, as far as possible, upon the reasonable grounds of practiced reflection. There is a constant tendency to fly from reason to a paradise of perfection or quietude. There is no easy salvation for humans, and it is a delusion to think that we can find it. Life is restless and outgoing. It can never be content with what is; it is always in the process of becoming. It is the *new* that we worship, not because it is better, but because it is a product of our own creative energy.

Our actions are mere random impulses until they are organized in creative work. It is the unity of effort and energy that gives vent to our dreams. Thus the good life uniquely involves creativity. This is the great source of joy and of exuberance. It is in our work that we best reveal ourselves, not in idle play or leisure—as important as these things are—but in the mood of seriousness. Yet creative work is a form of play and, if coterminous with it, can be among the highest forms of aesthetic satisfaction: planning a project, teaching a class, constructing a road, and performing a symphony are all forms of creative endeavor. Those who do not work lack the key ingredient of happiness. The "sinners" are the lazy ones who cannot, or do not, have the creative impulse.

Though the joys of creativity are legion, pleasure needs to be experienced and enjoyed in itself and for itself. The hedonic-phobic cannot let himself go. He is imprisoned in a cell of psychic repression. One needs to open the doors to the delights of pleasure, to the many wondrous things to do and enjoy: food and drink, art and poetry, music and philosophy, science and travel. But merely to seek pleasure without any serious lifework is banal. And to focus only on physical pleasures—important as they are—is limiting. One needs an expansive view of life, to enjoy many things, to cultivate one's tastes for the variety of life's goods. Robust hedonism is a form of activism; the world we live in and have created offers splendid opportunities for our enjoyment.

Among the finest pleasures of life are the joys of sexual passion and eroticism. The celibate has committed a sin against himself, for he has repressed the most exquisite pleasure of all: the full and varied sexual life that is so essential to happiness. We must, therefore, be open to the multiplicities of sexuality. We ought to act out and fulfill our fantasies, as long as they are not self-destructive or destructive of others; and we ought to be free to enjoy a full range of pansexual pleasures.

Important as individual audacity, courage, intelligence, self-power, and the fulfillment of one's personal dreams and projects are, the good life cannot be experienced alone, in isolation. The richest of human plans and joys are shared with others. Love in its truest sense is nonpossessive, a cooperative participation and friendship, and is the noblest expression of a moral relationship. We need to develop love and friendship for their own sakes, as goods in themselves.

But we cannot focus on inward ends alone, for the world intrudes in our domain of interests. We should develop a wider moral concern for those beyond our immediate contact, for the community, the nation, and the world at large. A person's creative work can and should involve others, and a sense of our moral obligations and responsibilities should develop that enlarges our horizons and enhances our universe. A beloved cause can give meaning and content to one's life. Though one works hard for progress, one should have no illusion about the possibilities of utopia; a willingness to tolerate ambiguity, even imperfection, is the mark of maturity.

Finally, each person must face death: life has meaning only if we realize that it will end. It is in viewing one's life as a complete whole that one sees it for what it is: what I accomplished and did well; whether I fulfilled some of my dreams and plans; whether I enjoyed life, made friends, fell in love, worked for a beloved cause, and so forth. I should have no false hopes about death, but I should do what I can to ward it off. Indeed, health is a first condition if one is to live well. We must not be deluded by a belief in immortality but should face death realistically. A free person cherishes the creative life as the ultimate good. But when death comes, one should accept it with equanimity, if with sorrow, and one should realize that in the face of death the only thing that really counts is what has been the quality of one's life, and what one has given or left for others.

Thus we may ask: Can we achieve the exuberant life? Yes, to some extent, but not by following the path that most philosophers and theologians have advised. The key to a full life is to open up to life—not suppress it or flee from it, but to give vent to our creative endeavors, to allow our imagination and creativity to have free play. We need to have confidence in our own powers and be willing to live audaciously. We need to be critical and skeptical of premature claims of truth or virtue, to use our common sense based upon reason and experience. We should not be afraid to enjoy pleasure or sexuality. Yet, at the same time, we need to develop love and friendship with others and a genuine moral concern for a better world. These are some of the ingredients that I have discovered contribute to the richness of life.

Each day, each moment, can be an adventure, pregnant with opportunity. With so many good things to do and enjoy, life can be interesting, exciting, and energizing. The *full* life is the goal. Though one has cherished memories, one need not look back; nor should one remain fixated on the present, indecisive and afraid to act. We need always to look ahead to the future: life is openended possibilities. We are not only what we are now, but also what we will choose to become. That is the confidence and the optimism that has inspired me. Whether others will also find joy in the strenuous life of challenge is, of course, up to them. It is there simply awaiting one's action. The point is that it does not depend simply upon nature or society, destiny or God, but on what each person chooses for himself.

2

BURSTING AT THE SEAMS

There must be something wrong with me. I am happy, exuberant. This has been true for as long as I can remember. Am I sick? Those around me seem to moan and complain, while I usually wake up singing and am joyful throughout the day. Life is so wonderful. I feel literally as if I am bursting at the seams.

Why am I happy? What does it mean to be satisfied—deeply—with life?

I ask this not only because I wish to plumb the depths of my own being but because I want others to learn what I have learned, intuitively and analytically, about the fullness of life and the opportunities for happiness.

I do not deny that despair, unreason, anxiety, meaninglessness lurk somewhere in the background. Yet these passions and problems have never bothered me as they have others. I have never, or rarely ever, been overwhelmed by despondency or *angst*. I have never lost my verve for life or the strong motivation to persevere.

I am told that menopause or prostate trouble awaits everyone, and perhaps someday I will encounter periods of depression. Perhaps I will undergo some great tragedy yet to unfold. Perhaps my accounting is still to take place, and I owe the universe some suffering. I have had my share of troubles. Yet they never were able to bow my back or buckle me under. I even found such traumatic experiences not without significance. Misery and pathos add intense, if dissonant, qualities to life experience. Others often emphasize the negative side of life. I accentuate the positive aspects. I am oblivious to the pall of gloom.

Instead I invariably feel exhilarated and find that there are not enough hours in a day to do all the things that I want to do. I am confronted by so many good things, interesting experiences, exciting possibilities. I want to do them all. I approach each with excitement. I admire Beethoven, whose paeans of *freude* provide my theme song: joy, joy, joy!; Picasso, whose intensity exudes hope, confidence, and vitality in his works of art; Michelangelo, who tempts nature with his daring and eloquent feats of artistic grandeur; Gulbenkian, the fabulous oil mogul, who when asked what he liked best replied, "everything!"; and Bertrand Russell, who lived fully as both a rational and a passionate being.

9

There are alternative ideals that have been drawn in human history, all promising the "good life." Is the humanistic model that I am presenting applicable to everyone? Or is it possible only for a small majority, a creative elite, Abraham Maslow's few self-actualizers—healthy, joyful achievers? In my view, although the full life is at root the heroic one, it expresses the essence of life itself; and this element is essential to the growth of human civilization. Without creative audacity, the drama of human history could not have developed as it did.

There are, as I have said, other ethical models that compete for our attention. There is the ideal life of the so-called religious saint: ethically motivated, self-sacrificing and ascetic, full of faith and virtue, dominated by overbelief and repression. Or there is the life of the contemplative meditator: withdrawn from the world of affairs into an inner world of expanded consciousness, whether rational or transcendental in emphasis. At the other extreme the life of the pleasure seeker beckons: suckling rosebuds and breasts, seeking sensual pleasures and hedonic tones. Against that stands the life of the stoic: wishing to suppress pain and sorrow and cultivating an attitude of indifference. Always with us is the conventional establishmentarian—whether bourgeois, bureaucrat, employee, housewife, or soldier—satisfying the traditional mores, fulfilling these tasks, doing one's duty in terms of his social station. And in opposition is the revolutionary: overwhelmed with the need for sacrifice and dedicated to the cause of utopian justice.

Some might say that the model of the good life that I have discovered is not to everyone's liking. Some may find it too difficult for them or too full of bravado. Perhaps people's proclivities in this direction are a function of their personalities, and to some extent are even genetic. Thus not everyone will find the activistic life suited to himself. Yet I believe that it is possible for many or most human beings to find some merit in the active life, for its chief excellencies are courage, the willingness to dare, self-power, resourcefulness, creativity, and intelligence; these qualities, though they play a role in daily life, are essential for any grand human achievement. Indeed, in each of the alternative models, such qualities must be present to some extent if we are to live and function. It is simply a question of emphasis. If we are to proclaim a way of life, create something different, bring into being a new idea or invention, or forge a frontier, then we need to dream, take a chance, seize an opportunity. These are the qualities that are uniquely and superbly human, the risk-taking that makes possible the great human thrust.

It is not "the human predicament" about which we should worry. Those who emphasize "the human condition" are often dominated by forlornness, fear and trembling (the "Augustinian-Kierkegaardian syndrome"), and the mistaken belief that salvation comes from the passive mood—from dependence on and acquiescence to the divine. Rather, we need to underscore the activist frame, which alone makes possible those social conditions from which a transcendental lotus-eater can withdraw. By *activist frame* I refer to the dominant virtues of modern life: the willingness to take destiny in one's own hands, to tempt fate and to turn it about to suit oneself. It is not the quiet release from decision, action, passion, or torment that is the goal of my life, but striving, seeking, meeting challenges, and overcoming obstacles. It is this that gives my life its special zest and vitality. It is this that makes me say that I am bursting at the seams.

Some will demur, saying that I am merely glorifying the values that dominate American society, that is, the achievement motive, entrepreneurship, success, pragmatic doing. And these values, we are told, may be eclipsed, ephemeral expressions of a phase of human history that will pass—much the same as Aristotle expressed the virtues of Hellenistic culture, Marcus Aurelius the values of Rome's, Aquinas the mood of medieval religiosity, or Bentham the utilitarian calculus of nineteenth-century Britain. Granted that our values reflect our cultural bias, so that we cannot disentangle from them entirely. Yet the heroic virtues that attempt to bend nature to our will, to express the stout spine, strong heart, or firm jaw, transcend our culture and typify resilient characteristics of the human enterprise. These Promethean virtues expressed strong impulses in the pagan hearts of the Greeks and Romans; they reappeared during the Renaissance and modern times (in opposition to the Christian virtues of submissiveness and piety); and they were proclaimed anew by Nietzsche at the beginning of our century. They are, in the final analysis, the qualities that make possible human achievement in every field of endeavor: art, science, industry, commerce, politics, civilization itself. They are central to the humanist frame.

It is audacity that distinguishes the human response from that of other forms of life on this planet. Humans are intrepid, insolent, and impudent. They seek to break loose from the constraints imposed by nature; they are high-spirited, restless, adventuresome, inquiring, inventive. Humans are condemned to invent their own futures; they are responsible for what they will become; they are forever full of hopes and aspirations, plans and projects. They are always involved in a process of discovery and creativity, seeking new paths for joyous existence. Humans simply cannot acquiesce to the universe, nor are they content merely to fulfill their nature; they constantly strive to exceed themselves and nature by bringing forth from imagination creative modes of thought, new artifacts and inventions that did not previously exist in nature (tools, instruments, symbols, works of art, objects, machines, technologies, institutions, and organizations of all sorts). They do not merely discover what nature is, but add new forms and combinations to it. It is in the agony and joy of work that we truly achieve our grandeur and forge our destiny.

The meaning of life is not to be found by withdrawing from its challenges, contemplating the universe in mystical transcendence, fulfilling our duties by moral sacrifice, or even achieving self-actualization; rather, it is created by us as we reach out, voyage, and adventure. In this process lies the drama, excitement, and exaltation of living the full life. Life has no meaning per se; it only presents opportunities for us to seize and act upon.

3

THE BOUNTIFUL JOYS

The pessimist bemoans life. This is a vale of tears, he cries. Human beings are impotent. He points to the toil of Sisyphus, the dilemma of Schopenhauer, the impermanence of things, and the finality of death. The humanist's rejoinder to the pessimist is optimism: *life is, or can be, worth living.* The real question to be raised is whether life is worth living on its own terms, without any illusions of immortality. Unfortunately, that question cannot be resolved entirely by reason. There are rational arguments that one can present to the forlorn spirit who is crushed by events and unable to cope with them. Religion is a method of adjusting by escaping into reverie and unreality. Ultimately, being able to live as a humanist may be only a question of courage and motivation, and if motivation is gravely impaired or absent, there may be little we can do to engender it. The ultimate courage is to be and to *become* in spite of existential reality, and to overcome adversity and exult in our ability to do so.

One can respond to the pessimist's catalogue of the evils of life by presenting an affirmative statement of its manifold possibilities and joys.

The fullness of life. The vale of tears is balanced by the summit of joys, the sorrows of life by its achievements, the depths of despair by the peaks of success. If life has tragic dimensions, it also has intrinsically worthwhile experiences. Though we may suffer grief at some moments, at other times we experience humor and laughter, enjoyment and pleasure. Although the priests remind us of the failures and defeats of human existence, humorists delight in fun, and we can savor and find pleasurable moments of experience. There is room in life for tears; but rather than submit to our fate, we can create a better life by exerting intelligence and effort, and by reducing or eliminating ignorance, hunger, deprivation, disease, and conflict. Many of the ills of life can thus be remedied and ameliorated; the goods can outweigh and outdistance the evils, and the tears can be balanced by joys.

Human power. We need a proper sense of our own powers. Although there are some things that are beyond our ability to eradicate or control—like death, if not taxes—the history of civilization illustrates that fortitude and intelligence used wisely enable us to overcome adversities. Earlier civilizations may have been unduly pessimistic about sin, corruption, and natural catastrophes. But science and technology enable us to understand the causes of phenomena and to find appropriate remedies for them. To the primitive mind, there appears to be no rhyme or reason to things. A flood washes away crops; a village starves. Perhaps we'd better sacrifice a child or a lamb to appease a god's anger—such is primitive "reasoning." And those who so reason submit to their fate in the hope that the gods will rescue them. For things he cannot control, a person feels the need of a divine order as a way to lessen his anxiety.

But we should recognize that although we may suffer misfortune, there is always the possibility of good fortune. Today's sorrow may give way to tomorrow's luck. The drama of human civilization also reveals the potentialities for untapping new discoveries and powers. It is by means of creative work that we can overcome adversity; we have the powers that will enable us to change things for the better. We need to gather our resources after defeat and strive anew. Human will *can* ameliorate adversity. The future depends on perseverance, ingenuity, and the indomitable human spirit.

The satisfaction of striving. Those who have emphasized the myth of Sisyphus have exaggerated the dilemma, because there can be significant enjoyment and enrichment in working to reach our goals. Performing a task repeatedly need not be painful drudgery, but can be a source of immense satisfaction—as athletes discover in endless hours of practicing for a sports contest. Indeed, perhaps it is the quest itself that is the chief source of life's enrichment. The lover pursues the beloved, the entrepreneur builds a new industry, the novelist spends years on a magnum opus. It is within the creative acts themselves that we find the stimulation. It is not what we achieve so much as the activities undertaken in achieving it. The means expended to attain our ends cannot be divorced from the ends themselves. We should not condemn all labor as a crushing burden. Indeed, having nothing to do in the Garden of Eden or paradise may be equivalent to a state of hell.

Expectation and realization. Arthur Schopenhauer posed a dilemma: we are either goaded by desire, hence restless and anxious; or once satiated we become bored and ennui sets in. Given this dilemma, life is really senseless and not worth living. Schopenhauer's dilemma can of course be rebutted. His attitude expresses the reactions of a jaded sensibility. What about the exuberant attitude, which finds the opposite qualities in life? There are great and exciting expectations and desires that stimulate us to action, and there are great thrills in experiencing and striving for them. When we finally achieve our ends there are the joys of consummation, the immense gratification in quenching our thirst, satisfying our hunger, and releasing our passions. Moreover, once we have attained our goals, new and interesting ones always emerge. Thus we stand between the pleasures of expectation and the delights of realization.

In answer to those who argue that everything in life is impermanent, one may respond that although it is true that nothing lasts, the flux of change has some redeeming value:

The many uses of history. First, the efforts of earlier civilizations are not entirely forgotten; they remain in human memory, in the artifacts, works of art, books, and monuments that have survived. They have become part of world culture, and we appreciate and profit from them. Some good that we do may survive us, and future generations perhaps will be indebted to us for what we have bequeathed to them. Using ethnology and archeology, we are able to partially uncover and reconstruct past civilizations. We can put them in broader perspective as part of world history, from the cave drawings of prehistoric men and women in France, Africa, and Australia, down to the present moment. The past thus becomes meaningful in the present, as each culture assimilates, appreciates, and reinterprets its past heritage for itself.

Still, the impermanence of things is an indelible part of reality. One can see this in astronomy, where the cosmic scene is a spectacle of the birth and death of stars and galaxies, all moving at tremendous speeds in an ever-expanding universe. Many of the things that have passed can be rediscovered in someone's present.

The appreciation of novelty. Second, there is always something new under the sun. We can see this in the world of manufactured objects, where we await with great anticipation the latest brand or model; yesterday's product is already outmoded, tomorrow's may be perfected. This is no doubt an illusion, yet last season's fashions, books, or styles give way to those of the upcoming season. The splendid walnut tree eventually perishes, but there are new trees to replace it. Caesar may die and all may mourn him, but Augustus will reign. There is the excitement of something new—which may at first shock us by its audacity. Granted there is grandeur in the classical styles, but these will be replaced by different modes of expression, themselves perhaps destined to become classics and to survive their detractors. Thus there is some virtue to impermanence. Uniqueness, individuality, and novelty all have some place in a pluralistic universe and can be savored for their own sakes while they last. Nothing lasts forever, moans the melancholic. Yes, I reply, but how lovely are the new sprouts emerging to take their place!

The tree of life. Last of all, we are reminded, are senility, death, and nothingness, which await every human being. That is a brute fact, and there is no escaping it. We can stave off death and prolong life by modern medicine, and in the future the human species may find new ways of extending life far beyond threescore and ten by proper nutrition, exercise, and medical therapy. We can hope that there will be biogenetic breakthroughs for future generations that will increase longevity significantly, so that men and women may live and enjoy life for many decades more in reasonably good health. We are reminded of death by the pessimists, and of life by the optimists. Given the fact of death, our main focus should be on life—not to pine about its termination, but to take its every moment to be precious.

This argument may fall on deaf ears. Some individuals are so turned off by life's challenges and responsibilities that they claim to find life distasteful, debilitating, and depressing. They are so weighed down by burdens that their only response is negativity. They are dismayed by and even angry at the exuberant person. They resent mirth or laughter; they are always serious. Some may, in moments of desperation, even contemplate suicide.

How do we respond to such individuals, who do not find life worth living? I suppose that at some point logic fails, and we cannot prove anything to them by argument—for the zest for living is instinctive and noncognitive. If it is absent, there may be some underlying physiological or psychosomatic malady gnawing at the marrow. The exacerbated tragic sense has many causes, and who can say with certainty what deep-seated cause has led to a distorted sense of reality? Extreme depression may be physiological, even genetic, in origin. But its origin may also be found in the frustration of one's basic needs. It may have its roots in homeostatic imbalance, the repression of the sexual libido, the failure of self-respect, the inability to find some creative work or a beloved cause to strive for, the lack of wisdom, or the lack of love, friendship, or community. Presumably, if these needs were satisfied, a person could grow and develop, and might find some creative basis for a meaningful and enriched life. If a person doesn't find his present life worth living, then perhaps he ought to put himself in a situation where he might.

Countless individuals have sung praises to the tree of life in the past and will continue to do so in the future. The fruit of the tree of life is wholesome and nourishing, and in eating it we find that its secret is that *life is intrinsically good*. This is the basic touchstone for the ethics of humanism. Each and every person needs to create the conditions that will enable him or her to live richly and joyously. This, in the last analysis, is the purpose of all moral and ethical rules and regulations. They are good and right not simply in themselves but also for their consequences—for what they make possible: wholesome, creative, happy lives. The common moral decencies and responsibilities need to be respected as essential to the very framework of life in the community. But the test of an ethical system is also whether it enables individuals to live exuberantly. Generation upon generation of human beings in the past have found life rewarding, and generation upon generation no doubt will continue to do so in the future. We need not escape to nirvana or seek salvation elsewhere—which is actually an escape to *nowhere*. The acts of creative living, including the sharing of life with others, is the summum bonum of the human condition. That is the response the humanist gives to the theist. There is nothing ultimate or absolute beyond the living of life fully: *it is its own reward*.

4

THE MEANING OF LIFE

ETHICS MINUS GOD

Does life have genuine meaning for one who rejects supernatural mythology? Can a person realize a significant life if one abandons faith in immortality or providence? Is life tragic because it is finite? Since death surely awaits everyone, is life therefore absurd? Faced with this existential dilemma, we cry out, "Why live?" Can we be happy? Is there a basis for moral conduct? What can we do if God is dead, if there is no immortal soul, and if there is no purpose immanent in nature?

It is important that we focus on the so-called problem of the meaning of life as it is posed by the theist. In answer to the theist, we may say that the existential question as framed by him is mistaken. We should not grant to the religious believer the validity of his challenge. Instead we should ask whether life is really meaningful for *him*. Does he not deceive himself by posing the theological–existential paradox and by assuming that only a broader purpose can save him? Is it not the theist who squanders life? In what sense would life be worthwhile if God existed, if the universe had a divine purpose—given the existence of evil?

The conception of an omnipotent God connotes the correlative notion of helpless creatures. "Man's chief end," admonishes the Scottish shorter catechism, "is to glorify God and enjoy him for ever and ever." What kind of life can be said to be significant if we are totally dependent upon this God for our existence and sustenance? The relationship of creator to created is analogous to that of master to slave. The religious picture of the universe is akin to a model prison, wherein inmates are beholden to the warden for their daily bread and their highest duty is to praise and supplicate him for life. The immortality myth warns that if we do not pledge allegiance to God's will, we shall suffer damnation. Is not the life of an independent free person to be preferred to one of eternal bondage?

No, replies the believer to these skeptical questions. God promises eternal salvation, not oppression, for the elect. But upon what condition? As Bertrand Russell has said, to sing hymns in praise of Him and hold hands throughout all eternity would be sheer boredom. What of the lusts of the body, the joys of the flesh, the excitement and turmoil of pleasure and passion—will these be vanquished in the immortal life? For the free person, Hell could not be worse.

The religious believer insists that humans are free, for we are created in God's image, capable of choosing between good and evil. The rub, however, is that only if a person chooses to obey the master will he be rewarded with immortal life. But the problem of evil turns this eternal drama into divine comedy: God entrusted me with the power and freedom of choice, yet He will punish me if I stray from Him. Why did He not program me during the act of creation so that I could not avoid knowing Him and following His guidelines? Since it is He who created me, why does He condemn me for satisfying my natural inclinations, which He implanted in me? Why does He permit suffering and pain, torment and tragedy, disease and strife, war and plunder, conflict and chaos? In order to test us, responds the theist. But why the necessity of the trial, with so much apparent vindictiveness? To punish us for the sins we have committed. If this is the case, why punish the innocent? Why cut down the seeming paragons of virtue, the valiant and the noble? For the sins they have committed but may be unaware of? Why visit pain and torment upon infants and children—in suffering cancer or a tragic accident? Are they paying for the sins of their parents? If so, is this not a morality of collective guilt? (And what if the children are orphans!) One who believes in reincarnation may attempt to rescue the case by insisting on a prior existence. Possibly children are made to pay for the sins that they have committed in an earlier life, though as an ill baby writhes and cries out, he does not remember those prior existences— as Caligula or Hitler—for which the child now suffers.

The rationalization continues: perhaps evil is due to our omission, not God's commission. We should discover a cure for cancer, for example, or learn to stop floods. But if God is all-powerful, why doesn't He intervene in cooperative venture? There is no natural evil, say some theists, attempting to resolve the problem; the only evil is "moral evil," they assert, the evil of humans, not God. But the inescapable inference is that God permits evil. Why does He not stamp it out? Why should not God be merciful and loving rather than legalistic and moralistic? Is He, as Hume suggests, like us: merely limited in power? Then why worship another finite being?

Some theists insist that evil may be only an illusion, and that from a larger perspective what appears to be evil may turn out in the end to be good. In the total divine plan, pain and suffering need not be bad. Why is not the converse true? From the larger point of view what appears to be good may also be only an illusion, and everything in the end irredeemably evil.

Thus the believer has woven a fanciful fabric of mythological imagination in order to soothe the fear of death and to comfort those who share his anxiety. This is an ad hoc rationalization aimed to settle his doubt, but it is ridden with loopholes more puzzling than the universe we encounter in everyday life.

Believers finally concede—from the Book of Job down to the present—that there are things beyond human understanding, such as the paradox of free will versus determinism and the problem of evil. Unable to resolve the contradictions, they end up in simple confessions of faith.

Should we not rather be prepared to deal with life as we find it—full of sorrow, death, pain, and failure, but also pregnant with possibilities?

But, insists the believer, people cannot be happy if they know that they are going to die and that the universe possesses no larger purpose. What is happiness? Does it involve acquiescence to another, dependence on a greater being, religious faith and devotion, credulity and piety? Why is religious masochism a form of bliss? It may release us from torment and anxiety, but it involves flight from the full realization of our powers. Not only, therefore, does religious theism fail to give life meaning, it fails as a source of happiness. More often than not it has exaggerated the pathology of fear, the anxiety of punishment, the dread of death and of the unknown.

The believer is tormented by his overextended sense of sin and guilt, torn by a struggle between natural biological impulses and repressive divine commandments. Can a religious believer who submits to a doctrine of sin truly be happy? For the humanist the great folly is to squander life, to miss what it affords, to not play it out. The cemeteries are filled with corpses who bartered their souls in anticipation of promises that were never fulfilled.

But can one really be moral, remonstrates the theist, without religious belief? Are we capable of developing moral virtues and a sense of responsibility without a belief in God as a presupposition of morality?

The answers here in part depend upon what is meant by the term *moral*. Morality for the believer requires the existence of a faith state, a pious appreciation of God's redemptive power. This entails the "virtues" of acquiescence and obedience, as well as the suppression of our natural biological desires, including our appreciation of sexuality, and even some degree of self-hate. We may deny, however, that many of the so-called "moral virtues" of traditional theism are either moral or virtuous. The highest virtues are in man's existing for himself; rationality, courage, self-interest, self-respect, pride, some element of self-centeredness are essential components of morality, which in the last analysis focuses on happiness. This being the case it is possible to be moral without belief in God.

But, asks the theist, if God is dead, is not *everything* permissible? Would we not be rapacious and misuse our fellow creatures? How, without God, can we guarantee charity and justice? The brotherhood of man presupposes a divine conception of individual dignity based upon the fatherhood of God. To abandon this postulate of the moral life would be to reduce the human race to hunter and prey and every form of barbarism.

Basically, these are empirical questions. There is no logical connection between the fatherhood of God and the brotherhood of man. A hierarchical church has defended in the past an unequal society with strict social class and privilege. Moral sympathy is not dependent upon theistic belief. The Crusades and the Inquisition, the massacre of the Huguenots, the Catholic–Protestant battles, as in Northern Ireland, the Jihad unleashed with fury, the Muslim–Hindu or Muslim–Jewish slaughters, are among the cruelties perpetrated by theists. Moreover, belief in God often deflects a concern for one's fellow humans to supernatural goals; faith supersedes charity. If one's interest is the afterlife, then there is a temptation for some—but surely not all—to render unto Caesar the things that are Caesar's. Churches have had little difficulty in suppressing progress and revolution. Franco, Salazar, and Pinochet were true believers, as have been those in power in authoritarian regimes in South Africa and Pakistan. Religious devotion is no guarantee of moral devotion. Rather, there is good evidence that moral concern is autonomous and rooted in independent phenomenological experience. The history of humanity demonstrates that atheists, agnostics, and skeptics have been as moved by moral consideration for others as have believers. Spinoza, Kant, Marx, Russell, Mill, Dewey, and Sartre have had deep and abiding moral interests and have not depended upon traditional religious faith to bolster their morality. On the contrary, they have demonstrated that morality grounded in human experience and reason can be a far more reliable guide to conduct.

WHY IS LIFE WORTH LIVING?

There are other sources of despair. I have in mind the "existential plight" caused by life's exasperating and sometimes tragic difficulties, failures, and conflicts. There are moments when everything seems pointless, when we wish to abandon all of our commitments, when we may even contemplate suicide—profound crises of self-doubt and frustration. We may ask: Why beat one's head against a stone wall? What's the use?

At some point in life many of us have suspended desires, interests, and ideals: the death of a loved one, a cherished friend or relative; intense personal suffering; a disease; defeat of one's country; failure; deception uncovered; injustice perpetrated. The young burdened with the choice of a career, the middle-aged facing divorce or financial ruin, the old enduring the pangs of loneliness—all know moments of desperation.

Yet in spite of adversities and frustrations, the humanist maintains as a first principle that life is worth living, at least that it can be found to have worth. Can one demonstrate why the principle ought to prevail? Why express the courage to be? Why not die? Why life instead of death? If we are all going to die one day, why defer the inevitable? Why stave it off? Why not *now*?

One cannot "prove" that life ought to exist, or that a universe with sentient beings is a better place than one without them. The universe is neutral, indifferent to our existential yearnings. But we instinctively discover life, experience its throb, its excitement, its attraction. Life is there to be lived, enjoyed, suffered, and endured.

We must therefore rely on ourselves and distinguish two major, though distinct, questions. The first is epistemological, and the second psychological. Epistemologically, one may ask, can we "demonstrate" the basic principle of humanist morality, that is, that life is worthwhile? As his first principle, the theist adopts belief in a divine order beyond empirical confirmation or proof, which is in the last analysis a leap of faith. Does the first principle of humanism rest upon equal footing? In a crucial sense, my answer is No. For life is found; it is encountered; it is real. It needs no proof of its existence, as does an unknown and unseen divinity. The question is not, "Does life exist?" This is known as intimately and forcefully as anything in our universe of experience. The question rather is normative: "*Ought* life to exist?" This first principle does not make a descriptive claim; it is prescriptive and directive.

There are different kinds of first principles. They are not all of the same logical order; nor do they function in the same way. There are first principles that assert actual truth claims about the universe: for example, the assertion that God exists, or that determinism is real, or that the dialectic is operative in history. All of these principles have to be judged by the requirements of evidence and logic. Those that cannot provide sufficient grounds of support fail. A normative principle, as distinct from a descriptive assertion, is a guide for future conduct. It does not talk about the world in descriptive or explanatory terms. It lays down recommendations for us to follow, values to uphold, ideals to live by.

It is no doubt true that the epistemological principles of deductive logic, which provide for clarity in inference and thought, and of inductive science, which apply to the criteria for weighing evidential claims, function in one sense prescriptively; they provide guidelines for clarity and truth. In the last analysis they are justified pragmatically: do they assist in the course of inquiry? But still these are not truth claims of the same order as the God claim, for they are not attributing properties to the world.

Theistic descriptive claims are bad answers to bad questions, such as: "Why in the universe at large should organic life exist?" This makes no more sense than asking why things exist in the inanimate world. "Why should there be something rather than nothing?" asked Heidegger. But in one sense this is a meaningless question, though no doubt for the religious consciousness a poignant one. The demand for an explanation of "Being in general" or for an answer to the "riddle of the universe" is inevitably elusive, because there is no such thing as "Being in general." There are a multiplicity of beings that may be said to exist—physical objects, organisms, persons. These entities are encountered in experience and may be submitted to analysis because they have discernible properties. The question *why* they exist with the properties they have may be accounted for scientifically; they may be explained in causal terms, as having evolved in nature and as conditioned by natural laws. To ask "*Why* Being in general?" on the contrary is both fruitless and pointless. To posit God as the alleged ground of Being does not advance inquiry. We can always ask why He exists. There are limits to genuine explanation, and certain kinds of questions and answers are beyond the range of intelligibility. The universe exists, in a distributive way, that is, there are particular things. These we may encounter and describe in experience. Similarly, the question "Why should there be life in general?" can only be treated empirically. Any response would be in terms of known physical, chemical, and biological principles. Life comes into being in our solar system and possibly elsewhere in the universe when certain physical–chemical conditions are present.

The question that is sometimes raised in moments of existential despair is "Why should I exist?" or in recent decades, because of the threat of nuclear holocaust, "Why should the human race exist?" or still further, in consideration of ecological destruction, "Why should life on earth exist?" We have no guarantee, of course, that any forms of life will persist. Indeed, there is some probability that life on our planet may in some distant future become extinct, and this applies to the human race as well, unless by ingenuity and daring humans can populate other portions of the universe. There is no a priori guarantee of eternal survival.

Whether or not the human race continues indefinitely, however, an individual cannot persist forever. Thus the question "why" applies here most appropriately. "Why ought I to live?" and "Can I prove that my life is better than my death?" ask the nihilist and the skeptic in a mood of despondency. The answer should be apparent by now. One cannot prove that one ought to; all such proofs are deductive. From certain assumed premises, inferences follow. But what is at issue is precisely the premise that life itself is worthwhile; and human experience is the premise upon which all our knowledge and truth is based. Nor does "proof" mean empirical certainty based upon verification, for in the range of experience there are no certainties. In a strict sense, that life is worthwhile is not amenable to a descriptive confirmation; it is not capable of being tested as other hypotheses are. Rather, it is a normative postulate, on the basis of which I live.

There is, then, a second question—not the epistemological demand for proof of life's value, but the quest for psychological stimulus and motivational appeal. What is at issue here is whether we can find within life's experience its own reward. Many persons in times of desperation and defeat lose the desire for life and cry in the darkness for assurance that they ought to continue. Can we provide the sustenance they seek? Surely not, as I have said, by means of any logical or empirical proof. For these persons the will to live has its source deep within their psychobiological nature. If it is absent, what can we say? Does this mean that the value of life is merely irrational preference and quixotic caprice? No—there is more than that. We can give reasons and point to overlooked facts and consequences in seeking to persuade a desperate person not to commit suicide. We can try to arouse an affirmative attitude, hoping that the person will find *some* redeeming features remaining in life, by considering the possibilities: the beauty of dawn and sunset, the pleasures of eating and making love, friends, music and poetry.

Life must have some attractions and stimulate some interests. But what if it does not? What if the pain and sorrow are too great? For some people life may not be worth living in every context and at any price. In some situations, a sensible person may conclude that death with dignity is the only recourse: an incurable cancer accompanied by great suffering, a burden to the family, a betrayal of incalculable wretchedness, the defeat of a person's most important aims, the death of a loved one, a life of slavery or tyranny—these things may for some be too crushing and overwhelming to endure. The point is, it is not simply biological existence that we seek; modern medicine keeps many people alive. It is the *fullness of life* that we want; if that is completely absent, a heroic exit may be one's only recourse. I may conclude that I would rather die on my feet as a free person than on my knees as a slave or on my back as an invalid without interest or passion.

The humanist need not answer the theist or existentialist by justifying the view that life is always worth living, that people must be motivated to believe this when they cannot. We can make no universal claim. What we can say is that most human beings, under normal conditions, find life worthwhile. But, I reiterate, it is not simply life at all costs that humans seek, but the *good* life, with significant experience and satisfaction.

It is nonetheless true that for the humanist the cardinal sin is death; survival is our highest obligation. Self-defense against injury or death is a necessary precondition; we tend naturally to wish to preserve ourselves. The continuance of life remains an imperative rooted within our basic animal nature. If life seems empty it is usually because our basic needs are unsatisfied and our most important desires are frustrated. When misfortune befalls a person and sadness is one's companion, a person may still respond that though daily life may seem insurmountable, and though one's spirits may appear suffocated by events, still one ought not to give in; one ought to fight to survive.

Why? Again—one cannot "prove" this normative principle to everyone's satisfaction. Living beings tend instinctively to maintain themselves and to reproduce their own kind. This is the primordial fact of life; it is precognitive and prerational, and it is beyond ultimate justification. It is a brute fact of our contingent natures, and it has its roots within, in an instinctive desire to live. The deepest sources of our being yearn for it.

5

THE FULLNESS OF LIFE

There is thus the vital normative principle, concomitant with the will to live, that we seek, not simply to live, but *to live well.* What we want is a full life in which there is satisfaction, achievement, significance.

What constitutes the fullness of being? What is the good life? Philosophers such as Plato, Aristotle, Spinoza, Bentham, and Mill have reflected upon the nature of the good life, as have prophets, poets, theologians, judges, psychiatrists—experts and plain men and women alike. Many contemporary philosophers have cautiously eschewed the question because they have been fearful of committing the so-called "naturalistic fallacy"; that is, assuming that their value judgments are objectively grounded in the nature of things—they are not. Granted the analytic pitfalls, it is still important that we revisit the question, for the nature of the good life is a perennial concern in every culture and every epoch. Even if there is danger that we are merely engaging in "persuasive definitions" of "good" and "bad," it is important that in every period some efforts be made to define the excellencies of the good life. Even if the moral life is not to be resolved by metaphysics, logic, or science alone, there are degrees of rationality, and our principles can be informed by reflective examination.

Thus we may ask, what are the characteristics of a life well-lived, at least for contemporary human beings? As I have said, what most men and women seek is not simply life or bare existence, but the good life, what philosophers have usually called "happiness." What precisely happiness is, however, is open to dispute. It is not an ideal Platonic quality resident in the essence of man or in the universe at large; it is concrete, empirical, and situational in form and content. It is a concept relative to individuals, to their unique needs and interests, and to the cultures in which they function. As such, happiness is in constant need of reformulation. Nor is it elusive or unattainable, as the theist believes; it is fully achievable if the proper conditions are present. Historically, there has been confusion about whether happiness refers to *eudaemonia* (health and well-being), to peace and contentment, or to pleasure and enjoyment. I wish to use the term in a somewhat different way to designate the *fullness of being—*

a life in which qualities of satisfaction and excellence are present. What would such a life entail?

PLEASURE

The hedonist is correct when he says that a full life should contain pleasure, enjoyment, excitement. It is difficult to achieve a full life if there is excessive pain or suffering, particularly over long periods of time. To live a full life, one must be able to enjoy a wide range of interests and experiences: delicious food, good drink, sexual love, adventure, achievement, friends, intellectual and aesthetic delights, the joys of nature and physical exercise; one's experiences must be marked by a reasonable degree of tranquillity and a minimum of protracted anxiety. It is a mistake, however, to identify pleasure totally with the full life, as hedonists have done. For one may have hedonistic thrills yet be miserable; one may pursue pleasure and suffer a mundane, narrow existence. The complete sensualist—an opium eater for example—may undergo intense pleasurable excitement but be mired in a state of melancholy, grief, or boredom. Although moderate amounts of pleasure would appear to be a necessary condition of the good life, pleasure is not a sufficient condition for the fullness of being; the hedonist indeed may be the unhappiest of persons.

There are, of course, many varieties of hedonism. There is, for example, the voluptuary hedonist, who flits from one sensation to the next in an intense quest for physical pleasures. But the voluptuary can rarely find life satisfying. Did Don Juan, Casanova, or Alcibiades lead full lives? Does the alcoholic, glutton, or addict? The search for new thrills and the focus on the immediacies of enjoyment usually mask an underlying insecurity and instability; they are often signs of immaturity and irresponsibility. Children scream and demand instant gratification; adults learn from experience that it is often wiser to defer gratification. The voluptuary's appetites for touch and taste constitute a vital aspect of the good life, but surely this is not the be-all or end-all of human existence.

Recognizing that such a life may lead to anxiety and pain, some hedonists, such as Epicurus, have preached the quiet pleasures, advocating retreat from the cares of the world in order to achieve a neutral state of *ataraxia*. They seek peace of soul and emancipation from anxiety. Quiet hedonism has often meant withdrawal from the adventures of life, a limiting of experience, a narrowness rather than a fullness of life. "A glass of wine, a piece of cheese, and a quiet garden" constitute a closed universe. Aesthetic hedonists, such as Walter Pater, likewise have emphasized the cultivation of taste, especially the enjoyments to be gained from appreciating works of art. But this model if taken exclusively is in the end precious, appropriate for a leisure class rather than for doers. Other hedonists focus on intellectual, spiritual, or religious pleasures. Still others, such as utilitarians, emphasize the moral pleasures of altruistic dedication—pleasures that presume some moral growth and development, and that compete with the physical pleasures of food, drink, sex. It is often asked: Which pleasures are "higher" on the scale of values and which are "lower"? Many moralists consider the biological pleasures demeaning, and the aesthetic, intellectual, moral, and spiritual pleasures superior.

Hedonists have located an enduring truth about the human condition: without some pleasure, life would not be worth living. But they make a cardinal mistake in isolating pleasure from the process of living. Pleasure is intimately intermingled with life activity and different kinds of experience; what we seek to attain in a full life is a vigorous mood receptive to the varieties of enjoyment, as Lucretius and Goethe recognized. Aristotle observed that pleasure is part and parcel of the good life, helping to complete and bring appropriate activities to fruition, but that the person who seeks it preeminently will probably never find it. Pleasure must accompany and qualify certain fundamental life activities. Pleasures cannot be measured quantitatively by any hedonist calculus, as Mill noted, but should be judged qualitatively. The pleasures of a developed human being have an appeal that infantile hedonists are unable to appreciate.

To come back to our earlier question: Which pleasures ought we to prefer? The basic biological pleasures, or the developed pleasures of an educated and sophisticated person? Efforts by moralists to prove that the so-called "higher" pleasures have a quality intrinsically superior to the "lower" pleasures seem to me to fail. A librarian who can appreciate good books, fine music, and art but not enjoy sex is not necessarily leading a fuller life than the bucolic farm boy or girl who cannot read or write but who enjoys the thrills of sexual delight. Granted that the person who knows only physical pleasures and has never cultivated other sensibilities is limited in the range of appreciation. But it is an exaggeration to maintain, as Mill does, that educated people who have tasted both the so-called higher and lower pleasures invariably prefer the former. If it comes to a choice between an orgasm or a sonata, most persons who are honest would seize the former. But it is not really a question of one or the other; in a full life we want *both*. To ask which ultimately we should prefer—an embrace or a moral deed, a steak or a symphony, a martini or a poem—is senseless; we want them all.

SATISFACTION OF OUR BASIC NEEDS

To realize the fullness of life requires some satisfaction of basic needs. Without it we are prey to malaise; there are certain norms of health that must be satisfied. The wisest men and women have recognized that health is the most precious of possessions, more important than riches or fame. Contingent upon our biological and sociocultural nature are needs that we must satisfy if we are to achieve health, whether physical or psychological.

Our basic needs are two-dimensional: *biogenic* in that they have biological and psychological origins, and *sociogenic* in that they are manifested through and conditioned by society and culture.

Biogenic Needs

1. The primary need of the organism is of course to *survive*. Threats in the environment must be overcome; injury must be avoided. The natural biological mechanisms of self-protection have evolved. They are fairly simple in some species, but more complicated in the human species. They are instinctive structures that operate constantly to preserve the integrity of the organism. Fear of death is the deepest of human forebodings; it is through this primal source that religions are sustained. Fear has roots deep within our somatic nature. It assumes profound psychological and sociological dimensions in civilization. Where the rule of the jungle prevails, any form of peaceful life is impossible. Civilization is possible only because it affords security and protection for individuals. Life need not be dangerous and brief; it may be enjoyable through a long life, but only if the social environment provides sufficient security.

2. A concomitant requirement is the need of the organism to *maintain itself and function biologically*. The simplest requirements are oxygen, water, food, and shelter. The human organism ingests materials from the environment in order to survive; the struggle for self-preservation is dependent upon satisfying these basic needs. The organism tends naturally toward a state of equilibrium; any rupture in it stimulates counteractivity to restore homeostasis and organic harmony. There is an organismic tone of the whole body that is essential for well-being. Social institutions come into being to serve basic biological needs; the economic structure of society, methods of production and distribution, makes available a range of goods necessary for survival.

3. Related to these needs are those of *growth*: the egg fertilized by the sperm, the fetus, infant, child, adolescent, and mature adult. At different periods of life different needs and capacities emerge. Each stage of life has its dimensions and expectations: there is exploration and excitement in childhood, impetuosity and idealism in youth, the perspective of maturity and the virtues of wisdom or accomplishment in old age.

4. *Reproduction* is essential to the species, though not to each individual. Nature rewards those who engage in the act of copulation, necessary for sexual reproduction, by intense pleasure. Our whole being yearns to love and be loved, to hold and be held, to fondle, embrace, and penetrate or be penetrated, to be one with another. The celibate faces a void, which he may try to fill but never can. The world is denuded for those who suffer sexual famine, and no degree of sublimation or substitution can make up for it. Although sexuality instinc-

tively serves a reproductive function, it exerts a more powerful claim upon us and plays a vital role in psychosomatic health.

Many philosophers who have written about happiness have overlooked sexual satisfaction. Happiness is not primarily, as the Greeks thought, a matter of cognitive reason; it requires deep-seated emotional satisfaction and psychic adjustment. Freud has made us aware of how we ignore sexuality at our peril. Unhappiness, neurosis, and pathology are bred in sexual frustration and repression.

5. The need to *discharge surplus energy* is another organic requirement. We see it most graphically in children and animals, as they play games and romp, but it is also present of course in adults: we need to relax and wind down. Amusement and entertainment, which release us from built-up anxieties and tensions, are expressive experiences that give a special quality to life. These are not simply frills, for organisms spill out overabundant reserves and expressive play is one way by which they do so. Surplus energy is also released by physical exercise and work. We feel vital after exercise, a walk or a swim; it is an expressive need that appears to be related to the tendency to reach levels of homeostasis and equilibrium. Reservoirs of energy need to be released for healthy functioning.

Sociogenic Needs

The biogenic needs apply not only to all forms of human life, but to animal life as well. But humans cannot survive, let alone live, as isolated individuals. The family, tribe, clan, and community—small or large in size—enable us to satisfy our needs and fulfill our interests. Our sociogenic needs help us realize our biological needs and allow them to develop a primacy of their own, but the mere satisfaction of biological needs is not enough for civilized persons. The fullness of life—its variety and quality—is always related to the cultural context in which we exist, and whether or not we flourish depends upon the materials of culture with which we work.

Each of our primary needs is transformed and extended by culture. Food and drink are necessary for survival, but their refinements—infinitely varied recipes, subtleties of preparation, cultivation of wines, sophisticated settings, appropriate circumstances—all are social inventions conditioned by our culture; and so our needs are eventually transformed by complexity. The same principle characterizes the relation of sex to society. It is a necessity of survival, but its nature is transfigured by considerations of love and passion, by its significance in the changing mores of marriage and divorce, and by its practice in alternative forms and its exploitation as commerce. The habits we develop are conditioned by the sociocultural context in which we live.

Thus both biology and culture converge upon the individual. Both chance and causality make us what we are. The challenge for each of us, though we are culture bound and time bound, is to make what we can of life, to savor its finite moments in history, and to transcend where we can the limits imposed upon us.

We can never go back; as culture challenges and changes moral patterns, we need always to make and remake what we are and to try to live authentically as best we can. Given all our idiosyncratic differences, there are nevertheless some general sociogenic needs that apply to all men and women, and there are excellences that qualify the good life. It is useful to try to spell them out, though they are no doubt limited by our culture. Other cultures and other times rejected them; they are nevertheless vital to us and perhaps to most cultures.

6. If literature and art, psychology and religion, and indeed all experience, teach us anything, it is *the need for love*. There is no doubt about its central importance. No one can live entirely alone, without the affection of other persons and without being able to reciprocate.

Love has two primordial roots: one, in the dependency of the young—in the mutual need and affection that develops out of parental care of the child—and the other in orgasmic sexual arousal and attraction. But there are of course other dimensions and levels, all revealing how dependent we are upon others; our very self-image is defined by the responses of others to us, as we define theirs. Among the finest and most enduring moments of life are those that we share with others. It is not enough that we receive love or appreciation; we need also to bestow it upon others. To want only to be loved is infantile and possessive; it is hardly conducive to growth. To genuinely want the loved one to flower, to be interested in the interests of the other—this is the perfection and reach of human love. We may ask, are parents willing to allow their children to become what they wish, following their own visions of truth and value? Similarly for the mature man or woman who wishes to be a full individual in his or her own terms. Will one's lover permit this? Reciprocal love is not necessary for survival, nor even for sexual enjoyment, but its presence is always a sign of a full life. Unless one develops mutual relationships and thus experiences the joys of life, whether with a beloved, a parent, a child, or a friend or colleague, one's heart withers, one's roots become dry.

7. Another precondition for a good life, related to love, is *the need to belong to some community*. Many today are alienated because they have discovered no goals that they can share with their fellow humans. In the long history of humankind, the extended family or the tribe, the village or town, have been able to nourish this need. No person who is an island finds life fully significant. During the feudal period each person had his station and duties, which, though unjust to those at the bottom of the social hierarchy, tended to give a sense of psychological security and some identity. Postmoderns tend to be rootless; they rarely have a beloved community with which they can identify. Unable to participate in common goals, they often feel as outsiders, alienated and anomic.

Belonging to some community has in the past assured interaction on various levels. A small group in which there were face-to-face encounters was the bedrock of the human relationship. As mass society changes and populations increase, as small units coalesce and are absorbed by larger ones, humans are able to broaden their sense of community and allegiance. One's community may include the state or nation, religion or culture; eventually it may include a commitment to humanity as a whole. Religion at its finest has attempted to inculcate a more universal devotion to that moral point of view that treats all humans as equal in dignity and value.

8. There is an important element in the quest for well-being that conventional religious creeds have often underestimated—self-affirmation and *the need to love one's self*. This is as important for our well-being as is love of others. I do not speak of those who are puffed up with pride, self-centered, and selfish, and need to be restrained for the sake of society, but of those who have too low an estimation of their talent and worth and therefore little self-respect. Indeed, they are often victimized by self-hate, though it may be hidden from consciousness, and they may assume different forms of self-deprecation, timorousness, excessive caution, or extreme forms of asceticism. A form of self-pride that is balanced and temperate, as Aristotle noted, is important for our well-being, and it is essential for healthy reactions to daily challenges. Every human being has something to contribute, but he cannot do so if he finds little value in his own individuality.

9. This leads to still another vital element in the full life: *creative actualization*. Individuals need more than to satisfy their basic needs; they need to bring into fruition their highest potentialities. This means that there should be a striving to develop. Unless this effort is made, the fullness of life will not be realized. The ideal of creative self-actualization is essential to the concept of happiness that I am delineating. It is the actualization of my basic species needs, those that I share in common with others, but it is also individualized, for it expresses my unique and personal idiosyncrasies, tastes, and talents. The injunction is for me *to be myself*, not what others would have me be; I must express my own nature in all its variety, and in doing so I create something new.

This is the activist's model of life; it calls upon us to expend energy, to realize what we can be—not what we are. Nature is in a process of unfolding. There is no complete, static human essence or nature that defines me and that I merely need to uncover and fulfill. Rather, I am constantly being made and remade in dynamic processes of growth and discovery.

I have certain native capacities, but these are largely unstructured; they can take various forms. The direction I choose depends upon the cultural context in which I act as well as upon my native abilities. To act is to bring something new into existence. The goal is creativity, the spring of life.

The full life in the last analysis is not one of quiet contentment, but the active display of my powers and of their development and expansion. The creative life involves exploration and curiosity, discovery and ingenuity, the delight in uncovering and introducing novel modes of expression. This life is one of forward thrust; the achievement motive dominates. To venture, to experiment— these are the virtues of the ongoing spirit, which untap and express hidden powers and implicit capacities and formulate or create new ones. It is natural to regret a wasted life—a child prodigy who fizzles out, a unique talent that lies fallow, a great person who is reduced by burdens—and to applaud a creative person, whatever his or her endeavor or area of excellence.

To succeed is not merely to attain one's ends; rather it is to *exceed* them. The model that I am presenting is contrary to the historically idealized quest for a state of eternal bliss. It proposes enjoyment achieved by full participation in life, not necessarily as defined by society, but as found in an individual's own search. Perhaps this exuberant approach is an expression of our own cultural bias. Other civilizations have emphasized the value of meditation and spiritual exercise. Is the incessant quest for achievement simply self-serving ambition? And is this not possibly self-defeating? Do we not in the process often lose the capacity to appreciate the immediacies of experience? Not as I conceive it. This creative model exults in the present moment. It does not necessarily involve a quest for public approval; creative individuals frequently move against the times. The achievement motive refers to ambition in more personal terms: our wish to excel by our own vision of what life can afford. The spirit of contemplation, like that of celibacy and the priestly mood, if overemphasized, may express fear, even neurosis, a withdrawal from the challenges of life. I do not deprecate contemplation as part of my nature, a source of intellectual joy and peace. What I am criticizing is the notion that the contemplative life is to be pursued to the exclusion of all else and that it is the highest form of sainthood. My model of the true "saint" is Prometheus, the creative doer. Some critics properly point to the banal values of the excessively competitive society. The option that I am emphasizing focuses on the strenuous mood, and we can use it to focus on our own ends, and to fulfill them whatever they are. It is the experimental and adventurous life of challenge and excitement.

AUDACITY, FREEDOM, AND REASON

The ability to live an autonomous, creative life involves audacity, a defining characteristic of human beings and a key to their greatness. The audacious life is a life of risk-taking. Human nobility is not simply that we can develop the courage to be, but the courage to grow and change.

There are fearful and weak people of little imagination and daring who warn that this or that is absolutely unattainable and cannot be done. But the advance of civilization is sparked by the decision not to accept the clichés of one's age, not to be penned in by nature or caged in by history. The Promethean figure is venturesome and bold. These are the virtues of the true heroes and geniuses of history, who have given us new ideas and inventions, new departures in truth and beauty, nonconformists who would not take no for an answer, independent spirits who have made up the roll call of progress.

All human beings have some capacity to be self-activated, provided they are willing to recognize their freedom and seize it, and not to become mired in limitations. I am not by this asserting that determinism is false. We are determined in part by antecedent conditions, but organic life expresses a form of teleonomic causality. There is no contradiction in affirming that we are both free and determined, autonomous and conditioned. Determinism is not a metaphysical generalization about the universe; it is simply a rule governing scientific inquiry. It presupposes that if we inquire, we will most likely discover the causal conditions under which we act. It need not deny that human life is self-affirming nor that we can create goals and strive to attain them.

The free person is autonomous because he is unwilling to forfeit existence to external events, but instead resolves to control them. One acts freely insofar as one can, recognizing not only the constraints within a situation, but also the potentialities. To be human is to be open to new possibilities; we are dynamic beings, our alternatives are discovered and created. We are what we will, and we can become what we dream. Not all of our dreams can come true—only a fool believes that they can—yet some can, if they are acted upon by reason and experience and applied to the realities of nature.

Though each person is unique, we are all faced with similar challenges to create our own futures; our lives are the sum of the projects to which we commit ourselves. The term "lifework" is here appropriate. A full life involves artistic vision and creation. The person with a career that he enjoys and finds rewarding is the most fortunate of humans, especially if he can blend labor and action, work and play, and can turn work into a fulfilling outpouring of the self, an expression and an adventure. Our lifework should be measured not only in relation to job or career, for there are many other significant sources of creativity: to build one's house, become involved in a cause, act in a play, travel, or become a chef are all forms of enterprise in which persons can express themselves in excellence. The full life is psychologically abundant, bursting at the seams, capable of exulting in consummatory experiences.

This does not mean that life does not have its defeats and failures. Our best-laid plans often fail. Our loved ones die. We are aware of the breakdown of means, the tragic conflicts of ends, the abandonment of plans, the moments of despair. Unless these events are completely overwhelming, a rational person can take them in stride. The creative person is capable of some measure of stoic wisdom.

Human freedom, however, is most complete when our actions are modified and controlled by reason. Can one who is irrational not be happy? Does not happiness basically involve emotional satisfaction? Philosophers have no doubt overestimated the rational life and underestimated the deeper forces in our somatic and unconscious behavior. Human beings surely may achieve contentment without developing their full rational faculties; they may lead enjoyable lives and even be capable of some degree of creativity. Yet one who doesn't develop one's rational ability is deprived; like the virgin who suffers sexual starvation, such a person is incapable of full functioning. Reason expresses crucial biosocial needs rooted in our cultural history, necessary if we are to develop fully as persons.

How and why? In a negative sense, because it is the method of overcoming deception. Human beings, as we have seen, are all too prone to credulousness, to seizing upon false idols. Without reflection, we become prey to quackery. Reason uses logical analysis and evidence to debunk falsehood and expose fraud and to restrain our own self-delusions. As such, it is an instrument of liberation and emancipation, a source of freedom from sheer fantasy.

In a positive sense our rational impulses have provided us with science and ethics. Reflective experience has a double role: in developing an awareness and understanding of the world and in formulating the values by which we live. In the practical life reason cannot exist independently of our passionate nature. It is the union of thought and feeling that is essential to happiness. Reason that is divorced from its biological roots becomes abstract and oppressive. Cognition that is fused with affection and desire in lived experience expresses the whole person. The development of our critical faculties thus best enables us to define and fulfill the moral principles by which we live. Although reason alone is never sufficient for the fullness of life, it is a necessary condition for its attainment.

6

THE ETHICS OF EXCELLENCE

The central question is whether there are standards of *ethical* excellence that a rational person can use in life. Is it possible to evaluate the wide variety of tastes and appreciations of autonomous individuals, and to adjudicate between them? Can we judge between various styles of life and apply to them the terms *better* or *worse*? If so, on what bases?

The first point to make is that all evaluating procedures are *comparative*. Few absolute standards can be discovered. All standards, thus, are relative to a class of persons and their performances. We can, for example, rank track-and-field athletes, but only in relation to the performance of other athletes. We might do this by first examining the Olympic records. Only those who have broken new records or been awarded gold medals, such as Roger Bannister, Fanny Blanken-Koen, Paavo Nurmi, or Rafe Johnson, would qualify for excellence in the field. Lance Armstrong, who won the Tour de France after conquering cancer, stands out for his exemplary performance. *Excellence* is a thoroughly relative term, applicable to human beings engaged in some activity and used to compare their capacities and achievements. Here we are talking about athletic excellence, not ethical excellence, but analogous processes apply.

Another test of excellence is *consistency* in performance. It is not a single success—important as that may be to record—but achievement over a period of time that most impresses us. A child prodigy, however great a talent, may burn out early and be heard from no more. Not everyone is a Yehudi Menuhin, who displays virtuosity throughout his life. Thus we say that Wordsworth and Whitman are great poets, that Mies van der Rohe and Frank Lloyd Wright are great architects, that Einstein and Newton are great scientists. Such individuals are considered geniuses in specific fields of endeavor because their work broke new ground. Their performances or discoveries came to be recognized as pre-eminent, towering, or unique, and eventually each individual was publicly acclaimed. Does excellence require public approval? These individuals are considered excellent not because they achieved recognition, but because of the intrinsic qualities of their work, which manifests creativity, innovation, discovery. They are noteworthy because they have exceeded our expectations and have made an outstanding contribution.

I should add that there are countless creative persons who have not been recognized during their lives but whose excellence and creativity are eventually acknowledged. Van Gogh, for example, was not recognized as a genius during his lifetime, and Nietzsche was reviled as an evil man.

No doubt we can also quantify some forms of excellence, as when a person receives a perfect score on an examination. Often the evaluative concept is qualitative and difficult to characterize numerically; yet the excellence gleams through, much as a polished crystal, and we are dazzled by its sparkling beauty. Standards of ethical excellence are relative to a person's own level of talent and accomplishment. A person may not be a genius, nor make new breakthroughs, yet working with the materials he has, a kind of excellence may emerge. In focusing on excellence, I should make it clear that we should not concentrate on only a small elite. We should not judge the quality of a person's life by his fame or eminence, nor by the criterion of whether he is a genius or has made significant discoveries or contributions to the world.

Excellence is a relativistic standard applicable to the individual on his own terms, given his personality, the biological and environmental factors in his life, and the social circumstances in which he finds himself. The life of nobility that I am talking about has a dignity and grandeur that befit not only monarchs and presidents but also persons of the lowest station. Excellence emerges whenever there is a harmonious blending and symmetry. Even through pain, suffering, adversity or tragedy—and perhaps in spite of it—the life has been worthwhile. Such a person does not live in a degraded state of failure and self-deceit. His life exudes exquisite qualities. His life is *precious*, to himself and to those about him. One doesn't have to paint a Mona Lisa to excel in life, but only to decorate one's own hearth. Nor does one need to build a monument; it can be one's own career nurtured with loving care. A person can express a kind of artistry and virtuosity in living, even if it is in modest circumstances.

Perfection cannot be attained by any person; all humans have flaws. It is in spite of a person's limitations and character defects that a kind of qualitative worth may still express itself. A human life, if well lived, is a wonder to behold, a sublime and illustrious entity, like a splendid oak tree or a stately lion. We need to appreciate what it means to be a human being, and not mistakenly believe that one has to be a genius or a saint—for we are all only human.

We come back to the question: from the standpoint of *ethical* value, in what sense is it meaningful to apply the standard of excellence? Can we apply the terms *exquisite qualities* and *high merit*? Yes, we can. Here we appraise the following: (1) the *kinds* of values that a person cherishes and that activate him, (2) the *style* of life that he has adopted, and (3) how he *relates* to other persons within the sphere of interaction. In dealing with ethical excellence, I am not referring simply to a person's chief occupation or career—as important and satisfying as that may be in achieving the good life—but to the total constellation of values and principles manifested throughout the entire life. A person can be a great physicist and lead a miserable life, a great mathematician and not know how to get his car started, a sensitive poet and a terrible husband. I do not wish to focus on the part-man or part-woman but on the total life of the developed personality. What are the ingredients in a life that enable us to say that the person is exemplary, or that he is capable of some nobility? What are the admirable qualities, the signs of perfection and excellence, that manifest themselves?

From the standpoint of the humanist, the fruition of life is to live well and to achieve some modicum of happiness. For the individual, happiness involves some sense of achievement and of having reached the fullness of one's being. A person's life is like a work of art. We are involved in the creative process of giving form and structure, unity and harmony, to our plans and projects. We have blended colors, tones, shapes, and forms, and affixed them to the canvas. Our life is in part our own creation. What results is due to the choices and actions we have taken over many years and decades. Is the end product our own doing? Are we able to bring the parts together, to complete our dreams and projects, and to give a kind of unity and coherence to our world? Not everyone can create a masterpiece, build a noteworthy career, or lead an exemplary life. Many persons have failed. Their lives are wasted; they are overcome by fear and timidity; they are drowned by years of sorrow. They can never find a niche for themselves in the scheme of things. And so, they are condemned not only by the fates (to speak metaphorically) but also by their own inability to achieve great things. By this I do not mean social expectations, but their own. How many failed careers, dissolute marriages, and lives of quiet desperation are there?

Could a person's life have been otherwise? Yes, perhaps to some extent, but if so, how and in what sense? The full ethical life, measured in personal terms, involves a sense of achievement and accomplishment, a conscious recognition that we have, however modestly, contributed to the world, expressed our talents, and done something useful and productive in terms of our own ideals. To be able to do so can lead to a joyful and creative life, the bountiful, outgoing, adventurous life. Happiness, in some sense, can be achieved by most men and women, but it depends upon what we do. It depends on our being able to fulfill our basic needs, but also on our being able to express our creative talents in whatever fields we choose.

There are, of course, great tragedies, unforeseen accidents, and calamities. Someone is struck down by the ubiquitous tide of events, and through no fault of his own is unable to complete his life satisfactorily. Thus luck plays a key role in life: being in the right place at the right time, or being absent from the wrong place at the wrong time. But still, what happens to us depends on what we do, how we respond to challenges, whether we deal with them wisely, how we plan our lives, the choices we make, the people we relate to, our interests and activities, our occupations and careers, how we adapt and persist in spite of adversity, and how we respond to new opportunities.

Some of the classical religious models, I submit, are in a profound sense antihuman and the source of deep-seated misery and unhappiness. I am referring to those systems of morality that preach withdrawal from this world, such as some forms of Buddhism, which advocate the extinction of desire in order to achieve a state of quiescent Nirvana, or some aspects of Christianity, which emphasize salvation in the next life. The Promethean ideal is to challenge the gods and the fates, to adopt the outgoing posture, to dazzle our own world with achievement. Living outside the Garden of Eden, having eaten the forbidden fruit, we need the courage to persist despite adversity. That is what human culture is about; it is the product of our hopes and inspirations, of our imagination and resourcefulness, and of our determination to fulfill our highest visions. The sum and substance of the creative life is expressed in the heroic virtues: the unwillingness to accept defeat, and the determination to create a new world in which we realize our aspirations.

The key to the life of excellence is not found by simply satisfying our needs, or even in fulfilling our nature, but in exceeding it by leaping forward and performing challenging deeds. Ethical nobility best exemplifies itself by taking the first step into the unknown when all others fear to do so, by lighting a candle instead of suffering the darkness, and by seeking to reach new horizons for ourselves. A creative person is capable of *existential* choice, is willing to master his or her fate as far as possible, to dream of new frontiers, and to expend the effort to bring all of this into being. The creative person is not fixated on the past nor is he overwhelmed by the present moment, but instead he focuses his energies on attaining his future. He does not bask in Being nor is he mired in Nothingness, but he is eager to enter into the exultant process of Becoming, for that is the dynamic key to life.

In writing these lines, I am not unaware of the possibility for some skepticism, for I have described a style of life that has been emphasized in certain cultures but not in all. It is expressed in contemporary American and European life, where creative scientists, artists, entrepreneurial builders, and high achievers are praised. But not all cultures have focused on this; some have sought other ideals, such as religious quietude or spiritual release. Is what I am presenting universal in the sense that it expresses a common human capacity, no matter what the culture? Not all individuals in all careers are capable of high achievement. Yet I say it applies to everyone. Would it apply to the computer typesetter, farm laborer, or factory worker, who has a job to do that leaves little room for creativity? Some individuals seem to exult in the adventurous life of challenge, while others would prefer comfort and security. Is the ideal I have presented only available to a creative elite?

These objections are worrisome, for, if true, they would mean that the exuberant life is an expression of my own personal predilections (or even physical makeup), and though I may find such a life exciting and ennobling, others may find it stressful and tiring. Is there any objective justification for it, or is it simply a matter of taste? Some of these criticisms appear to have merit. Perhaps I am only talking to those individuals who have a Promethean temper and who can find grandeur in a life of risk-taking and exertion. Yet, in support of my argument, I submit that if one scans the entire human drama, one finds that creativity plays the key role as the mainspring of civilization, and that each person can contribute to creative development, no matter how modestly. It is the creative urge that marks the indomitable human spirit, the fact that men and women are not content to remain in a state of repose but can strive to master events and turn them to advantage. The human animal is a builder and a doer, and is by its very nature creative. I readily concede the need for order and harmony, for savoring the immediacies of experience, and for times of release and relaxation from the strenuous life. Nonetheless, creative activity and the achievement motive are deep impulses within the human species, the sources of greatness and inspiration, which enable us to transcend the limits of our nature and to build culture. Many theists war against such impulses; they wish to save us from the ambiguities and challenges of living by postulating an eternal life of blessedness. But insofar as they try to deny the creative adventure they are antihuman and the enemies of human realization.

EXCELSIOR

Can I be more precise? What constitutes ethical excellence? It is not simply a life of pleasure or enjoyment but one of creative achievement. Is it possible to delineate the qualities and characteristics that such a life of excellence entails? Perhaps the term *excelsior* best describes this state of creative fulfillment. No one can attain perfection, and yet there are degrees of magnificence that each and every person may discover and express. I shall adopt *excelsior* to mean a concrete, empirical state, one that can be achieved here and now. One does not have to wait for nirvana or salvation in the next world.

First, we may distinguish those states of excellence that apply to the individual as he seeks personal realization and exuberant achievement. Second, there are excellences that apply to the individual as he relates to other human beings within the community, for no one can fully achieve a state of excelsior without sharing values. I will deal with this in part III.

I. Excellence Primarily in Regard to Oneself

1. *Autonomy.* Among the highest human excellences is a person's ability to take control of his own life. This means the willingness to accept responsibility for his own future and the recognition that it is the person who will

ultimately decide how he wants to live and what he wants to become. This is not to deny that by living in communities we make cooperative decisions, but since we have only one life to live, we should not waste it by refusing to make our own choices or by forfeiting that opportunity and allowing others to choose for us. The autonomous person thus has some sense of his own independence. Such a person is self-directed and self-governing. His autonomy is related to the affirmation of his freedom.

Can one control one's own destiny? Can one change or redirect events? Is one so structured by impersonal forces that one can do nothing other than submit to them? The great failure in life is an individual's acquiescence to fate, the willingness to escape from freedom, and the refusal to make choices about one's own vital interests. Theists demean human power when they maintain that we are nothing in ourselves but are dependent upon God at every turn. They insist that we can do nothing outside of God's dictates. We cannot overcome the tragic character of the human condition; the only solution is divine salvation.

The humanist differs with this pessimistic appraisal and psychological retreat by providing a positive alternative. We can cope with the problems of living. But we need to deal realistically with the world as we find it and not turn to a mythological deity for help. Only by extending our best efforts can we hope to overcome adversity, conflict, tragedy. We need to be willing to do what is necessary to understand the processes of nature and to seek to redirect them for our own purposes. If we are to succeed, we need to have some confidence that we can make a difference, that our activities will be effective, and that at least we will try.

Thus autonomy is personal freedom extended to control the events that impinge on our lives. I am not talking about our ability to influence other people or society at large, but to control our own private life and the acceptance of this as an ongoing project. One must think: I am at the center of choice and decision, and I must decide what I wish to do with my life. I will make my views known, and when possible I will attempt to act upon them. This involves courage, audacity, and verve.

The opposite of this attitude is conformity, withdrawal, and in its extreme, fear and trembling. Here one is defeated before one begins. A person feels that there is nothing that he can do except submit to Fate and the Furies. Yet a person with an autonomous, self-affirming, assertive outlook refuses to give in without a fight. The autonomous person has pluck, energy, and some strength of will, which enables him to forbear and to prevail.

Autonomy is not antisocial; indeed, the open, democratic society encourages the growth of autonomous persons. The best society is one in which people are willing to accept some responsibility for themselves and to behave intelligently in making their choices. Autonomy does not mean that I may not work in concert with my wife or husband, sister or brother, mother or father, friend, colleague, or fellow citizen. Insofar as I am autonomous, I can respect other persons as equally entitled to autonomy over their lives.

2. *Intelligence.* Classical philosophers have emphasized the essential role that reason plays in the good life. In doing so, they have perhaps underestimated the significance of the conative and passionate dimensions of human experience. Aristotle delineated five intellectual virtues that he thought contributed to rational excellence: philosophical wisdom, scientific demonstration, intuition, art, and practical wisdom. Our intellectual abilities are far more complex and extensive than that. I have in my book *The Transcendental Temptation* catalogued twenty-one such intellectual qualities, including everything from abstract intelligence and logical ability on the one hand, to technical skill, artistic virtuosity, and mechanical dexterity on the other.

Aristotle perceptively recognized the significance of practical wisdom in making ethical choices. One can possess high intellectual skills and manifest significant intellectual attainment in one area and lack it in others. It is difficult to find one person possessing all the intellectual talents. From the standpoint of the ethical life, however, the most important quality is that of practical critical intelligence. Common sense, or native understanding, enables us to cope with the dilemmas encountered in life and to make sensible choices. I call this *good judgment*, the ability to evaluate alternatives and make intelligent decisions.

Whether this ability is a gift of the gods (that is, genetic) or a product of experience, capable of being cultivated by education and training, has been debated by philosophers. Why are some people able to hit the bull's-eye, as it were, and to know the best thing to do in a situation, whereas others are *taugenichts* (good-for-nothings), poor fools constantly embroiled in disasters and unable to make wise choices? Practical wisdom is probably a result of both talent and training; fortunately we can learn to improve our capacity to engage in critical thinking and apply it to ordinary life. What I have in mind here is *prudential* intelligence, that is, the ability to make plans, fulfill projects, and reach decisions after a deliberative process. This includes an estimation on our part of the costs and consequences of alternative actions. Cognition becomes constitutive of the process of choosing. The ethics of excellence depends upon our ability to make *informed* judgments based upon the knowledge of good and evil.

We had better be honest about this excellence. No one is perfect, and even the most rational person may at times succumb to passion. It is surely appropriate to fall in love, cheer the home team, or enjoy oneself at a banquet. Intelligence provides an ideal model, a comparative method for evaluating values and principles and balancing competing claims within a situation. Critical ethical intelligence is not purely formal or abstract. Its content is concrete: one should not counter reason against desire. It is not a question of cognition mastering or dominating desires, as the ancient Stoics would have it, for all motivation involves our wants and is deeply biopsychological in content. Our motives, fused with desires and reasons, stimulate us to action, not to thought alone. All that awareness can do is bring about an equilibrium between the various phases of our psychological impulses. Intelligence itself is a biological state. It is not an interloper; it is an intimate part of our entire physiological makeup, though only one ingredient in the preferential process of valuing. Nonetheless, we may say that we ought to prize intelligence as an excellence, for insofar as it can play a causative role in helping to modify intentions and interests, it can contribute to a better life. It is essential, for it is the fullest and the most complete expression of what we are as human beings.

Intellectual activities are a deep source of enjoyment and enrichment. This is surely the case with pure research, the quest for scientific explanations of how nature operates, historical investigations, philosophical understanding, and so on. Many individuals have dedicated their lives to intellectual pursuits and have discovered the intense satisfaction they can afford. Aristotle recognized that one needs some measure of leisure in order to pursue the life of the mind. Every man and woman is capable of some degree of intellectual activity, whether it is going to school, reading books, listening to lectures, or trying to discover something for themselves. There is a fascination in attempting to solve problems and puzzles; some of the most challenging games test our mettle as we become engrossed in their solutions. Humans are curious animals and we wish to know. Some people are so eager to be well-informed that they wish to learn everything they can about a certain subject. They may travel or read widely; they may wish to meet new people or go to exhibitions or lectures. This expression of our intellectual interests points to the fact that we place a high value on knowledge, both for its value in our lives and as a source of enjoyment.

3. *Self-discipline.* This is an important virtue to develop. It is related to intelligence and good judgment, but it goes beyond them. It applies to the life of desire and passion. Unless one can control one's emotions and direct one's efforts to constructive purposes, one's energies are apt to be squandered and dissipated in unproductive and self-defeating activities. One is in danger of being obsessed with a given pursuit, like the food addict, who eats to exhaustion, or the nymphomaniac, whose desire for sex is uncontrollable. The habit of self-discipline needs to be cultivated by education and training. Once achieved, moderation is used in satisfying one's desires. Self-discipline also enables a person to channel his efforts creatively in order to achieve his purposes in life. Discipline draws upon intelligence and practical wisdom. It fuses thought and desire. More than a cognitive state, it applies to the character of the whole person. It involves strength of will and the determination to persevere.

The undisciplined person is prey to every haphazard whim and fancy; his lusts and cravings dominate him. One may be overwhelmed by desires for sex, food, drink, drugs, or trivial entertainment, to which one may give in with abandon. Self-restraint is an essential guide for mature individuals, who are able to resist the lure of momentary temptations for long-range goals. It may entail some measure of stoic resignation, but it also involves the ability to face adversity and the determination to overcome challenges. This does not mean that a person does not enjoy life or ever give in to desires. Rather, he seeks to balance the various desires and decide which ones will be fulfilled. To lead an effective life, one needs to guide and control external events, but also to learn how to master and control one's inner drives so that they do not dominate.

4. *Self-respect.* The ethics of excellence involves the development of a decent respect for oneself. We are constantly being told that we ought to respect other human beings, our elders, the law, and those dependent upon us. This may be well and good, but in the process some individuals forget that they are entitled to the same kind of care and consideration they confer on others.

The focus on self-respect can become exaggerated if an individual develops an overinflated sense of his own worth. These are the egotists and egoists. I am not talking about them, for their self-concern has been inflated beyond reasonable measure, and society has a right to complain about this and guard against them. These individuals often behave in an infantile fashion, which may lead to megalomania and self-glorification.

Contrasted with this state is absence of self-esteem and an impoverished sense of identity. Having been beaten down by others, perhaps overcriticized by censorious parents or teachers, a person may rebel and flout even the most reasonable demands of society, or, on the contrary, one may withdraw, lacking any sense of independence. Such a person simply conforms to what is expected. I find that a deep and abiding concern of college students is whether their talents compare favorably with those of their peers. Poor or average grades or parental disapproval can arouse great anxiety. The students have an underlying fear that they may not succeed in life.

Some individuals, lacking self-confidence, give up early. Unfortunately, such individuals often find it difficult to live fully, because they lack minimal respect for themselves, their talents and abilities, and what they can achieve or attain. Those who lack self-assurance may constantly need to prove themselves, and so they wear themselves out in fruitless efforts to seek approval in the eyes of others, and they abandon what they would like to do in life. The opposite of self-respect is self-hatred. For some individuals self-hatred can so corrode their sense of worth that they constantly criticize themselves for failures or defeats— or even for their inability to succeed gloriously. They may be perfectionists, never content with the tasks they have chosen or their level of accomplishment. They have no inner peace. They may even give up in quiet desperation, seeking to find some quiet haven that will afford them warmth and security. Despite the lip service paid in our culture to openness, tolerance of differences, and emphasis on individuality, there is an appalling pressure to conform, which is not conducive to self-respect.

No one can succeed in everything he undertakes in life. One tries one's best, hoping to learn from defeats. But the person who lacks self-respect can never accept failure: he turns against himself. Although he can make allowances for those who fail, he will not do so for himself. He may love others, but he doesn't love himself. Christianity certainly helps to foster this self-guilt by advocating values that are completely unobtainable on earth, such as perfect virtue, and then castigating its adherents for not obtaining them.

The humanist responds to the perfectionist: you are the only person you have to live with all your life, from the beginning to the end. Hence, you might as well come to terms with yourself, enjoy yourself, and think well of yourself. Although hopefully you can recognize your virtues and limitations, you may need to make some allowances. This doesn't mean that you are not accountable for your errors of omission and commission, or that you should not constantly strive to improve.

Some self-respect is necessary for building one's identity and for expanding one's powers of autonomy and independence. Pride in oneself is not a sin. Self-effacing humility is not an appropriate response for a free, autonomous person capable of some action in the world and desirous of deserved respect.

5. *Creativity.* The creative person exemplifies the most eloquent expression of human freedom: the capacity for originality. Creativity is intimately related to autonomy and self-respect, for the independent person has some sense of his own power. He does not submit to the obstacles encountered in nature, but is able to invent or to bring into being something new. One not only can apprehend new possibilities but also bring them to fruition.

Creativity has many different facets. One often thinks of the creative scientist on the frontiers of knowledge who makes some monumental discovery or proposes some new and daring theory. Creativity is also the driving force of the great artist or sculptor, who is able to take the raw materials of nature and impose new forms that fulfill his creative vision. The poet, novelist, and composer, using the materials of language or harmony, weaves captivating works of art that inspire us. Similarly, the inventor or engineer creates a new instrument, machine, or device. Statesmen who draft constitutions, builders of new industries, and explorers of uncharted seas, continents, or galaxies all express similar creative impulses. The designation *creative*, I reiterate, should not be confined to exceptional geniuses, for it applies to ordinary people who display talent for innovative behavior.

In one sense, all organic life has creative dimensions. The first union and fertilization of egg and sperm and the processes of creative growth that flow from it illustrate the creative processes intrinsic to organic matter. Wherever there is learning and adaptation by life-forms to environmental problems, there is some degree of creativity.

Creativity is one of the defining characteristics of the human species. No one is entirely without it, for it is the necessary means by which we overcome adversity and adapt or respond to stimuli in the environment. There are, however, degrees of creativity; perhaps it best manifests itself in teleonomic activities consciously directed. Creativity involves both insight and imagination. It appears wherever thought strives to solve problems by introducing alternative means, and manifests itself wherever we seek to combine old materials in new ways. It is the key stimulus to culture building. Insofar as each person is unique, some creativity is expressed in idiosyncratic behavior and in how one learns to cope with and adapt to the world on the everyday, pedestrian level.

There are degrees of excellence attached to creativity. Some persons are more adept than others at discovering new possibilities. They are overflowing with new ideas; they have fertile imaginations. Unfortunately, someone can be a creative genius in one field of endeavor, or show enormous talent and achievement at one time, yet lack the creative outlook outside his field or for the remainder of his life. Thus we should focus not on narrow creativity in a specific area but on the creative life in general, which is approached adventurously and openly.

The uncreative person tends to be a conformist, prone to follow rituals or be obsessive in observing rules. A creature of habit, he is unwilling or unable to try something new, resisting change or novelty. The creative person, on the contrary, is a fountain of ingenious ideas. He is fruitful, constantly bubbling over with new thoughts, schemes, and plans. A problem with one form of creativity is that people have brainstorms but end up as visionary dreamers who never implement their ideas. An effective creative person is one who can follow through. He is not simply an ideas person but a doer, able to realize his dreams. To be effective, a person's ideas must be grounded in reality. The great creators of history have not simply had random flashes of insight, but have been able to express them, give them form, and ground them in reality. They do not simply conceive or apprehend in their inner souls alone, but can give birth to their offspring. Creativity thus involves a generative process of organization and realization. Many creative persons are not on the frontiers of knowledge, nor do they contribute to civilization's advance. They may not be gifted with special talents, yet in their chosen areas they are creative: finding and following new recipes, redecorating a room, planting a garden, repairing the roof, breeding horses, or teaching a course. I am talking not about pseudo- or pop creativity, which follows the whims of fashion, but about genuine creative expression. The creative person has some confidence in his powers and willingly meets the challenges of life with self-assurance and zest.

Creativity ought to be encouraged in the young and nourished and cultivated throughout life. Unfortunately it has its enemies. Creative persons often arouse envy and jealousy, and because they are at times unpredictable, they may be difficult to live with. If allowed to vent all their enthusiasms, they can be exhausting to those around them.

From society's standpoint, the most important use of creativity is its application to work. Some forms of work are drudgery. The creative person is able to make his work exciting. One's work is not separate and distinct from the person, but flows forth as an expression of one's own interests. Drudgery most likely ensues when means are disconnected from ends and one is given orders to fulfill that hold no interest. A slave or peon has no mind of his own, or at least is not permitted to introduce his own purposes and fulfill them. His labor is thus humdrum, rote, or mechanical. Creative activities thrive best in a free environment, where people's efforts are directed toward their own goals. Given the division of labor, it is often difficult to permit creative persons free rein to luxuriate in their inspirations. One needs to work to make a living, and this work may be boring, yet it needs to be done. That is why developing opportunities for creativity in the marketplace is important. But if this is not entirely feasible, then the expression of creativity in leisure time becomes all the more important for the ordinary person. A creative person, in any case, is resourceful, in that he can deal with life's problems, using both imagination and effort to achieve what he wishes.

6. *Motivation*. Some individuals are highly motivated. They are always ready to undertake projects without wasting time or engaging in delaying tactics. They are resourceful in both ideas and deeds. Other individuals are lazy and ineffective. They never seem to have sufficient energy or interest in doing something, but get by with a minimum of effort. They have low levels of motivation and hence low levels of activity. They do not wish to stand out. They would much rather rest quietly in a garden than weed and plant it or venture outside of it. They seem to withdraw from the hustle and bustle of living.

Motivated people, on the other hand, are self-directed. They have courage, stamina, and the will to do something, and are not loath to dirty their hands and do the things necessary to get the job done. There is an old saying: "If you want something done, ask a busy person." A lazy person never succeeds because he lacks the determination and drive to do so.

There is an excellence that characterizes well-motivated individuals. They are able to gather together the things they need in order to attain the goals they appropriate as their own. They have autonomy, self-discipline, self-respect, and a capacity for creative, inventive, and adaptive response. But they also have the ability to fulfill their goals, whatever they are. Individuals often shy away from tasks they do not like or that are given to them by others. They are only happy when they are doing what they want to do. Unfortunately, some people are limited by narrow horizons and restricted interests. They demonstrate, not only at work but even at play, that they have impoverished imaginations. Low levels of motivation characterize them. They never seem to find themselves. Their drives are wanting. They never develop a career—for them a job is a job, not a *profession*.

Well-motivated persons *profess* a specialty or expertise and are committed to it. They are achievement oriented. But more, they find some pride and satisfaction in their accomplishments. Underachievers are bankrupt as persons. They are easily bored, which means that they are boring. Their reactions are infantile, for their only interest seems to be "having a good time." Unless they can point to some contribution they have made to their own lives, some deeds or accomplishments that are creative and rewarding, they are underdeveloped and will clearly have a lessened sense of self-respect. Well-motivated persons are dependable, for you can count on them to get something done. Unmotivated persons are given to sloth and indecision. In extreme cases, they may literally end up as bums.

7. *Affirmation.* Living the full life depends, to a great extent, on a positive outlook. This means having some degree of optimism, believing that life can be good and bountiful, that it can be ameliorated and improved. Opposed to this outlook is negativism, pessimism, and a tragic sense that life is difficult, that things cannot be changed and will only get worse. There always seem to be impossible Bastilles to storm. This attitude is defeatist and depressive.

Affirmative persons take life as a challenge. They look upon it as an opportunity. They wish to do many things and to experience widely. Exuberant happiness cannot be achieved without some sense of one's own power and the ability to solve one's problems. The attitudes of affirmative people are apt to be cheerful ones, for these people look to the future with high expectations. Their attitudes also express humor, laughter, and an appreciation for fun. If we have self-respect and some creativity and are well motivated, then our outreach is ongoing and there is a willingness to explore, experiment, innovate. Optimists tend to look at the positive side: they focus on the good in people, not on their faults. Living is exciting; horizons are unlimited; there are not enough hours in the day to do all the things they want to do.

Pessimists are forever focused upon the tragic aspects of life. They worry about, without seeing solutions to, the problems of the world—hunger, suffering, pain, and sorrow. They are timid and fearful of what people will say about them. Thus they are permeated by negativity, paralyzed by fear, and more apt to retreat than to advance.

Affirmative, outgoing, optimistic, buoyant people find life to be joyful. There are so many wonderful things to accomplish, so many future achievements that beckon. Life is full of great promises and opportunities: whatever ills encountered now can be improved upon and ameliorated. Optimists are never bogged down by feelings of impotence, but instead have a sense that human effort can be effective, that we can make this a better world in which to live. A new turn of events is taken as a propitious opportunity, a bright prospect for success. Optimists willingly meet new challenges with anticipation and enthusiasm. They are full of the will to live, to overcome, and to attain new heights of creative enjoyment.

8. *Health.* High on the scale of excellence, perhaps even first, is the realization of personal good health. Perhaps it is a truism to emphasize health (though philosophers have often overlooked it), but any realistic view of happiness must take health as its starting point. If one is to live and live well, one

must be in reasonably good health. If one is grossly handicapped, sick, or in constant pain, one may not be able to function well nor be able to accomplish all that one wishes. Yet many individuals have been able to live significant lives in spite of debilitating pain or physical handicaps. In situations of poor health, people should attempt to do the best they are capable of doing. It is interesting to note that many professed humanists lived long and comparatively healthy lives. What's more, they remained active until their deaths. John Dewey pursued a vigorous career until the age of ninety-three, and Bertrand Russell, who died at ninety-seven, was arrested for demonstrating against the atom bomb when he was in his nineties!

There are important principles we should follow if we wish to live healthy lives. It is particularly essential that health education be an important part of our upbringing and that children should learn from the earliest age about their bodies. The widest dissemination of scientific knowledge should be readily available. This means that there should be adequate information about (1) proper nutrition; (2) the importance of daily exercise in maintaining physical and mental fitness; (3) ways of avoiding unnecessary stress and attaining periods of relaxation and rest; and (4) exercising moderation in the life of pleasure. All of this is within the range of preventive medicine. For the humanist, the neglect or abuse of the body is immoral, particularly by those who seek the idle pleasures of hedonism or who waste their talents in indolence and sloth. This means that drug addiction or gluttony in food or drink—growing obese or eating or drinking to reduce one's anxieties—are also to be condemned.

The test of whether an action is good or bad lies in its consequences. The emphasis in medical science has been on diagnosing and treating illnesses once they occur, and though this is vital, we also need to understand how to avoid risks to health and prevent illness. We now know that the excessive intake of alcohol, cholesterol, or cigarette smoke is dangerous, and only a foolish person ignores the warnings. In any case, every individual is responsible for his own health. The body is the most important possession that we have, and it is our responsibility to see not only that it is not abused and that preventive measures are observed but also that proper care is taken once an illness develops.

The achievement of good health is not simply physical or biological; it involves an important psychological dimension. Psychiatric disorders are the bane of human existence, the source of anxiety and depression, misery and unhappiness. The treatment of the whole person is essential: no doubt many mental illnesses have their origins in biochemical malfunctioning. Psychiatry needs to seek the causes of manic depression, schizophrenia, and other debilitating illnesses. Which of the various methods of drugs or psychotherapy are most effective in treating mental or emotional disturbances remains to be determined. Severe cases of psychosis may have a biochemical basis, so the sick individual may not be helped much by counseling, although his family may benefit from it. Such illnesses are tragic in their destructiveness, rendering the victim unable to cope by simple acts of willpower.

The fulfillment of a person's psychosexual needs seems to be an important factor in health. Does the satisfaction of libido fantasies and the avoidance of repression enhance a person's ability to enjoy life? The answer appears to be yes, though of course within reason. It is difficult to discover a single model of sexual realization, for tastes and enjoyments are wide-ranging. Different individuals are "turned on" by different fantasies. What appears odd or vulgar to one person might be exciting to the next. Richard von Krafft-Ebing, who in the late nineteenth century catalogued "deviant sexual practices," devoted an entire chapter to foot fetishes. Without delving into intricate questions here, I merely wish to state that the capacity to satisfy the sexual libido, culminating in orgasmic release, seems to be an important contributing factor to health.

9. *Joie de vivre.* The French terms *joie de vivre* and *bon vivant* refer to joyful living. All work and no play is not the be-all and end-all of life. The affirmative outlook, important as it is, focuses primarily on the future. Yet the present moment is intrinsically worthwhile, and we need to appreciate fully the immediacies. The *capacity* for enjoying life is an important excellence; it manifests itself in the hedonic and the erotic. The ability to enjoy pleasure without excessive guilt or the sense that it is evil is a positive virtue. I am thinking primarily of those pleasures in personal life, innocent and robust, that do not injure or harm others.

Many moralists have exiled hedonism, eroticism, and the *bon vivant* from their moral universes. Theists have railed against the body and condemned sexual pleasures. In so doing, they betray their own *hedonic* or *erotic phobia*, which expresses a disease of the soul. Various terms describe the failure to appreciate hedonism: asceticism, self-denial, repression. The inability to savor the delicacies of life is a corroding psychological malady and can be a source of neurosis and misery.

There is a wide range of pleasures that we should enjoy as part of healthy living. First are those that involve the satisfaction of our basic urges and needs: food, drink, sex. Built on these are the developed pleasures of moral, altruistic, intellectual, aesthetic, and even spiritual joys. A person with *joie de vivre* can find pleasure in a wide range of activities. He can enjoy a feast, drink heartily, make love, read books, travel, listen to music, work for a cause, enjoy sports, poetry, the arts—indeed, experience everything that is worthwhile.

However, excessive concentration upon hedonistic delights, abstracted from the activities of life and to the detriment of other excellences, is not conducive to the well-lived life. The glutton, fleshpot, drug addict, or libertine mistakenly focuses on the immediacies of enjoyment as the sole end of life. Fixation on the hedonic-erotic is infantile and destructive to the total personality, especially insofar as it dominates other creative activities. The hedonist is the prisoner of his own pleasure-seeking desires; there is an inner tyranny at work.

One must steer a course between two extremes: on the one hand, theistic morality, which rails against the body and makes war on natural enjoyments, and on the other hand, amoral hedonism, which abandons all self-discipline and allows us to become prey to our cravings. One cannot fulfill all of one's fantasies. Self-restraint and moderation are signs of personal maturity. Still, the satisfaction of one's sexual needs must be rated high on the scale of values, and this means some orgasmic pleasure and sexual release. Masturbation is a common method of sexual enjoyment. Kissing, petting, sexual foreplay, and sexual intercourse involve the fullest expression of the libido, for these relate to other persons.

No doubt the strength of sexual passion is connected to the need of the species to reproduce itself. But in human affairs, reproduction is no longer the primary reason for sex; the desires to achieve pleasurable orgasm and to enhance love and intimacy are the chief motives. These matters become enormously complicated, given the wide range of pleasurable activities people seek; thus what is "normal" or "natural" is not easily determined. Romantic love is no doubt among the highest of human pleasures. Infantile forms of love wish to possess or even use the other person as a source of sexual gratification. The intensity of psychosexual longing can drive men and women to madness and desperation—especially in the case of unrequited love (as in *Carmen*)—but also to the most rewarding forms of fulfillment. In one sense, an individual is never fully realized unless and until he or she is capable of achieving some kind of romantic attachment to another.

Are humans polygamous and is promiscuity to be accepted? Humankind has long since discovered that jealous rivalries for sexual partners could lead to constant warfare. The institution of marriage, a monogamous relationship, with divorce as a safety valve, is a sensible solution. Although sexual pleasure can be derived from the physical act itself, one soon discovers that some kind of emotional attachment provides the most enduring form of satisfaction, especially when it is based on sincerity and trust. Sexual enjoyment appears to be more complete when it is experienced in a loving relationship with another.

Love is twofold: first, it helps to actualize our deepest yearnings, needs, and desires, especially to be loved by another human being; and second, if we are able to love another person, we wish him or her to prosper on his or her own terms. There is a general concern for the good of the other person, not for the reflected glory that he or she brings. Mutual love is both sexual and altruistic.

10. *Aesthetic appreciation.* Included in our capacity to enjoy life fully is an appreciation for the finer things of life as perceived by the senses and enhanced by the intellect. The term *aesthetic* best describes these pleasures, which include the fine arts, poetry, drama, literature, and music. One's ability to appreciate great beauty enriches life. Unfortunately, some individuals never seem able to develop an understanding of the arts. They may be tone-deaf or color-blind or

uninterested, totally unable to enjoy classical music, art, literature, or the theater. The appreciation of aesthetic values is a product of education, and parents should expose their children to these values at relatively early ages.

Appreciation presupposes a kind of growth and development of the personality: one admires the natural beauty of a brilliant sunset or a beautiful woman, and this does not require training. But the highest reaches of the arts require some exertion. To learn how to read requires early effort, and what a great source of satisfaction and joy it is to the person who masters it.

One's aesthetic sensibilities need not be limited to the arts, for tastes can be cultivated in other areas—in fine delicacies that the gourmet appreciates, in exotic varieties of flowers, or in embellishments in fashion. The aesthetic touch can be added with finesse and expertise to almost any field of human interest. The connoisseur of fine wine is able to discern subtleties that bring pleasure to his sense of taste. A simple farmer may not be able to tell the difference between a chablis and a bordeaux, but he may have a subtle and distinctive appreciation for breeding blue-ribbon horses or show dogs.

7

MEANING AND TRANSCENDENCE

THE VALUE OF LIFE: THINGS LEFT UNSAID

All living beings undergo continuous processes of replenishment and renewal. Within each species is the constant striving to persist and to reproduce its own kind, in spite of the surrounding forces in the environment that tend to denude or destroy it. All forms of animal life seek food in order to survive and procreate—though most apparently are unaware of the tentativeness of their existence. In the end nature prevails and every single representative is vanquished: the leaf withers and the lilac dies; the sapling that grows into the magnificent elm eventually rots and decays; the young stallion is reduced to a decrepit horse.

And what of human personality? We are creatures of intelligence and imagination. We are aware that life is finite. We see that the infant, the child, the young person, and the mature adult, all full of possibility and power at one time, eventually grow old and die. Pubescence, adolescence, and senescence are all inevitable phases of life. Human beings thus have knowledge of their inexorable demises, and also of the tragic character implicit in the human condition. Life is full of danger: as soon as one is born, one is old enough to die. There is the sudden accident or the incurable disease, which can overtake friend and foe alike. These bitter pills are difficult to swallow. Most people will not or cannot in the final summing up accept their ultimate demise. Out of their anxieties about it grows the quest for transcendence and religious faith.

That life is or can be good and bountiful, full of significance and pregnant with enjoyment and adventure, is also apparent to those who have the courage to overcome the fear of death and achieve something in the world. Modern civilization, education, science, and technology have helped us to minimize disease and extend the years of a life of rich enjoyment and harvest, without worrying about our ultimate destiny or God's plans for us. Yet lurking in the background of the consciousness of every person is always the potential for despair, the ultimate dread of one's

53

own death. No one can escape it: we are all condemned to die at some time, no matter how we may strive to stave it off.

My father was struck down at fifty-nine of a heart attack, in the prime of life, but he told us at his bedside that he knew he was dying. He kissed my mother and said that his life in summation was happy. My mother, always ebullient, loquacious, beaming with life, on her deathbed at ninety-five told us that she did not want to die. She refused to accept her approaching end with equanimity. Her mother, at eighty-three, suddenly gasped her last breath in her daughter's arms and was dead without warning before she knew what happened. Her youngest daughter died of a terrible cancer at the age of fifty. Regardless of how we feel about death, each of us too will someday reach, even after a life of fullness and exuberance, a point of no return.

Let us reflect on the human situation: all of our plans will fail in the long run, if not in the short. The homes we have built and lovingly furnished, the loves we have enjoyed, the careers we have dedicated ourselves to will all disappear in time. The monuments we have erected to memorialize our aspirations and achievements, if we are fortunate, may last a few hundred years, perhaps a millennium or two or three—like the stark and splendid ruins of Rome and Greece, Egypt and Judaea, India and Peru, which have been recovered and treasured by later civilizations. But all the works of human beings disappear and are forgotten in short order. In the immediate future the beautiful clothing that we adorn ourselves with, eventually even our cherished children and grandchildren, and all of our possessions will be dissipated. Many of our poems and books, our paintings and statues, will be forgotten, buried on some library shelf or in a museum, read or seen by some future scholars curious about the past, and eventually eaten by worms and molds or perhaps consumed by fire. Even the things that we prize the most—human intelligence and love, democratic values, the quest for truth—will in time be replaced by unknown values and institutions—if the human species survives, and even that is uncertain. Were we to compile a pessimist's handbook, we could easily fill it to overflowing with notations of false hopes and lost dreams, a catalogue of human suffering and pain, of ignominious conflict, betrayal, and defeat throughout the ages.

I am by nature an optimist. Were I to take an inventory of the sum of goods in human life, they would far outweigh the banalities of evil. I have outdone the pessimist by cataloguing laughter and joy, devotion and sympathy, discovery and creativity, excellence and grandeur. The marks made upon the world by every person and by the race in general are impressive. How wonderful it has all been. The cynic points to Caligula, Attila, Cesare Borgia, Beria, or Himmler with horror and disgust; but I would counter with Pericles, Aristotle, da Vinci, Einstein, Beethoven, Mark Twain, Margaret Sanger, and Madame Curie. The nihilist points to duplicity and cruelty in the world; I am impressed by the sympathy, honesty, and kindness that are manifested. The negativist reminds us of ignorance and stupidity; I, of the continued growth of human knowledge and understanding. The naysayer emphasizes the failures and defeats; I, the successes and victories in all their glory.

The question can be raised: How shall we evaluate a human life and its achievements—in the long or the short run? What is the measure of value, the scale of hope? From one's immediate world there may be boundless opportunities. Look at the things that one can do, if social conditions permit a measure of freedom and if one has developed the creative verve: one can marry, raise a family, follow an occupation or career, forge a road, cure a malady, innovate a method, form an association, discover a new truth, write an essay, construct a space vehicle. All are within one's ken and scope, and one can see a beginning, a middle, and an end. One can bring to fruition the things one may want, if not in one's lifetime, then in the lifetimes of those who follow and their children's children. France, the United States, Russia, China, and the New Zion are social entities that human beings have created. The despairing person groans that they have disappeared or will disappear *in the end*, in the long run, if not today or tomorrow, then ultimately. He complains about the ultimate injustice of our finitude. One may know that that is true and even come to accept it. But we are alive today, and we have our dreams and hopes, and the immediacies of experience and achievement can be enormously interesting, exciting, satisfying, and fulfilling.

Can we enjoy ourselves today and tomorrow without worrying about the distant future? No, says the nihilist. He is unable to live in this world; he is fixated and troubled by its ultimate disappearance. "How can life have meaning if it will all end?" he complains. Out of this grows a belief in immortality and ultimate survival.

"Why not make the most out of this life, if that is all we have?" I respond. Indeed, this life can be full of happiness and meaning. We can make a comprehensive list of all the goods and bads and of all the values and nonvalues. For every evil that the pessimist antihumanist presents, I can counter with a virtue; for every loss, a gain. It all depends on one's focus. A person's world may be full of the immediacy of living in the present, and that is what he may find rich and vital. The life world involves one's yesteryears. This includes a human being's own small world—the memories of one's parents, relatives, colleagues, friends. It also includes the history of one's society and culture—as memorialized in the great institutions and traditions that have remained. But more, one's life world shares the recorded histories of past civilizations and the memories of great minds, artists, geniuses, and heroes, as bequeathed to us in their writings and works that remain. There is also the residue of things far past, which, uncovered by science, tell of the evolution of the human species, as the strata of earth and rock dug up reveal more of our history and that of other forms of life. It also encompasses the physical universe, extending back billions of years. The eye of the cosmos unfolds through countless light-years in the telescope of the astronomer: the formation of the rings of Saturn and moons of

Jupiter, the birth and death of countless suns and galaxies. And what does our present include? Everything here and now on the planet and in the immense cosmos investigated by science. But what does the future hold? We can contemplate our own futures: tomorrow, next year, twenty years, or fifty. How far may we go? We can make plans, but we cannot foretell what will be—if anything—one century hence. Of this we may be fairly certain: the universe will continue to exist—though without us or our small influences affecting it very much.

Thus one can argue the case from two vantage points. First, there are the life goals or scene of action that an individual, his family, and culture experience, its dimensions of space-time, its phenomenological range in immediacy, memory, and anticipation. And this can be full of significance. Does life have ultimate meaning per se? No, not per se. It does, however, present us with innumerable opportunities. Meaning depends on what we give to it; it is identified with our goals and values, our plans and projects, whether or not we achieve them and find them interesting. There is the fountain of joyful existence, the mood of exhilaration and the satisfaction of creative adventure and achievement—within varying degrees, realism no doubt admonishes.

Millions of people, however, do not find life interesting, are in a quandary, and are overwhelmed by the problems and conflicts they encounter. Life apparently leaves them with a bad taste: it is ugly and boring, full of anguish and sorrow. They bemoan a cloudy day, complain about the humidity, rail against the past, are fearful of the future. The tragic dimension of life is no doubt exacerbated by those who suffer great loss or a severe accident. But nature is indifferent to our cares and longings. A raging fire or cyclone may indeed destroy everything we have built and love; and we are forced to submit to adversity. There is thus the desert of despair, the emptiness of lost zest, the collapse of meaning. In some social systems human beings are their own worst enemies, unable to live or breathe freely, imprisoned in the gulags of their souls.

Yet, within the life world we occupy, we are capable of intensity, enjoyment, and interest if we are able to express our proper freedom as independent, autonomous, and resourceful beings, and especially if we live in an open society that encourages free choice. The spark of the good life is creativity—not escape, retreat, or complaint—and the audacious expression of the will to live. *My will be done*, says the free person—not "thine." Yes, it is possible—comparatively and reasonably—in spite of the demands and obstacles presented by nature and society, to achieve the good life. I am referring not to a life of quiescent withdrawal or simple self-realization but to the active display of one's talents and powers and the expression of one's creative imagination. One may dig a deep well where none existed before, compose a lullaby, invent an ingenious tool, found a new society, teach a class, pick up and move to another area, succeed on the job or change it. It can be fun; no doubt there may be some sorrow and tears, but basically it may be worthwhile.

I am willing to argue the case with the naysayer on the level of the phenomenological, contextual life world. "What is the matter with you?" I may ask. "Are you sexually repressed? Then satisfy your libido. Are you tired and unhealthy? Then examine your nutrition and exercise. Do you hate your work? Change your career; go back to school. Is someone sick? Try to find a cure. Are you lonely? Find a lover or companion. Are you threatened by your neighbor? Form a peace pact or establish a police force. Are you troubled by injustice? Don't just sit there; help mitigate or stamp out evil. Enact new legislation. Come up with a viable solution." Human ills are remediable to some extent, given the opportunity, by the use of intelligence and the application of human power.

But it is the second vantage point that troubles so many: the argument from the *long* run. If I do not survive in the end, if I must die, and if everyone I know must also die—all of my friends and colleagues, even my children and their grandchildren—and if my beloved country or society must perish in the end, then is it *all* pointless? What does my life really mean then? Nothing at all? This quandary and the despair that such reflections can generate is no doubt the deepest source of the religious impulse, the transcendental yearning for something more. Can one extend one's present life world and those of one's loved ones and community indefinitely in some form throughout eternity? People ask in torment and dread, "Why is there not something more to my existence?"

My wife, who is French, sometimes raises these questions when we are alone in bed late at night. And I have heard others raise similar questions. At some point there is the recognition of one's finitude, as one gradually realizes that one is growing old and is not eternal. The lines on one's face and the sagging body point to the fact that one's powers are not eternal. Prayers to an absent deity will not solve the problem or save one's soul from extinction. They will not obviate the inevitable termination of one's life world. They merely express one's longings. They are private or communal soliloquies. There is no one hearing our prayers who can help us. Expressions of religious piety thus are catharses of the soul, confessing one's fears and symbolizing one's hopes. They are one-sided transactions. There is no one on the other side to hear our pleas and supplications.

WHY HAS SECULAR HUMANISM THUS FAR FAILED TO TAKE HOLD?

It is at this point that one may ask whether the primary reasons why thoroughly secular philosophies that accept human temporality have not succeeded better than they have are psychological and existential. Why do religious institutions, even the most blatantly fraudulent and immoral, persist in spite of the growth of science, near-universal education in advanced countries, the possibility of an end to poverty, and the untapping of years more of healthy living?

Is there something genetic and sociobiological in the human species? No doubt there are many powerful social causes to explain the persistence of religion: cultural lag, ethnicity and tradition, communications media that present religion as true and that go unchallenged, religious indoctrination and institutionalization, the union in some cultures of religion and state power, and in others with economic power.

If one looks back to the Enlightenment and the Age of Reason, we see that men and women dreamed of using science and education to achieve human progress. They believed that in time superstition would disappear. The philosophers of the eighteenth century deplored the ignorance and dogmatism around them, the sinfulness and hypocrisy of the clergy and the churches; they believed that reason, if applied, would overcome blind religious faith and superstitious credulity.

That this has not happened is all too apparent. For even highly educated men and women—doctors and lawyers as well as beggars and thieves—are wont to believe in salvation by some deity. The end of poverty, the overcoming of disease, and the attainment of affluent standards of living are no guarantee of liberation from this fixation. The churches and temples may wax and wane in influence and appeal, but they do not disappear. And new forms of transcendental religiosity are created overnight to replace those that weaken in their messages. Why does religious tradition have such a profound influence? Why does the weight of the past bear so heavily upon the present that even otherwise rational and skeptical persons find it difficult to resist its allure?

There is no confirming evidence for the existence of a God, and the so-called arguments to prove His reality are inconclusive. We have been through a protracted debate between philosophy and theology, science and religion. Philosophers have won each point of the debate in each battle. There is no conclusive evidence for a divine source or purpose for the universe and no proof of God's existence save our own wish fulfillment. Moreover, the major monotheistic religions—Christianity, Judaism, and Islam—all rest on myths of revelation. Yet the theologians appear to continue to win the wars. For each succeeding generation seems to be impervious to the victories of skeptics and the defeats of theologians in the past, and it invests its own meaning in the old religious forms and institutions or creates new and even more irrational ones. Why is this so? Why is the message of Christ risen, Mohammed as the prophet of God, Moses on Sinai, or extraterrestrial divinities and demons of the occult still persuasive for each generation anew?

Is it because these prophets promise that there is indeed *more* to this life as lived and endured in the phenomenological life context and in the universe? And if so, do many or most souls *need* something more? I reiterate my question: Is humanism forever condemned to be a minority point of view of a relatively limited number of skeptics, one that is unpalatable to the broad mass of humanity? Or are there other options?

THE QUEST FOR TRANSCENDENCE

Do human beings *need* to believe that there is something more, something that transcends this vale of expectant promises and ultimate defeat? This is the great challenge for the secular humanist, who is forever beset with extravagant claims of the supernatural, miraculous, mysterious, noumenal, or paranormal realm. Is what we encounter in our perceptions all that there is? Of course not, for we make inferences, develop hypotheses, uncover hidden causes. Knowledge is a product of observation (direct and indirect) and rational inference. Both experience and reason are drawn upon in ordinary life and in the sophisticated sciences to establish reliable knowledge.

We surely should not exclude—antecedent to inquiry—any claims to knowledge about nature or life, however radical they may at first appear. One cannot reject dogmatically new dimensions of experience or reality or refuse to investigate their authenticity. The history of science and philosophy is replete with unwarranted, a priori rejectionism. Yesterday's heretic may become today's hero, and today's martyr, tomorrow's savior. One must be open to the possibilities of the discovery of new truths and the nuances of fresh experiences.

The transcendent has had many synonyms. Philosophers such as Plato have sometimes used it to refer to "ultimate reality." Plato distinguished reality from the realm of appearances; sensations and observation only denoted the world of objects and particulars in flux. There was a deeper Truth, he said, which only reason and intuition could plumb: the world of universal ideas, in terms of which the contingent world of concrete fact is dependent. The world of Being remains sheltered to the senses, yet it subsists behind it and can be known only by dialectical investigation and reason. Kant referred to the *noumenal* so as to distinguish it from the *phenomenal*: the noumenal lies beyond the range of our phenomena; the phenomenal is knowable, and it obeys regularities and laws as structured by the Forms of Intuition and the Categories of the Understanding. Science is rooted in the phenomenal world, as ordered by the mind. But the "real" world is itself unintelligible to our understanding. We can only get a glimpse of the noumenal, perhaps in our moral life.

We are able to define and stabilize perceptions and ideas by language. Words clothe fleeting sensations, emotions, and thoughts, and give them form and structure. We are able to communicate to others the world we experience and interpret it by relating it to a common world of symbols. But language has many social functions. It enables us to interconnect symbols and to make assertions about the intersubjective world. What lies beyond the rubric of our syntax? Are we imprisoned within walls? Does the mystic intuition enable us to leap beyond the limits of linguistic discourse?

There is some ground for arguing that the world as we experience it and talk or write about it in language is not necessarily as it appears, and that there is something beyond, which the parameters of the human mind and language cannot presently comprehend or describe. The growth of human knowledge belies any conceit that pretends that what we know is fixed or has reached its final or ultimate formulations. For no sooner is a theory or hypothesis enunciated and maintained as true than its limitations may be seen, and newer, more comprehensive ones may emerge to replace it. Any effort to limit or fix the body of knowledge has thus far met with failure. On the other hand, we cannot thereby conclude that nothing we know is reliable or that the world as we view it in ordinary life and science is mere illusion and deception.

This apparently is the position of those who use the term *transcendence* with a supernatural and divine meaning, as it has been for many latter-day uses of the term *paranormal*. The term applies in opposition to two modes of knowing: (1) the appeal to evidence and the testimony of the senses and (2) the use of rational intelligence to develop theories and evaluate hypotheses. It also suggests that there are other ways of knowing—mystical, intuitive, and revelatory faith, all of which claim to give us a glimmer of the transcendent and allegedly supplement our use of experience and logic. Transcendental meditation, prayer, and faith states allegedly open up the possibilities of a new form of awareness. They supposedly bring us to the brink of a nonordinary reality. The same applies to the alleged world of extrasensory perception or psychic phenomena.

By using such techniques, the mystic or psychic claims to be put in touch with another realm that transcends the categories of everyday life, language, and science. This is termed the "higher realm" of being. It shows, the mystic claims, that there is indeed "something more" to life and reality and that this gives proper meaning and perspective to this life. It is the source and ultimate destiny of humans, especially in the long run, says the theist.

The questions then are clearly drawn. Is there a transcendent realm of being existing beyond this world? Is it unknowable to ordinary experience, logic, and science? Is it knowable *only* by the intensive use of methods of transcendental and mystical revelation, nonsensory perception and insight?

It is at this point that the scientific humanist and the mystic are at loggerheads; there are not only different theories of reality but also different methods of knowing. The basic questions posed here are: What can be known? Are there limits to human knowledge? Are things that are unknown indeed unknowable? If this is the case, we have two options. First, one may barter one's life to an unknown destiny, affirming that because of the limits of knowledge and the need for something more the transcendental stance is a meaningful response. Is this affirmation of belief a reasonable position? Or is it open to criticism and disapproval? The second option is to adopt the stance of the skeptic, that is, to suspend knowledge and deny that such forms of reality are knowable or meaningful and to live life fully and on its own terms.

8

THE HUMAN CONDITION

Humanist accounts of decision making in ordinary life have been fairly optimistic, for humanists are confident that rational solutions can be given for many or most problems in life. Ethical judgments are amenable to resolution by reference to given sets of descriptive facts. There is a kind of prudential wisdom at work, and an internal logic governing wise choice. Moreover, a "moral point of view" is reasonable because of the social nature of the human species. For many issues in life one can select with little trouble, and the process of decision is relatively simple. In such cases, one's choices are usually made by reference to a given framework that is brought into the situation. One refers to one's existing values, motives, wants, and desires and seeks to bring these into terms with the social structure of expectations, rules, and norms. Hence some stability in choice is possible. Shall I take the car or walk? Shall I buy a Klee or a Miró reproduction? Shall I vote Labor or Tory? Shall I join the Hay Fever Sufferers' League? What should I send my mother-in-law for her birthday?

Yet there are times of great trouble and stress when decision problems enter into the very framework of the value structure of a person or society, and when one's most fundamental norms are at stake. At this point one's choices may be said to be both free and in bondage. If a person critically questions or rejects the normative patterns of conduct, his own de facto valuings, and the rules of his community that have guided his life until then, he is left, in a sense, to create a new state of being. At such junctures an individual may recognize the awful character of a voluntary decision that is unlimited and unconditioned by his usual values and expectations. But he can also recognize the frenzied drives that his brute passions and instincts can unleash in the void. Only then might he see that his values and norms in a sense have an irrational basis and that his conduct involves affirmations that seem to be "absurd" in their foundations.

"Practical wisdom" accepts the framework that is given and acts from within, making choices in terms of the existing circumstances. It abides by the golden means of temperance, prudence, and caution. It seeks an equitable solution to its problems. In being "reasonable" one selects the "higher" pleasures

61

over the "lower," and the "moral" life over the "immoral," the "sensible" over the "wild," the "virtuous" over the "vicious." For here one seeks to fulfill oneself in the context of civilized sociocultural rules. But once we are forced to renounce the standards and norms of social order or to flout the socially approved character traits, we find that our lives are unbounded, yet they remain restricted—for, we ask, where else may we turn?

An honest philosophy recognizes full well that the basic structure for our choices is ultimately "arational"; that is, nonrational, but not necessarily irrational. But if we were to act on this insight—that is, if our choices were to be emancipated from the social-reality principle and be based upon pure impulse and desire—the results might be chaos, and only terror might strike the heart. Fundamental decisions—those concerning death, divorce, choice of a career, war, or national disaster—can call into question the whole basis of our structure of rules and valuings. And this is what the moral skeptic is disturbed about when he demands an "ultimate justification" for his values.

This is the posture assumed by the radical, utopian, or reactionary in politics, who does not accept the given state of values and rules but wishes for something entirely different from what now prevails. To the moral skeptic or political reformer who calls into question the whole framework of present beliefs and actions, there appears to be no easy answers. Why accept the status quo, as the man of practical wisdom advises? Why not overthrow the whole structure and start anew? For those who have experienced such a state of existential indecision, the problem is real and pressing. For those who have actually wrested themselves loose from their habitual behavior patterns and lived in such a state—by turmoil, conflict, and conversion in their personal lives and careers, or by devotion to political radicalism, or by changing cultures midstream in adult life—such decision problems are all the more drastic. It is well and good for people who have never questioned fundamentally, or indeed have never lived on two sides of life, to advise prudence in choice, to deplore moral or political skepticism, and to claim that existential questions are meaningless. It is possibly necessary to have lived in two cultures to understand one, or to have transvalued and renounced one's former values to understand what they were. For it is in such moments of anguish, when we can discover what appears to be a minimum of guiding lights for choice, that our illusions and myths are seen for what they are, and that we may cry in the night, alone. It is when we become skeptical, cynical, sophisticated, emancipated, or debauched that we may see things in their true outlines. The bohemian anarchist or anomalous individual is condemned to the social wastelands. But perhaps it is only such nonconforming individuals who can see the ultimate irrationality, nonrationality, and sometimes futility of many social rules and conventions.

It is doubtful whether our academic professors and philosophers today always see things in a clear enough light, for they have roles to fulfill in society and commensurate statuses, and these frequently destroy their sensibilities. Many have become schoolmarms instilling received opinion in undergraduates. They may succeed, at best, in teaching students to question gently and politely some of the dominant shibboleths and hosannas. They have become men and women of practical wisdom, that is, they are frequently more concerned with the advancement, prestige, and success of their own careers than with truth. Philosophers have become specialists in the academic division of labor, and this has determined in part their attitudes and beliefs. The dialogue is within and among philosophers of the same craft.

But to stand outside the existing framework of values and to look at it critically gives one a different perspective. Socrates was barefooted and bareheaded, a free-roaming intellectual. Spinoza, Kierkegaard, Hume, Locke, Marx, Nietzsche, Mill, and Santayana were, at least, not professors. Our intellectuals today are all too often institutionalized. They are committed to their professional roles within the academies and to corresponding ideologies of prudence. They are not free-floating, but are involved on the inside; all too infrequently do they peer from without.

The existentialists' attitude affects few Englishmen or Americans. "We all know that we have to die one day, why do they have to keep reminding us of it?" complained the English philosopher A. J. Ayer about existentialism. Existentialism by no means presents the whole story. Its attitude on methodology and science presupposes a special moral posture, one that we put to the severest criticisms for its subjectivism, and it minimizes or overlooks the role of knowledge of nature in decision-making. Yet European existentialists, such as Heidegger and Sartre, were aware of the revealing moments of human freedom and of the relationship between the human being and Being. They are witnesses to the sand upon which we mortals stand. In the existential perspective, our basic decision problems are not easily resolvable. And in such situations (though any situation, for them, is potentially existential in character), all too few of the usual standards are operative. There are no holds barred, and we seem to be thrown on our own, to make ourselves as we see fit.

If we are honest and receptive to all possibilities and to all points of view, when we find innumerable alternatives—intellectual, passionate, and instinctive—one course of action may seem as good as the next. And the future that is to be made seems to be contingent on nothing but our imagination. Our decisions are engendered and propounded in terms of our commitment to our social and cultural existence and to our habits of character; once a decision is made, a whole line of consequences may follow, changing the entire situation. Yet at any moment, existentially, we can enter the arid desert of nonacceptance; we can suspend and reject all of our commitments. Our basic values and norms in the final summation seem either to represent our conditioned social habits, our unconscious motives and blind feelings, or to be the product of capricious subjective choice, with one option apparently as good as the next.

This bitter truth about basic things, though seemingly desperate, does not leave us entirely alone. Even here there are some guides available to the individual. There is practical reason, and the norms and standards it presents. There are basic needs that the wise person may seek to satisfy and to take account of in reaching his decisions. Rationality does provide us with some help in reaching decisions, for it can give us understanding of ourselves and our needs. The individual need not be entirely helpless or lost in a sea of subjective indecision; given his desire to live and his social existence, decisions follow. In most of our moments we presuppose our values and act in terms of them. Existential puzzlement occurs only sometimes, perhaps only a few times in life. Life is not riddled with crises to the extent that some would have us believe.

Yet we are capable of entering a mood of desperation, at least philosophically, and we can ask the most basic questions about our existence: (1) "Why live?" and (2) "Why accept social and cultural life?" The questions that are framed in this mood are questions of normative justification. In answer to question 1, we must admit that the fact that there should be life rather than death is in a sense an absurdity—that is, we can give no reasons for our existence. We find ourselves here, alive, functioning, without being responsible for our own creation or having given our consent. As I have argued, that we should live is not amenable to rational proof or justification.

That life in the universe at large is better than nonlife cannot be proven. Life has evolved. It is found, given, encountered. From the standpoint of living things, there is a kind of instinctive tendency (in normal cases) to maintain life. For those who do not accept it, the door is always open to leave. Some may grieve our early departure, but nature is indifferent to one more lost person; we shall return to the dust from whence we came. That there should be life rather than death, hope rather than despair, meaning rather than meaninglessness—these things are of moment only to human beings, not to nature. A person on the verge of suicide or death may seek some consolation for life, and he may yearn for a justification for its continuance. But none can be given, other than that most beings have an instinctive urgency to live. This is its sole justification—that life desires life, and that in living, a kind of interest, satisfaction, zest, joy, and happiness may be discovered. It is an odd organism that deliberately seeks its own destruction, although that obviously does happen. Yet even here the death wish is more a distortion of normal homeostasis than anything else. Thus the option posed between life or death is not between equal alternatives, for there is a primal unconscious tendency on the side of life. To entertain the idea of death is only possible for a fairly sophisticated being. Hence the balance is heavily weighted that an organism will naturally tend to accept life.

But to accept life—that is to strive, endure, suffer, and enjoy—already provides some clues in answer to question 2, why society and culture? For if one is to live, to survive and grow, then certain needs must be satisfied. And here society and culture fulfill their functions. Biogenic needs are the products of a long evolutionary process. Sociogenic needs have developed more recently in the drama of human life. Both may be overthrown, though the denial of biogenic needs may lead to disease and death, and the denial of all sociogenic needs may also lead to disease and death or anguish and turmoil. If we fear death, disease, anxiety, then we conform in some sense to the social structure of normative rules and we find it prudent to do so. But it is essential that our culture not be at variance with our biology, and that it satisfy our root nature without unduly repressing it. This is the ultimate test of culture: its long-range ability to satisfy our biogenic needs.

Society and culture too, from the wider view, may seem absurd, and that we should willingly be tamed by its restrictions may seem oppressive. Why be civilized? Why adopt the stamp of our age? Why be Etruscan in ways, fashions, attitudes, and beliefs—or Spartan, Hindu, German, or American? What we are is a product of the causal conditions operative in the species at large and of the special historical circumstances and events that have converged upon us. We have little control over the explanatory laws relevant to human conduct, although if we understand the relevant conditions we may be able to act accordingly, circumvent them, or bring new ones into being. Similarly, the social and cultural framework of rules and institutions has already preformed and molded our personalities before we become aware of what is going on. We are its helpless creatures conditioned as babes by society and culture long before we are able to turn upon it, criticize it, or change it.

But can we return to the presocial jungle? This is a live alternative only for the romantic or visionary. To abandon social and cultural rules entirely is not possible. Memory and habit will not release us; we cannot erase language, the social vehicle of our judgments. Of course, there is always the alternative of changing cultures—of moving from one culture to another, from a modern culture to a primitive one or vice versa; or we can move from one sector of a culture to another—we can change classes or cities. But it is virtually impossible for us to abandon sociocultural rules altogether, for men and women are creatures of society and are imprisoned within its walls. There is a root biological dependence for survival on the care of at least one other person: child dependence seems implicit in the species. It is, of course, possible for people to become disassociated from rules, but extreme instances of this may end up in mental institutions—they are unable to function in their social environments. There have been recorded cases of people who were civilized and then returned to their primitive tribal ways, as in Brazil, for example, where missionaries Christianized some savages, brought them to live in England, and allowed them to return to the jungle again, only to find many years later an almost complete reversion to primitive ways.

No, *we* cannot very well return to the presocial jungle. The question I am raising—"Why be civilized?"—is meaningless for the civilized person. It is like the question, "Why live?" And, as I have said, there is no rational or ultimate justification for life. One lives because there are tendencies within that strive for survival; when these are not present, one gives up the battle and dies. Similarly, there have developed civilizing tendencies and characteristics that impel expression. To deny them if we could is to accept death in a sense—the death of a new part of ourselves that has evolved and been built upon our basic biological nature. I can no more retreat completely from society and culture than I can from life. Both are enigmas, though we are closer to seeing the evolution of the former than that of the latter, for the processes of accretion are enormously more rapid in the development of culture than in the development of life.

Once I recognize the value of some sociocultural organization as instrumental for satisfying my basic needs and desires and for creating new ones, the real question I face is this: "Which part of society or culture shall I accept and which shall I reject?" We know that we can modify some of our practices. There is a hierarchical order of events at work at each level. The individual is a result of complex physicochemical and sociocultural forces, all of which have converged and left their traces upon him. A person is, as it were, a residue of things past. But one can intervene on various levels, most directly on the level of individual choice and memory. One's nervous system as a particular mechanism bears the imprint of one's own experiences. There are choices to be made, as we have seen. In a sense there are three aspects to an individual's life: physical–chemical–biological, sociocultural, and individual personality.

The question that the individual faces is usually a proximate one: what to do here and now in regard to this framework. But, once again, he can call into question the whole framework; and I reiterate, there may not be an ultimate answer.

Here philosophy may be relevant, and here an important function of philosophy, and especially eupraxsophy, may come into play—at least it has done so in the past, for it enables us to stand outside the framework and to see things in their proper perspectives. It reveals the presuppositions of our knowledge and action. This function of eupraxsophic inquiry is often overlooked, even though it expresses our highest consciousness and awareness. Most human beings are so immersed in biology and culture, so engrossed in the day-to-day cares of social life, that they forget to stop, take a breath, and inquire: "What does it all mean and how does it fit together?" They have forfeited their lives to the trivial. Their values are the values imposed by the "they" of social living. The mad pursuit of money, sex, honors, rewards, and success can demand all of one's energy and devotion, especially if one operates only within a narrow context of life. Alas, when we take a coductive[1] look at the domain of values, from the outside as well as the inside, we frequently sap these values of some of their potency and vitality.

Spinoza pleaded for the development of an attitude that could see things whole and under the "eye of eternity." Such a perspective, he thought, might emancipate us from the narrow desires and passions of ordinary life. All things, he thought, were modes and affections of the same underlying "substance," "God," or "nature." This is the metaphysical or philosophical insight: once our plans and desires are placed under the focus of eternity and within the broader context of the universe at large, they diminish in intensity; once our present cultural valuings and rules are compared with other cultures past and present, they are minimized in urgency and enthusiasm. Perhaps philosophy is a bad thing, for if taken seriously it may take the wind out of our sails, dry up our gusto, and lessen our conventional motivations. Too much reason may at times hamper rather than facilitate decision, as the Sophists recognized.

The philosophical attitude has been ridiculed precisely because it is hesitant and reflective: while the average person jumps in and acts, the true philosopher sees the futility of haste and may avoid jumping and acting. "Fools rush in where angels fear to tread." I am not here talking about the specialist in philosophy, the logician or analyst. I am referring to the eupraxsopher who is the critic of value and culture and who is aware of hidden presuppositions. For he preeminently sees things in the coductive light for what they really are, from the outside as well as the inside. Such an approach also enables an individual to recover himself, freed from the tyranny of the nonessential and the irrelevant.

Such an individual may be able to free himself from illusion. One can see, for example, that science is primarily a way of life, one that rests upon the inculcation of a distinctive attitude or that presupposes its own rules of behavior, evaluations, and prescriptions. Reductionism, holism, coductionism, determinism, historicism, and other general methodological principles are really prescriptive rules governing inquiry, even though they are tested by their fruitfulness in inquiry and their effectiveness depends in some way upon nature. Moreover, to be interested, as the scientist is, in clarity, truth, impartiality, knowledge, objectivity, or open-mindedness, rather than music, art, intuition, mountain climbing, or surf sailing, is to affirm a way of life.

To advance the cause of scientific research in society is to express a moral imperative. Scientific research, like most other human enterprises, requires some dedication and commitment. But dedication and devotion are moral qualities, and the whole system of science rests upon decision and choice. The same is true of logical and semantic analyses. Theories of meaning, too, are normative and prescriptive in part, for language rules fulfill human purposes. Logical analysis thus involves instrumental activities. This is not to impugn such philosophical activities; indeed, such strategies of research may be effective. But they are strategic programs, and the deeper truth recognizes that all enterprises, whether philosophy, logic, science, art, politics, or lovemaking, presuppose basic norms. All systems in perspective, even the most descriptive in intent, may be seen to rest on our valuations. That we ought to lead the reflective, conceptual life rather than the affective, aesthetic, immediate life perhaps is not amenable to any final justification or proof. There are differences in culture and attitude that have conditioned our points of view, and there are sets of values and rules that we already possess and that determine our postures.

The inferences to be drawn from philosophical skepticism may not be precisely as philosophers have drawn them in the past. We cannot deduce a moral conclusion or imperative from our picture of the situation. We cannot even recommend a final attitude. Attitudes and states of character fluctuate with historical circumstances. It may have been well and good for the Athenian gentleman to follow Aristotle's golden mean, to be liberal, temperate, magnanimous, of slow gait, low voice, and proper pride. Or, indeed, for the medieval man to assume the role of the monk or the courtier, or the nineteenth-century educated person to be a hedonist and utilitarian. It is wise, one may argue, to be rational, intelligent, and objective in one's decisions, no matter what the time or place, as most philosophers have usually claimed. But these are only hypothetical imperatives.

We should not go overboard and claim that the rational life is the ultimate or final ideal. One may also argue that the life of reason is a positive evil if it seeks to deny or reduce the life of passion, and that the substitution of cognitive symbols for emotions and feelings may be oppressive. Reason in a sense may be repressive, for, while ordering our instinctive passions, it may leash them as well. The growth of the cortex and its attendant symbolic power may in a sense be an abnormal growth, for in the place of brute nature it may impose cultural standards. The life of a virgin schoolteacher may in the nature of things be no more noble than that of the nymphomanic Messalina. I think that we may deny that any one way of life is eternally justifiable, even that of the philosopher. I would explicitly question the sanctimonious admonishments of moralists that we ought to be temperate in our desires, or the impugning of the pleasures of the flesh. If life, at root, is "a tale told by an idiot—full of sound and fury, signifying nothing,"[2] and if society and culture are like games—sets of rules that we adopt to play at life—then perhaps we ought to get the most out of life. The pleasures of sex, food, and drink may be as important to a person as the cultural pleasures of art, philosophy, and pinochle. And, if it all means nothing, then any course may seem as good as any other. I am not here necessarily accepting Bentham's remark that pushpin may be as good as poetry. I am merely denying that we need assume that poetry is always better than pushpin. For practical reason, deliberation and calculation about our long-range desires and plans are in order. But for coductive reason, the deliberative process itself is prescriptive at base, and it is the whole person, not the part person, who must live.

Similarly, while we stand inside of society we may be concerned with social justice, that is, with providing a set of rules that will most equitably satisfy the distributive needs of the individuals who make up that society. Here, too, however, from the standpoint of coductive reason, there may be something transparent and empty in taking this as the primary end of life. Those of us who are social reformers or are socially interested feel compelled to take part in the public affairs of the day. As political men and women we decide and act, and the game of politics may very well take all. There is a kind of religious devotion to the ideal of social betterment. But there seems to be no ultimate basis or justification for moral obligations, either. Our rules in society delimit the rules, rights, and duties that we perform. If we are to perform our functions in a reciprocal way, then we must obey the rules, even if they are only the loose and indefinite ones of morality.

Moral rules, like all others, are teleonomic and instrumental. We build up feelings of sympathy and love for other human beings, and we develop a sense of belonging to a community. We may inculcate a sense of sin, guilt, or conscience about certain acts and support these feelings by custom, education, and law. But we are unable to find any infallible justification for basic moral rules. Their justification is practical and hypothetical, not absolute or categorical. A father or mother feels that he or she must sacrifice for the child, and a grown child for the parent. And this is true as long as we wish to imbibe the game of cultural life, and to live and function. But one can find no ultimate standards or guides that will solve the problem of morality. Because of our social and cultural commitments, some morality is necessary. But society and morality are not intrinsic to the nature of things. And one can, at least theoretically, abandon or resist both.

I have been arguing all along that, within the structure of a level of being, a person accepts events and relations as given. But it is from without that the level is placed in its proper framework. People who have always stood outside of a warm house and peered through the windows cannot fully understand what is being experienced inside the living room by the fireplace, or so we are told, but I fear that people on the inside are equally blind if they never open their windows or peer out.

From inside the house one can say this—science in knowledge, logic in meaning, and reason in practice are the most effective instruments for living. Because we live in a common world of objects and events, and because human beings share relatively the same problems and needs, it is best that our actions and beliefs be based on reasonable methods. Cognition is a need because it enables us to establish our lives in terms of external reality. Theoretical science and practical science at least enable us to find public knowledge and public rules with some objective ground in nature, and in terms of which we can communicate. If all activities are prescriptive, this does not mean that all are equally effective. One cannot defend all systems of beliefs as equally valid because they all rest upon faith, as some religionists have vainly attempted, for there are fundamental differences between the hypotheses of science and those of religion. Faith as tenacity or as will to believe, that is, faith based on little or no empirical support, is surely different from faith grounded in empirical evidence and experiment. The internal truth claims of the reigning mythologies are not verifiable, but the truth claims of science are. Thus while both science and religion express prescriptions when viewed from the broader existential context, still in regard to their internal cognitive claims there is a vast difference.

Hence we must defend the marvelous inventions of scientific method, logical clarity, technological thinking, and practical wisdom as being in closer touch with nature than other ways of behaving. We must grant that the scientific method presupposes certain values, which are required in some sense if we are to live and function in nature. From the standpoint of social and national policy and especially for the underdeveloped countries at present, scientific technology offers the best hope of competing in a postindustrial world; it is indispensable for survival. Thus one must defend the scientific method: no matter what our desires may be, if we wish to satisfy them, then science and reason best provide the instruments for satisfaction. Or, at the very least, one may argue in this way: if the way of life that we should adopt is an open question, then we must presuppose conditions of free inquiry in order to resolve the question—but this again is a basic value presupposition of science.

Thus, in the last analysis, science and practical reason have a pragmatic justification and vindication (as Herbert Feigl observed) because they are most instrumental to life activity, individually and socially. Any philosophy applicable to contemporary life must now take them as the main guides for valuational choice. This is the most important commitment of our times. Moreover, in addition to their instrumental values, both science and practical reason have a kind of intrinsic quality and value of their own, an attraction and appeal that only those who have experienced and used them can best appreciate.

Yet we still have two brute facticities to confront: the fact of life and death, and the fact of society and culture. Who is to speak of them, for them, and about them? Only the existential eupraxsophic consciousness is willing to face the true human condition of life and death. These brute elements are implicit in human existence—over and beyond our instrumental effectiveness—and this should be apparent to all who are willing to reflect on the nature of existence, and it is especially revealing to all who have divested themselves of their cultural myths, whether those of the ancient god of Immortality or, in our contemporary scene, those of the bitch goddess: success or consumer gluttony. These religious myths may serve psychological and sociological functions; they may provide a balm, peace of mind guaranteed, and social cohesion. These functions are often foreign to the literal scientific person, who takes these myths (especially the theistic) for literal nonsense, although he himself may worship at his own mythological altars.

The truly eupraxsophic person is one who dares to face the nature of life and death with courage, the person who has a sense of both the rich possibilities and the inevitable finitude of life—and few of the devotees of organized religions are metaphysically aware in this sense. It is a mistake to think that theism has a monopoly on insight. On the contrary, humanism is capable of a deeper and fuller understanding of the human condition. The true religious response is a response to the demands of the external world. It develops usually when we come to realize in full shock, and usually in times of crisis, the flux of human existence, and when we recognize that, though the fondest human dreams may be realized, alas, "vanity, O vanity," they rest upon quicksand. In the words of the author of Ecclesiastes: "All go unto one place, all are of the dust, and all return to the dust again."

The tragedies implicit in the temporal historicity of life, the death of each human being, the fact that all humans are unclothed, naked, and alone—this is the awesome bedrock fact that confronts the sensitive consciousness. The existentialists were not the first to discover this fact of nature and life or the pathos of suffering and dread. Yet all too few persons are willing to see life and death for what they really are; they put death out of their minds, and, like the other animals, ignore it, or they think that it is a problem only for the old to worry about. We see others die, not ourselves. Yet life and civilization are mere mortal events, which will pass like all else.

Along with this awareness of the transience of life—and it takes true courage to face it—there is another fact to be faced: the recognition that there are powers and forces external to and independent of us, the recalcitrant given. There is a source of our being that we cannot control, but that we can only come to terms with and accept. Some mistakenly call this "God," or attribute its power to mysterious demons and mythological entities. Others attribute it to "causal laws" and to the fact that we are only a small part of vast systems of events. In any case, some recognition of our dependence upon the tide of events and the limitations of our powers is present in the eupraxsophic response, and this usually leads to some stoic resignation and perhaps a degree of "natural piety."

These facts of life and death, of transience and dependence, I think all can accept. They can be easily confirmed by scientific observation, and they are as true for the atheist as for the theist. And these facts do not disappear by claiming that the whole problem is a pseudo-problem or cognitively meaningless. True, there may not be a solution, but there is still a real predicament that we face. Yet men and women frequently do not wish to face their transience and impotence. They cover it up or disguise it. The cares of society and culture dominate our consciousness. Civilization builds symbolic worlds, and we are taken up by new events. We are concerned about making a living, getting married, writing a novel, playing the stock market, investigating the causes of a disease, supporting the party, or contributing to economic growth, to democracy, or to world peace. And, in our haste, we frequently overlook our brute animal existence.

The existential human condition is often not faced; it is usually forced upon us in times of extreme crisis or change. When it is faced, and faced hard, the truth may chill us, and so we construct false mythologies to avoid it: the immortality myth of the good life promised later on, or the utopian myth of the good life on earth for humankind now. But the scientific method can confirm neither, nor can it guarantee that our vain hopes are inscribed in the womb of nature. The assertions of traditional theistic religions, that God exists or that there is an immortal soul, are at best expressive or imperative utterances that have not been verified and are unverifiable. And the messianic promises of social reformers or psychological therapists that unlimited social progress or psychological happiness is just around the corner awaiting us with certainty are also seen to be idle chatterings in the wind.

We huddle together in society and create smoke screens for the protection of life against the cold wind and death. Nature cannot sustain them—and with the dust they will eventually vanish. As we expand the frontiers of space exploration, new challenges will confront the human species. Our organic existence will be given new dimensions as we learn to travel in a wider universe. But the new discoveries awaiting us cannot alter the ultimate human condition or the impermanence of life. There are some things we can ameliorate and change, and there are many problems we can resolve—but who except the completely self-deluded can believe in their final solution or in our ultimate salvation? Whether humankind eventually destroys itself or propagates the solar system and stellar systems beyond is the frightful yet exciting option of the future.

I do not wish to seem overly pessimistic. I think that it is important for us to unify our scientific knowledge, particularly our knowledge of human beings. I submit that a science of human beings is both possible and necessary, and that there are no unalterable or a priori obstacles, as far as I can see, to the understanding of human nature. Neither the appeal to motive, historical, or teleonomic explanations as special kinds of explanation, nor the fact of free intention or decision, nor any alleged mind–body dualism can invalidate the scientific explanation of human nature. The fact is that the human organism is a teleonomic animal capable of decision and action, and science can trace the conditions of such behavior. Moreover, this knowledge enables us to improve our practical know-how and our power for making decisions. Our prescriptions and rules are more effective if based on descriptive knowledge. Science itself is not purely descriptive but has a prescriptive basis. But this does not undermine its claims or make it totally unlike other human interests. It merely places it in its proper valuational locus.

Moreover, scientific rationality is probably the most effective value system available in the world today, and it is one that we should be committed to, individually and socially, for the good life. It provides the best means for individual happiness and social progress.

Yet in looking at our ethical life we find this paradoxical fact. The human species is a product of nature, and as part of it we are governed by the same causal conditions that are found elsewhere in nature and that we may be able to understand. Yet we are decision-making organisms—choosing, selecting, valuing. We become aware of our own choices and reflect upon their direction, and we have a creative role in their formation. But here nature is ironic—a cruel joke has been played on human striving. As conscious beings we are able to understand full well the status of our values: they have an animal basis and a sociocultural fulfillment, yet they are transient, historical, and changing. We can satisfy some of our longings—for love and health, for happiness and equanimity—with various degrees of effectiveness. But the special human condition is that we, through eupraxsophy, can recognize the instability of all human desires and their ultimate terminal character, as well as the instrumental nature of our sociocultural rules. We should, I suppose, be grateful that indifferent and blind natural processes enable many of us to achieve fourscore and ten, and perhaps more. We should be grateful that, in spite of a nature that is blind, we nonetheless are able to see and understand.

The important power of coduction as a rational principle of understanding is that it enables us to stand both inside and outside the processes of life: we can appreciate things in their proper contexts, but also see their functions and interrelations. Objectivity in knowledge, meaning, value, and decision is contextual; at bottom it is a product of culture, not nature. We can justify, vindicate, or plead our special causes. We can defend our basic ground rules and persuade others to accept them. But prescriptive rules in the last analysis are affairs of a teleonomic animal who has evolved an edifice of society and culture, an animal who, if overly conscious, can undermine its animality altogether. Rather than make us free, the truth may deaden our zest for living, for it will present to us bluntly and coldly the instability of life and the impermanence of values and social rules. As skeptics we can rise above the illusions of our age. But we can also sink into the morass of hopelessness and nihilism.

All that human beings have is life. What we make of it, or what it makes of us, is all that counts. Society and culture have emerged in part to facilitate our animal desires, but they can also be a mask for deception. Humans develop knowledge. Through knowledge we may discover what we are, what we need, what we desire, and what we can have. But knowledge is the instrument of desire, and desire of life; yet life ultimately ends in death. Life while lived can be good and bountiful: love, devotion, kindness, knowledge, achievement, success, well-being, happiness, economic growth, and social betterment are all possible within limits. But all good things must pass, and life has its bitter end. Some may develop feelings of resignation toward these brute facts. Some may panic or lose nerve. In any case, the facts should be allowed to speak for themselves.

The eupraxsopher who has left the cave of illusion can see human nature and life for what they really are. Yet each of us must partake of the game of life. As rational inquirers we must deal with knowledge, meaning, and value, though in so doing we presuppose the rules applicable at the various levels of inquiry. As a practical being one can lose oneself in the whirlpool of life, while as a philosophic being one can understand the ephemeral basis of life (though, unlike Plato, we have no solace in eternal essences). This is the constant paradox of life: reason that is holistic in scope and practical in action is possible, but it is at variance with reason that is coductive and existential in scope. Reason in science and practical wisdom enable us to live and enjoy the fruits of the good life. But reason in eupraxsophy places things in their proper, and broader, coductive focus, and in its revealing light we see full well the opportunities we face yet also the transient character of all human existence and the teleonomic and animal basis of knowledge, meaning, and value.

In spite of all this, life is still worth living, and we have within our power the possibility of living fully, even exuberantly. To waste this opportunity or to flee from it is the highest form of human tragedy. The human condition is such that all too often it is fear and trembling (to paraphrase Kierkegaard) that overwhelms us—not the courage to be (Tillich) or the heroic passion to leap over the abyss (Nietzsche). Unfortunately this tempts many men and women to place themselves in bondage to the false illusions promised by priests and prophets and to abandon their own sense of power.

PART II

INDEPENDENCE

9

POWER

STOICISM

If we are to achieve joyful exuberance, the first point to recognize is that human beings have some power and control of their own destinies. We can live a full life, but only if we are able to expand our sense of power, not necessarily over other humans, but over ourselves. But, we may ask, what is the full extent of human power? Dare we exaggerate our capabilities without risking psychological defeat? It is well and good to emphasize the potentialities for creative autonomy, but should we not recognize that there are boundaries restricting what we can do? Is it not foolhardy to adopt the audacious stance, to proclaim the power of choice, to tempt nature or stand against the universe, seeking to bend it to our will, when all of our plans will be defeated in the end—by death, if by nothing else?

Life teaches the bitter lesson that the fondest of human dreams are often shattered. We learn the sorrows of unexpected tragedies, accidents, disease, pain, failure, defeat, conflict, and that the obdurate realities of nature often frustrate our deepest desires and play havoc with our best-laid plans. Certainly we can dream, but we can never match our dreams with realities. Nature constantly resists human efforts and often subdues them.

The religious consciousness is aware of the failures and defeats of life, particularly of the facts of human transience and death—and we are faced with the problem of evil. How live in the face of adversity? How forbear when the cruel twists of fate can destroy us: a premature death, an unforeseen natural disaster, a plane crash, a sudden heart attack? A slight miscalculation can wreck the noblest of human endeavors.

How bear the slings of outrageous fortune? How does a lonely individual face the taunts and torments of existential reality? How can we live in the face of the overwhelming sense that there are vast powers in society and the universe at large beyond our control?

The Stoics offered consolation by cultivating an inward attitude of apathy or indifference. They were impressed by the "inevitable necessity of all things" and by our own insignificance in the face of it.

Epictetus, a former Roman slave, begins the *Enchiridion* by saying:

> There are things which are within our power, and there are things which are beyond our power. Within our power are opinion, aim, desire, aversion, and, in one word, whatever affairs are our own. Beyond our power are body, property, reputation, office, and, in a word, whatever are not properly our own affair. Now the things within our power are by nature free, unrestrained, unhindered; but those beyond our power are weak, dependent, restricted, alien. . . . Aiming, therefore, at such great things, remember that you must not allow yourself any inclination, however slight, toward the attainment of the others; but that you must entirely quit some of them, and for the present postpone the rest. . . . and if it concerns anything beyond our power, be prepared to say that is it nothing to you. Remove (the habit of) aversion, then, from all things that are not within our power, and apply it to things undesirable which are within our power.[1]

Living in a vast empire, seemingly beyond anyone's control, the Roman Stoic, whether emperor or slave, felt that he had to perform such duties as were expected of him. He could not retreat from the world, as did the Epicurean. He could withdraw instead into himself by the suppression of unnecessary feelings of involvement. He could lessen anxiety and worry about the unexpected tragedies. There is an important element of reflective awareness here, and it suggests a kind of nobility of spirit. Yes, we say, we need the courage to bear adversity, to go through life without being crushed by its misfortunes. All wise persons learn that there are some things over which we have some control, and that there are some things far beyond human control, but that we can contain our inward thoughts about them. It is important that we recognize that tragic events occur: the death of a child, the defeat of one's country, the failure of a crop.

Yet there can also be an overemphasis on passive acceptance. The Stoic solution was to "follow the way of nature" in order to achieve virtue. But moderns have learned that nature is not fixed and society is not closed to human purpose and that we are able to modify the natural world and reform social institutions.

We have discovered that there often are powers that we have though we may be unaware of them, that situations have latent possibilities, that there are untapped potentialities that can be actualized, that we can bring into being new instruments to achieve our desires, and that we can vastly extend our range of interests and activities.

KNOWLEDGE IS POWER

The development of modern science and technology marks a radical break with the past, for it makes possible an enormous enlargement of human powers.

For the philosophers and scientists of Greece and Rome and the philosophers and theologians of the Middle Ages, the goal was to try to make the universe intelligible to thought. Even a figure such as Spinoza, serving as a bridge between the Middle Ages and modern science, was impressed by the order of nature. The highest human good, and the source of blessedness and salvation, was for him the intellectual love of God or nature, an appreciation of its logical structure. Joy was in knowing that the vast panorama of events fits a marvelous causal order and that man is part of the scheme of things.

For Bacon, however, knowledge is power. It is not enough to understand the universe; we must apply our knowledge for human use. If the Greeks developed a theoretical approach to nature, we have developed an experimental one. Thus modern technology is an effort to apply the principles of the sciences to practical uses; and modern humans have learned that knowledge is an instrument and force and that we can do things with it. It is western civilization that has had strong confidence in human powers—much more so than those in the underdeveloped societies, who too often believe that we cannot change anything.

It is not enough to behold in mystic vision or rational insight the wondrous order of nature, but we must use this knowledge to satisfy our interests and goals and to create new ones. With scientific knowledge many of the mysterious tragedies that befall human beings—disease, accidents, premature death, famine—can now be averted. We can understand their causes, and we have a method of correction and cure. Thus our sense of power is for us far greater than that in earlier centuries. Knowledge is not a sign of the inevitable necessity of all things but a clue to the pregnant potentialities that we can unlock and the vast new powers that we can develop. As the human species enters the Space Age, the possibilities of adventure for the soaring human spirit are virtually unlimited.

Many people feel that modern technology has now gone too far, that we have opened a Pandora's box that can destroy us, that technology is irretrievably polluting the environment, and that it is a new demon that we must guard against.

I note these familiar facts because it is our sense of power, freedom, and autonomy that is at issue. We cannot be audaciously happy unless we have a sense that we can guide and control our lives and that of society. Courage and persistent effort are possible only in this perspective.

If we believe that the world is predetermined and that our destiny and fate are beyond our control, then our response is to seek some measure of peace from the forces that would dominate us. We can know God and submit to His power in love and adoration, accept the "inevitable necessity of all things," or seek release in mystic contemplation; but our own efforts and concerns are of little avail. Fatalistically we say, "Whatever will be will be," and we are unwilling and unable to resist the tide of events. Thus there is in an extreme form a deep-seated religious sense of our powerlessness, helplessness, impotence: we can only prostrate ourselves before nature or God or the universe.

Yet the full life is tied up with a sense in which we are aware of our own power as people; that is, the belief that we *can* control or influence our lives to some extent, that we *can* modify or redirect the forces about us, that there is some energy at our disposals to do so, and that we can take pride in achieving what we set out to do. Call it naïve optimism, if you will, but it is the central humanistic virtue.

OVERCOMING FEAR

Any theory, whether based on religion or science, that denies voluntary human choices or action flies in the face of human experience. We have power over our conduct to the extent to which our behavior is motivated; that is, insofar as our choices are our own and follow from our own wishes and desires, plans, and interests. In classical philosophical language, our behavior is free if the moving principle is within us rather than caused by external forces or unconscious drives. Our purposes are influenced and modified, of course, by the conditions under which we act; yet at the same time we have something to say about how we act, and at the very least, can alter the conditions under which we act.

There are two key factors in a purposive process: (a) we have an idea or wish as an end goal, and (b) we engage in activity or work to bring it about. Creative thinking continually intervenes in the initiation of new goals, in the kinds of adaptive behavior that we engage in to achieve our ends, and in the invention of new means and instruments to bring them about. In all of these senses humans are not passive recipients but dynamic agents. We have something to say about our futures, for we can think up new projects and plans, create organizations and techniques that did not exist before, and rearrange and reorder the materials of nature in novel ways. Our abilities to do this depend only upon whether or not we have rich and fertile imaginations.

We can see creativity at work in the public and private lives of individuals as they introduce goals and plans and go about resolving them. Thinking is both imaginative–creative and coping–adjustive. Teleonomic choice is the fundamental process in human life; that is, what will happen in the future is a result of the purposes that we initiate and try to bring about: going to the supermarket to purchase groceries, enrolling in law school, building a condominium, developing a career, writing an article, moving to Arizona, investing in the commodity exchange, or helping to build a space colony.

Now some of the things that we resolve to do, we can do. There are few obstacles; the means are readily available; the end is clearly in view. Our daily decisions fit into this means–end continuum. I decide to wallpaper the bedroom, and so I select the paper, get the brushes and paste, and go merrily about my business, completing the job in one afternoon. Similar factors apply for choices of longer duration. I plant a vegetable garden in the spring, care for it throughout the summer, and harvest it in the fall. Or I begin a book, spending many months or years researching and writing it. Now in some of the projects that I wish to bring to fruition, I may encounter great difficulties. The glue is too thin and the paper peels. There is a hailstorm and my vegetables are ruined. I am unable to complete my book, due to distractions.

Often I may experience great obstacles: the means I use may be inadequate; consequences that were unforeseen may ensue; contingent events may intrude. Indeed, that is often the plight of the human condition. The path may not be easy and smooth, but rutted and full of dangers. Some people seem to have an excess of "bad luck"; a whole set of circumstances may trip them up; they may make blunders. Thus the dreams they cherish may not come true, though those of their neighbors do. Their plans may be thwarted by natural forces—the resistance of brute facts—or by human and social forces beyond their control. Woodrow Wilson was unable to complete his term as president because of ill health, or to see his belief in a League of Nations bear fruit in the United States. Franklin Roosevelt was felled by a fatal stroke on the eve of victory in war. Lyndon Johnson was unable to bring a close to the Vietnam War; every policy he initiated seemed to spell disaster. Robert Kennedy was struck down by an assassin's bullet, cutting short his drive for presidential power. Richard Nixon and Spiro Agnew, at the height of their power, after an unprecedented electoral victory, were brought down by forces that they were unable to master or comprehend. And Ronald Reagan lives his last years with debilitating Alzheimer's disease.

The frustration of our plans constantly tests us. Not all of the things that we want can come true. Our fantasies exceed our capacities; our best-designed projects sometimes are destroyed by fortune and the tide of events. We may encounter unrequited love, electoral defeat, financial ruin, public ridicule and shame, or illness, or we may perform badly. These are the realities of the human condition, and everyone—the great and the small—suffers them to some degree. The whole point to life is this: Can I overcome the adversity, or will I be crushed by it? Eli Black, head of the vast business conglomerate General Brands, leaped to his death in the midst of financial difficulties. Anthony Eden resigned from office after the Suez fiasco. General Robert E. Lee surrendered, recognizing that the South's cause was hopeless. Golda Meir gave up the reigns of power in Israel. By emphasizing *perestroika* and democracy, little did Gorbachëv realize that he would destroy the entire Soviet system.

In one sense what will happen depends on the strength of our will and our willingness to persevere. The hero of Ernest Hemingway's *The Old Man and the Sea* is determined to snare his fish and hold on to him at all costs, in spite of tremendous difficulties, and in the end he succeeds. Napoleon, after being exiled to Elba, returned to lead a mighty army to Paris for one last attempt at conquest, and all the monarchs of Europe shuddered at his daring. Lindbergh flew across the Atlantic alone on an uncharted path. Beethoven continued composing though he was crushed by an onrushing deafness. Helen Keller learned to communicate and to develop as a person in spite of being deaf, mute, and blind.

The world mourns a departed leader and applauds the hero as a public figure. But we all know that our private lives are filled with the same vivid qualities and that the human adventure includes adversity, defeat, and frustration, as well as success and victory.

It is the drive of the individual, the unflinching persistence of the will, and the enduring strength of character that are the dynamic factors in achievement. We do not always succeed; we need to adjust our dreams, learn from our mistakes, adapt to circumstances. Human intelligence and courage need to be artistically blended by creative endurance.

The achievement motive can motivate strongly. But in addition to ability, sagacity, skill, and training, success requires some resolve and patience, tenacity and persistence, and the absence of excessive remorse. In a sense, then, whether we achieve our ends is a function of whether we have tapped our power. Why some persons have confidence in their powers while others do not is a difficult question. But the actual pursuit of the exuberant life depends upon the quality of boldness, and it involves the conviction that if you try something you can do it. One phrase that has remained with me since elementary school is my teacher's early advice to me: "Never say you *can't*. Get rid of that word from your vocabulary." Others have agreed. "They can because they think they can," observes Virgil. "No one knows what he can do till he tries," agrees Publius.

Why do some men and women lack the ability to try while others are willing to take chances and risks? Some individuals have learned life's lesson "nothing ventured, nothing gained." Yet others will never venture and will instead prefer safety and security. Some are overcome by indecision. Unable and unwilling to decide, they let events slip through their fingers, impotent to act or to conquer them. In the process they become mere spectators, rather than actors, debilitated by uncertainty and indecisiveness, overwhelmed by caution and trembling.

Fear is the source of human weakness, and insofar as one is afraid to act, to undertake something new, one is unable to become an autonomous person.

"He who hesitates is lost." Yet many not only hesitate, they never act. Human beings are divided into two classes: those who are willing to act and those who are not, the courageous and the fearful, the achievers and the might-have-beens.

Often related to this attitude of fear is one of self-hatred, which only exacerbates a person's feelings of impotence. Some degree of self-respect and self-love is essential for any human accomplishment. But if we inwardly believe that we will fail in what we do, or if we are afraid to act, the result is often demeaning to us. And as life goes on and we get older, our sense of self-worth may be further weakened. Lacking confidence in what we can achieve, we lack confidence in our worth as a person; we are inwardly self-critical and self-destructive; we turn upon ourselves, and the process of self-immolation feeds upon itself.

The opposite of fear and impotence is a feeling of personal worth and power; only these feelings permit us to continue to develop our sense of power. One can overcome excessive stoic resignation about the universe or one's personal limitations only if one has a sense of one's own proper freedom. One can extend the limits of one's own action and of the things within one's power. To be human is to be free; freedom is the chief source of human fulfillment. But what does it mean to be free? It does not mean that my actions are uncaused or unconditioned by events around me. It does not mean that I can act counter to the deterministic forces in nature. It means only that I am to some extent self-determined and that what happens to me, to those about me, and to my society also depends upon my efforts and actions, on what I add to the situation, and on what I decide to do. I am thus responsible in part for my destiny. Impotence signifies that I am unable to do anything, that I cannot succeed, that my efforts will fail. Potency points to the belief that I do have the capacity and opportunity to act in the world. Powerlessness is corroding and destructive of human personality; potency, a dynamic source of vigor and motivation. To say that I am free means that I have my own ideals of what the future should be like and that I can take steps to realize them in the world of action. *My* ideas have consequences. *I* can change things, alter them for the better. I *can* achieve the good life for myself.

RATIONAL CHOICE

Obviously there are limits to what one can do. Those who refuse to recognize limits are foolish; they may be inordinately power hungry or completely impractical. Overweening ambition or egoistic omnipotence is as much out of touch with the world as self-defeating impotence, for nature dictates that if we are to succeed in our goals that we have a realistic appraisal of what is objectively possible. We learn from bitter experience that impulsive behavior, imprudent policies, or taking unnecessary chances may have disastrous consequences. If one's dreams are not based upon a cognitive analysis of the real world, they are likely to be shattered. Practical wisdom can help us to ferret out nonsensical proposals from hard-nosed ones. Merely to want something and to resolve to get it is never enough. We need intelligence to appraise the circumstances in the situation in which we act, both as to the possibilities *and* the limits. Of course, we may be lucky, but to gamble constantly in life is to risk the probability of being crushed by the wheels of fortune. Our risks must be hedged. A risk should be taken only if there is a presumption of success. To dash in without planning and without properly examining the terrain is not a sign of bravery but of ignorance. As Aristotle pointed out, courage must be harmonized with intelligence; without it, it is simply rashness or foolishness. One can be the master of one's fate—yes. But one should not be so childish as to come unprepared. Courage without calculation is stupidity. Thus our plans and projects often are impossible or unlikely to succeed, and it is wiser not to act— we learn that from experience.

Freedom does not mean that I can do whatever I want, only that what I choose to do or not to do is a function of a deliberative process. And deliberation is a major ingredient in making actions succeed. Choices that are a product of a process of reflective inquiry are most likely more effective than those that are not. They are choices based upon a consideration of the facts of the case, of the possibilities and limitations, the means at my disposal, the alternatives that are available and can be created by me, and an appraisal of the likely consequences of various courses of action.

I may choose not to act, to forbear, to hold back, to adopt a cautious stance. But such a reflective choice also expresses my power as an autonomous agent. The converse of inaction, so typical of the powerless, is hyperaction. This can become an illness: to try to run in many directions at the same time, to refuse to stop to catch one's breath, to be continually high on projects without end, not to be able to sit still a minute, to begin new tasks without finishing previous ones. If there is a vice that most threatens the hyperactive personality, it is the attempt to do too many things at the same time. Some individuals are able to succeed: they become the Leonardos of action; others become merely squanderers undertaking too many projects but doing none of them well. They never seem able to enjoy life. Always on the run, they are unable to savor the delicacies and subtleties of experience. They are vulgar pragmatists, judging life only by its consequences in action, forgetting that many of the good things of life should be intrinsically enjoyed for their own sake and that utilitarian values can often smother sensual delight, the joys of repose and rest, meditation and tranquillity.

The end of life is not simply action for its own sake; the full life involves an integration of action with other phases of experience and an appreciation for hedonic tones and erotic sensitivities. Thus one should not do merely for the sake of doing, but doing should be related to other qualities of immediate experience, which can interpenetrate harmoniously in a full life. Action will lose its intrinsic worth unless it is related to the unified functioning of consciousness. One of the major sources of unhappiness for the hyperactive person is the inability to enjoy life's pleasures. One should live not simply to act, but to appreciate the joys of experience. There is also some danger that the strenuous mood of affirmation and achievement, in blotting out the virtues of rest and repose, may make the action-oriented person more liable to stress. Prey to ambition, overwhelmed by conflict and competition, such a person is especially prone to anxiety conflicts. It is important, therefore, that the action-oriented person place his action in a broader framework. Of significance here is the need to cultivate some stoic virtues, for individuals who play the game of life so hard that they cannot bear to lose are often consumed by anxieties of failure. Granted that one should try hard; yet one should not be overly apprehensive of defeat, nor allow self-recrimination or self-flagellation to torment oneself.

It is not the active life but the worry that may accompany it that is destructive to balance and health. One should strive to succeed, but if one fails—well, the appropriate response is to make allowances and say that one will do better next time. To be able to withstand adversities, to survive psychologically in spite of failures, is the best preventative of this kind of stress. To be able to achieve some self-acceptance, one must to some extent be able to see oneself in perspective, as a bystander, to laugh at one's mistakes, and also to be able to forgive them. Those who are excessively hard on themselves because of their failings not only are difficult to live with, they cannot live with themselves.

The Stoics were mistaken in their view that human power is thwarted by nature—we can extend our sense of what we can do far beyond what they thought we were capable of. Yet some Stoic consolation should still accompany our actions. Some philosophical wisdom is a necessary antidote for the vicissitudes of fortune.

PERSONAL FREEDOM

Personal power and freedom are essential if one is to live a full and creative life. Yet the extent to which an autonomous life is possible may not depend simply upon *my* attitude and resolve, but also upon the kind of society in which I live. There are some societies and institutions that excessively smother individuality. Autonomy does not thrive where the cultural soil is alien, where there is excessive repression, a solidified class structure, strict laws, hidebound traditions, or a dominant collectivist–communal ethic. Even in closed societies there is a need to develop some talented leaders within the elite who are capable of decision and action, if they are to govern effectively, though the great mass of people may be prevented from doing so.

Thus, insofar as individual autonomy is essential for the good life, libertarian values should prevail. Social regulations, though necessary, should never dampen individual choice. We surely need laws to fulfill the common good, but we need at the same time to maximize opportunities for individual achievement, allowing individuals to express their talents, interests, purposes, and careers as they see fit without excessive interference. A free person says: I cannot live in a society that unduly limits my power. I cannot breathe or create. I can thrive only where I am free to think, feel, and act in my own terms. A free society is thus a precondition for individuals to be able to fully express their powers.

Regretfully, there are far too many individuals who are willing to forfeit their freedom to social demands. They lack the courage to be what they want to be because they are fearful of what others might say and are unable to withstand criticism. The superego suppresses the desire of the ego to express itself. This is due in part to the distaste that many individuals have of not being liked; this reluctance makes them easily succumb to negative criticisms. They mean well and they cannot understand why others impugn their motives.

A person needs to discover, however, that although criticisms, especially if unwarranted, may be painful at first, eventually one can learn to bear them. One should abandon the belief that one can satisfy everyone. The hope is that we should learn to live with others harmoniously, to profit from their criticisms, where constructive, and to correct our mistakes. But we should not excessively worry about whether or not we receive universal approval, which is an impossible goal anyway. Individuals who are willing to abandon their independence also capitulate their claim to happiness. They are vanquished before they start.

10

COURAGE

THE COURAGE TO BECOME

There is a moral virtue or excellence intrinsic to the very nature of the human condition, and this is basic to the humanistic outlook. The goal of human life is surely to survive, but it is also to flourish, that is, to fulfill our dreams and aspirations. To achieve anything, to defend our stake, or to extend our vistas requires a quality of character that is pivotal to all human enterprises. I am referring here to *courage*, the endeavor to persist, fortitude, the active will-to-endure, the achievement motive, and the stout determination to fulfill our goals and exceed our natures. The opposite of courage is failure of nerve, the tendency to cower or retreat in the face of adversity. Emily Brontë expresses the resolve of the courageous person: "No coward soul is mine, no trembler in the world's storm-troubled sphere."[1] The human prospect thus depends on what we will or will not dare to do, how we will respond to challenges that we encounter, and how we will face death.

The human species differs qualitatively from other species on this planet, which seek primarily to satisfy their instinctive needs. We differ from them on a scale of magnitude, for we are not simply passive products of natural forces, responding to impulses within our biological being, but rather interactive participants in the world about us. Other species respond to stimuli in their environment, and they seek to adapt in order to survive. We differ from them because we are builders of culture. As such, we enter into the natural, sociocultural environment, and we constantly endeavor to change it. Human evolution is not a result of blind or unconscious biological and genetic forces but a function of sociocultural factors. These enable us to intervene in nature and modify or redirect the course of evolution.

"Man is condemned," observes Jean-Paul Sartre, "to invent man," and so we constantly alter the conditions of our being. Human history is not fixed; we are not simply determined. What will be depends upon the natural order but also on contingency and what we resolve to undertake. Our transactions within nature are such that we seek objects and activities in order to satisfy our basic biological needs and desires; we build upon these by constantly creating new needs and desires. We introduce new objects into nature, and we create new worlds of cultural reality: farms and canals, roadways and dams, bridges and tunnels, governments and constitutions, industries and empires, sombreros and sonatas, mosques and museums, and computers and satellites are all products of human imagination and ingenuity. They are brought into being to satisfy our interests. But these cultural artifacts in turn stimulate new desires and needs, and they take on a life of their own. Over and beyond our basic biogenic needs, complex secondary sociogenic needs emerge that intrigue and entrance us and redefine our natures.

We are surely constrained by our genetic endowment, but we are malleable within it, and we can modify and exceed it. We seek food and shelter in order to survive, and we engage in sex in order to reproduce. However, we also bask in the fineries of cultural existence; we develop the arts and sciences, we engage in sports and play, and we become deeply immersed in the subtle web of civilized life. Architecture and engineering, medicine and therapy, music and poetry, war and peace, religion and mysticism, and philosophy and mathematics may attract and consume us. Although we need nourishment in order to live, there are infinite varieties of diets, from soup and nuts to beef and potatoes, granola and tofu, macaroni and bourguignon, truffles and patisserie, beer and wine. Sexual reproduction is essential for survival; nevertheless, we embroider sexuality with the nuances of romance, and we delight in the diverse tapestries of taste and passion that we weave to enjoy sexual pleasures and enhance orgasm.

All of this is nourished by motivating principles in human life: the will to live and the desire to satisfy our desires, but also the persistence to fulfill our plans and projects, however unique or idiosyncratic they may become. The constant reaffirmation of our desires and interests spills out into the world. Our goals and aspirations are products of our needs and our deliberations, and they are achieved by using technological skills. The arts and sciences, techniques and know-how that civilizations discover are transmitted from generation to generation, and they constantly change—the wheel and wagon, horse and carriage, railway and sea vessel, and automobile and superjet provide us with improved means of travel. The hunter's knife or the surgeon's scalpel enables us to perform various kinds of operations. Our world is a product of our dreams and of our determination to fulfill them.

Courage is essential to the human drama. It is related to creativity. Humans are capable of creating new ideas and constructs; they are able to invent and innovate. The human being is not a passive mind or soul but an active organism capable of inventive behavior, able to enter into the world and reconstruct it. Art does not make explicit what is only implicit in the womb of nature, as Aristotle thought; it brings into being new forms of reality. It transforms nature. Rube Goldberg's contraptions wonderfully illustrate the inventions that imagination is able to produce. Although we are creatures of habit, conforming to social rules and customs and stirred by instinctive passions, we are also able to conceive of new futures and to take new departures to realize them. Many conservatives resist change and abhor novelty, but the human species is by nature radical in innovation. We have created the wheel, the water paddle, and the windmill to enable us to experience new activities; the club, arrow, ax, spear, and rifle to be used in combat; the fireplace, stove, and microwave oven to cook and bake; the harp, flute, violin, and piano to play music; the symbols, words, metaphors, and sentences to allow verbal and linguistic expression; the papyrus, book, printing press, telephone, television, and computer Internet to communicate with others.

The stimulus that incites all such creative actions is the affirmative expression of the human spirit. It is the will to live that is the spring of motivation, the spark of inventiveness; and it is the drive to achieve our goals, whatever they are, that is essential—whether in pursuing a love partner, amassing a fortune, winning a ball game, completing a treatise, erecting a bridge, achieving political power, or engaging in humanitarian efforts to help others.

Living involves many dimensions: the will to survive, the drive to succeed, and the creative urge to achieve are all present. This is as true of the religious absolutist as of the pessimistic skeptic in the everyday contexts of choosing and acting. In response to the nihilist, one may say that there is no need for him to get out of bed in the morning, and he may as well turn over and die. But he does get out of bed, at the very least to write skeptical tomes and persuade others about how it is all so useless. Even a playful nihilist requires some effort.

The affirmation of courage is not simply the "courage to be," as Paul Tillich called it,[2] but the *courage to become*, because it is the latter, not the former, that is the essence of the species. Tillich affirmed the courage to persist in the face of nonbeing and death. But it is the courage to *become* that best expresses the dynamic character of human existence. Our task is not simply to survive, but to forge our own realities. We have no clearly defined essence to fulfill, only an existence to create. Humans are able to conceive or invent their own destinies. All other species have natures, which they seek to realize. Human nature is in the realm of consciousness, freedom, autonomy, and creativity. We are free to decide who we shall be, where and how we shall live.

Accordingly, the first principle of humanism is related to our lack of ontological moorings. The fact that we are free means that we must choose what we are and where we will be—within the confines, of course, of the time-space framework and in the context of our social institutions and cultural milieu. And this is the same challenge of choice for the solitary individual pondering his or her own future, as it is for the tribe or nation-state debating how to formulate its policies.

The constant task of the human spirit is to overcome the desire to escape into another world, to continue to live in spite of adversity, to withstand the tides of fortune, to express creative acts, and to redirect our efforts in the future. This requires the expression of the courage to both persevere and to become; and what we choose to be, or where we will live, or what we will do tomorrow, the next year, or the next decade depends upon our determination and resolve. Accordingly, the *vitality of courage* is the stimulus and motivation that enables us to fulfill our interests, desires, and values, whatever they are. We have the power to be and to become, and the key question is whether we are willing to seize the opportunities, take destiny into our own hands, and assume the responsibility for our future being.

Anti-humanistic transcendental theism is the polar opposite of humanistic freedom. For there is a collapse of courage, a failure of nerve, an escape from freedom, and a retreat from reason into the myths of consolation. Transcendentalism is unable to face the reality of human finitude. It is unable to accept the finality of death. It is an expression of human weakness. *Weltschmerz* (pessimism) gnaws at the inward marrow of the self, and fear and foreboding may overwhelm a person. Theists may be aware of the views of pessimistic nihilists that all is for naught in the end. They refuse, however, to accept this final verdict, the paradox of evil, the cruel blows of fortune; and so instead they willingly barter their freedom and reason for the myth of salvation. In an act of self-denial, they proclaim, "Verily, we are nothing without God." We are ultimately impotent, unable to fathom the universe. We passively submit to the eternal spirit in the hope of escaping from the brute onslaught of existence. We will become selfless. We will submit in prayer and obedience to the ultimate forces that we cannot fathom and do not comprehend. "God, do not forsake us, we are yours, body and soul," theists plead.

Perhaps the theist's response to nothingness is offered out of a love for humankind: unable to accept life's injustice and unfairness—the death of a child, the tortured suffering of an elderly person dying of an incurable cancer, the collapse of the economy, or the defeat of the army. And so theistic religion provides balm for the aching heart. It is moral poetry meant to soothe the void and the sorrow. What does it all mean? "It makes no sense without Thee, God," the believer sobs within his heart. An earthquake or tornado destroys a church, and a hundred people praying within on a Sunday morning are maimed or killed. Believers do not know how to interpret this, and so they redouble their supplication to God. Nature has struck a cruel blow, they cry after an earthquake, and by a convoluted logic proclaim that only God had saved them. If a prophecy fails, they may, if they lack self-confidence, only reaffirm their original commitment to the prophecy.

This makes no sense to pessimistic nihilists, who confront the same abyss but cannot take the leap of faith to overcome it. Facing nothingness, they affirm that nothing is true, that all is vanity, that human existence is meaningless, having no ultimate significance. If pushed to the consistency of their logic, if it is all senseless, they should not embark upon any long-range plans, nor seek to realize any projects, small or grand, pedestrian or noble.

Neither the theist nor the nihilist can escape from the demands of daily living. One cannot simply flee to God now nor blithely choose to exit from this life and die. In order to live, of necessity one must exert some effort and, at a minimum, exercise the courage to endure. The theist, at least, is no longer worried about death, or so he says. God is in heaven and all is well. One can exert enormous labors in the world to fulfill this religious mythology: build cathedrals, achieve secular goals, even conquer new continents, though in the end this metaphysics is based on a mistaken appraisal of the human condition and a false belief in ultimate salvation. No such saving grace is available to pessimistic nihilists.

The ontological challenge to humanism has been laid down: Can humanism, in the light of existential reality as seen by the pessimistic nihilist and in the face of human finitude, nonetheless inspire us to undertake magnificent deeds and express high idealism? Can atheists build empires, create philosophical systems, compose operas, and discover scientific theories without the illusion of immortality or God? That is, of course, the basic question to be asked of humanism. I reiterate that the first principle is *courage*, and its antithesis is fear and cowardice. How will courage be stimulated; what will be the motive to action, the inspiration to undertake plans and projects, not simply to live, but to desire to prosper and excel? It is clear that empires have been built by nonbelievers—from Greece and Rome to Renaissance city-states, from Chinese and Japanese empires to liberal and secular states of the modern world. Pointing to these facts of history may not be enough for theists, who crave something *more* to sustain them and something dramatic to inspire them, nor will it motivate the nihilists, who abandon all dreams of empires as foolhardy.

THE INSPIRATION OF HOPE

The answer to this question is that courage means nothing in and of itself, unless it is accompanied by its fair companion *hope*. But what shall we hope for, what prospects and promises shall we seek to fulfill? If the human condition were irremediably hopeless, courage would have little attraction or appeal. The old adage: "Where there is life there's hope,"[3] takes on special significance, as does Alexander Pope's observation that "hope springs eternal in the human breast."[4] For in living, doing, desiring, and striving, our hopes are a constant stimulus to action. Hope is enmeshed with the very fabric of that which we prize and value. We wish to fulfill our goals; we strain to reach them, and our wishes are intertwined with and fueled by our hopes.

Our hopes are causative of our futures. They generate our activities and feed our passions. The future depends on what we resolve to undertake: wish is father to the fact. Living involves ongoing processes of desiring and aspiring, and it is replete with efforts exerted by us to realize our hopes. Not all of our goals can be effectively reached. Many of our hopes flounder unfulfilled; they may be dashed by things beyond our control, by impenetrable obstacles placed in our way. Yet there are always new desires to motivate us and new dreams to stimulate us to action. A mother hopes that her daughter will marry well, a father that she will become a teacher or lawyer. A student hopes to earn good grades in school, a general to succeed in battle, a minister to be able to persuade his flock, a poet to be recognized by her peers. We thus are constantly stimulated by a plurality of wishes, desires, and hopes. Many are minor and small in scale; others loom large in ambition and scope or are grandiose and majestic in magnitude. Many may only wish to bake a cake; some will aspire to conquer a continent.

Dreams, hopes, and aspirations are the stuff of which life is made. Yet both the transcendental theist and the pessimistic nihilist view this life as tragic. Many have an exaggerated fear of ultimate failure and defeat. Theists in particular have a distorted sense of their own impotence. If we are all alone in a vast impersonal universe, they believe, all would be without meaning. Why strive to do *anything*, why love or forgive, seek to pacify or mollify, to create or achieve if, *in the long run*, it all leads to ultimate nonbeing? Thus the sense of death may overwhelm the existential consciousness. Such a morbid view of the ultimate defeat of human life for both the theist and the nihilist may generate an attitude of hopelessness. The mood is not unlike that of the gazelle that, stalked and finally seized by the lion, collapses in fear, resigned to its fate, awaiting death in the jaws of the predator.

For theists hope is essential to the faith, but their hope is for an eternal life. For humanists this is a false hope based on wishful thinking, unsubstantiated by evidence or reason, a mere leap of faith to satisfy psychological cravings. For Dante, human existence is hopeless only if one is condemned to hell. *"Lasciate ogni speranza, voi ch'entrate"* ("Abandon hope, all ye who enter here") is the sign over the portico of his Inferno.[5] The skeptical pessimist shares the theist's appraisal that in a universe without divine purpose, life would be devoid of meaning. Should a person lay awake nights worrying that the sun will cool down in five billion years and that all life on earth will eventually become extinct?

CAN HUMANISM INSPIRE HOPE?

My response to this question is that *hope* should not be generalized or capitalized. There is no sense of absolute Hope shining as a beacon light for all to aspire. There is no cosmic Prospect for the human species. This is the fallacy of monotheism, which postulates God as the source of cosmic hope, a false belief in things unseen. There is no metaphysical basis for hope. Like "being" or "existence," hope has no content per se; it should not be viewed as a purely abstract concept. Rather hope should be interpreted pluralistically. It is multifarious, of virtually infinite varieties, as diverse as the idiosyncratic values and desires that people have. Its content is psychological and sociocultural. Hope implies the expectation and anticipation that what we want will come into being. The hopes of people vary, just as their individual personalities differ. Many hopes are as specific as, "I hope my fox terrier wins the championship at the dog show," or "I hope that it doesn't rain tomorrow and ruin my new white shoes." Or it can be socially contextualized: "We hope that our Roumanian team wins the Olympic Gold Medal," or "We hope for an early economic recovery," or "We hope for a bumper crop." Hope is always prospective, pointing to a future that we wish to eventuate, or that we work hard to bring into being: "We hope the next season will show an improvement in sales," or "We hope a great number of our students are admitted to good colleges."

Hope has both a cognitive component and an emotive basis. Hopes that are purely emotional often are capricious, as in the case of the young girl who dreams of Prince Charming sweeping her off her feet, or the couple who hopes to afford the mansion on the hill. All too often such dreams are pure expressions of wishful thinking. Thus we should recognize the importance of a cognitive or intellectual element in formulating and framing our hopes. I say that "I hope that I will graduate from medical school next year." This is not unrealistic if it is based on an accurate appraisal of my capacities and the opportunities for success. Or I may say that "We hope to reach a negotiated settlement," as when Palestinian and Israeli delegations work hard in hammering out a peace treaty that they can live with.

Presumably our hopes are concrete and contextual: they are a function of who and what we are, where we live, and the kinds of social conditions that prevail. If I am a beggar, I may be unable to buy the things I desire. If I am deformed, the girl or boy of my dreams may not be mine, and unrequited love may ensue. If I am without musical talent, I may hope to be a great musician or a conductor, but without any realistic chance of achieving it. If I am working in the coal mines of Yorkshire in the nineteenth century, or am a coolie in China during the Fu Dynasty, my options may be severely limited. Thus the range of human aspirations in one sense is relative to an historical epoch. If I have a debilitating disease, which confines me to a wheelchair, what I will do depends on objective constraints imposed on me. On the other hand, if I am reasonably healthy and live in a free, open, democratic, peaceful, and fairly prosperous society, I may have open horizons as a young person to become a computer scientist or a teacher, an engineer or an architect, a nurse or a business executive.

Related to hope is *power;* that is, we must have both the capacity and where-withal to realize our goals—otherwise they are simply dreams. Our ends depend on the means at our disposal. Some ends are purely vain and there is little or no hope of attainment, or they may not be genuine. Hopes are also a function of my freedom and of whether I am permitted the opportunity to attain my goals. If I live in a class-ridden society, my chances of improving my economic status may be severely limited by social barriers. However, our sense of power also depends on whether we have the determination and drive to seize the opportunity and change the circumstances within the social environment. In two provocative books, *Profiles of Genius* and *Profiles of Female Genius,*[6] Gene Landrum notes that innovative and creative people often face insuperable odds. He found this to be true not only about the founders of new industries, but also about great statesmen, explorers, military leaders, artists, poets, and scientific achievers—from Edison, Picasso, and Einstein to Catherine the Great, Golda Meir, and Ted Turner. Such people will not take *no* for an answer, and they will not easily accept defeat. Everyone around them may advise caution or retreat or may point out the hazards and the dangers of precipitous action. Yet these people are willing to persevere in spite of the naysayers. They have the Promethean qualities of audacity and verve. They are willing to take chances.

Promethean personalities have a passionate, volcanic lust to achieve. They are visionaries, possessed of prodigious energies. Often their extraordinary drive for achievement is a result of frustration, deprivation, and traumatic experiences that might dissipate or burn out other personalities. The Promethean's temperament is highly competitive and aggressive. He is not only a risk-taker, but also a thrill-seeker. Such a person can live with uncertainty and unpredictability and is able to tolerate novelty. He is often impatient and impulsive in achieving goals. According to William James, it is only by risking our persons that we live at all. Often enough our faith beforehand in an uncertified result is the only thing that makes the result come true.[7] Such individuals are highly charismatic, enthusiastic, and inspirational. They exasperate, but also motivate, those around them.

Perhaps there is a genetic and glandular difference between at least two types of individuals: those who seek comfort and security and are fearful of change versus those who relish adventure, challenge, and overcoming obstacles and are willing to take chances. It is the latter who exert strenuous efforts to achieve grandiose goals; they become the captains of industry, the great entrepreneurs, the founders, discoverers, and creators of new ways of living, whether in the arts, the sciences, or practical life. It is here that hope emerges as the companion of courage. For where there is a glimmer of a new frontier to be developed, the men and women of great courage will leap in boldly and fearlessly. They have the stamina and backbone to persevere. They are defiant of conventions and are inured to what others will say. They are willing to confront danger; they can bear up under great pressure. Many are daring and dauntless in their response. Unflinching, they leap forward in perilous endeavors. They are adventurers creating new worlds for us to live in. Many innovators are condemned by society as heretics or radicals; but if they do succeed, then they are heralded as the heroes or heroines of civilization. According to Emerson, "Self-trust is the essence of heroism."[8] And so those who do not falter need self-confidence and self-assurance if they are to see their dreams and hopes come true. Though they may have inner doubts, they exude self-confidence and have high self-esteem. They do not allow their self-doubts or lack of self-respect to consume them. The quality of pride is a virtue for the achiever: pride in their work and a sense of satisfaction in what they are attempting to achieve; they are the titans of experiment.

Opposing them are the cowards, pusillanimous and fearful souls who are unwilling to take risks. Timorous and weakhearted, they are suspicious of new ways of life. Lacking in self-confidence and fearful of change, or seeking a life of comfort and peace, they commonly resent great achievers—those who flout the sacred cows and stand out as different. Superstition, faith, and credulity are the last recourses of the craven. They are often prey to every charlatan promising them the Absolute Truth or Ultimate Salvation. They need God, a master, or a dictator to tell them what to do, if they are to survive the challenge. They prefer the security and consolation offered by the priests, rather than the challenges of using critical intelligence. Arthur Schopenhauer once observed that if you want comfort, go to the priests; if you want truth, to the philosophers. One reason why religious civilizations have burned heretics, from Socrates to Bruno, is that nonconformists do not accept the unquestioned dogmas and beliefs of society. Nietzsche castigated Christianity because he thought it was a religion of slaves—all those who lacked the will-to-power; and he attacked socialism as an expression of the resentment of the weak against the strong, as an effort to restrain them, and as a fear of greatness. The Communist totalitarian Soviet state likewise feared initiative and dissent, and so it sought to silence Sakharov and Solzhenitsyn.

Courage and hope are essential to the human spirit. By "human spirit" I mean the spirit and vitality of human beings who are willing to make their mark upon the world. Is it that I am exalting the masculine qualities of boldness and audacity? Is it the phallic symbol, the male thrust of the erect penis entering the vagina, that I admire? Do I denigrate female acquiescence, passivity, and submission? No. This sexist attitude is a holdover from a bygone age of patriarchy, where women were held in bondage to men. *All* men and women, I submit, have to some extent the capacity for creativity, the verve to accept challenges, the desire to express ideals, dreams, hopes, and aspirations in the real world. Women, as well as men, if given the opportunity, can excel. What I am focusing on is the "human spirit," and by this I do not mean some ghostlike and ethereal soul of the mystic removed from the world, but the spirited expression of our talents in the world. One can talk about a "spirited horse," meaning a valiant and courageous animal—though there is an effort by his trainer to break his will and domesticate him. There are also spirited human beings—in spite of the effort of dogmatic theists or totalitarians to dominate and tame them by tranquilizing them with metaphysical systems of false hope.

What I am presenting here is the *eupraxis* (good practice) of humanism: the virtue of courage, the emphasis on human power, the willingness to create and seize new possibilities, and the capacity to exercise freedom of choice. This is not only an ideal for rare or exceptional *übermenschen* (supermen), or the sole prerogative of privileged elites. All human beings, I submit, are able to tap their own personal potentialities to some extent. All persons have the capacity for self-reliance and the virtue of independent action. Creative heroes and heroines exemplify the highest reaches of excellence; Beethoven came from a poor family, Abe Lincoln was born in a log cabin, Mary Ann Evans (George Eliot) lived in a paternalistic and sexist Victorian social environment, Einstein became a refugee from Nazi Germany, and Richard Wright emerged from a deprived background in Mississippi.

For the humanist, Prometheus stands forth as the exemplar of the heroic figure, for he challenged the gods in their own abode. Prometheus deplored the wretched lives that humans lived. Out of love for humans, he taught them to reason and to think, and he made it possible for them to cease living in bondage and to become able to achieve a better life. It is this act of audacity expressed by the Promethean myth that the humanist admires because it heralds human power and independence. Should we seek to model ourselves after Prometheus instead of Buddha or Jesus? If we do, then confidence, the stout heart, and defiance are key human virtues—not humility and self-effacing passivity. It is the heroic virtues of the daring, unflinching, adventurous, and enterprising human being who climbs mountains because they are there and builds castles because they fulfill his dreams. He is relentless in the pursuit of his goals.[9] We need, however, to balance courage with other values. I surely do not mean foolhardy rashness, but courage based on a rational appraisal of our goals.

Implicit in the courageous posture is the virtue of autonomy, a recognition of self-power, a need to cultivate our individual creative talents. By courage I do not mean simply the exemplary talents of the hero-warrior displayed in battle or the strenuous exertion of the Olympic champion in competition with others. These are among the highest peaks of human excellence. Rather I mean the display of the courageous qualities of vitality and affirmation in even the pedestrian activities of life. Included in this is the willingness and the ability to endure defeat. No one is entirely able to fulfill all of his desires or succeed in all of his ventures. Perhaps the greatest test of courage is to bear defeat without losing heart. The supreme test of endurance is whether we can resolve to persist and whether we are willing to undertake new challenges in the midst of adversity. This brings us back to hope. We cannot be courageous if our situation is totally hopeless. But is the human condition ever completely hopeless, or are there not some redeeming virtues to life still remaining?

Is there a metaphysics of hope? If we take the historical point of view, and if we recognize the finitude of our reach, is not life hopeless in the end? My answer is that it need not be, for life while lived can be good in and of itself, and the achievements that we create can have their own intrinsic worth aside from any eternal quality they may have. Where there is some hope, where the situation allows us some free choice, and where we are not completely hampered by our station and its duties, we are capable of some considered enthusiasm. Life, in spite of difficulties, still can be good, and we can find some measure of hope in our future, some worthwhile qualities of experience to enjoy. There still are some promising options. Thus we can be sanguine if we expect that some of our goals can be achieved. We can hope to uncover some redeeming virtues and some reason for a positive attitude. Indeed, under optimal conditions we may even overflow with exuberance and buoyancy, because our bright prospects augur well. Of course, in most situations a naïve optimism is inappropriate. We perhaps need a realistic appraisal of the real possibilities and some reflective evaluation of what is likely to ensue. The best course is balanced optimism. The opposite of this is undue pessimism. Is this latter attitude ever justified? Surely one must distinguish between extreme and balanced pessimism.

One must concede that sometimes a person's situation may become hopeless—as when he discovers that he has an incurable cancer and that he has only a short while to live. The best response to this is that every moment is precious; we should live each moment fully and still seek to savor its delicacies. Is this possible when the barbarians enter the gates, rape our women, and kill our children, or when I lose everything in a devastating earthquake or an economic collapse, or when I am awaiting imminent death?

Bill Rourke,[10] a young man whom I knew, developed multiple sclerosis. He suffered for over a decade. This cruel and debilitating disease finally rendered him almost completely paralyzed. He was in constant pain. To the very last, he was at work on a book, which he hoped to finish. He could complete the book, he told me over the phone, only by dictating it to his wife. At last he died, his work incomplete, though he had strained every nerve and fiber to bring it to completion. His wife tearfully reported to me that in the last days Bill, a steadfast atheist, converted to Catholicism, the religion of his youth. A strong and committed atheist, his life had become hopeless, and out of suffering he succumbed to the myth of consolation and embraced a supernatural metaphysics of hope. There are no doubt countless others like him. But for the humanist, this is a desperate act of a despondent person who, cruelly buffeted by forces against him that he could not control and whose spirit was engulfed by the tides of fortune, finally surrendered.

Is there hope for the timorous souls of the world? Yes, responds the courageous person; wherever there is a breath of life there is hope! Do not surrender your dignity as a person to the purveyors of false hope. Unfortunately, for some people, their fears overwhelm their resolve. "Cowards die many times before their deaths; the valiant never taste of death but once," observed Shakespeare in *Julius Cæsar*.[11] No doubt, courage is a product of feeling as well as of belief, and the wellspring of motivation lies deep within the marrow of one's being. Alas, not everyone can stand resolute at the last moment until the end. Awaiting death, some people may finally give up the struggle. The response of a free person in such a situation is: if I am dying an incurable or painful death and there is no quality of life left, I would opt for active euthanasia and suicide. But Bill Rourke was surrounded by devout Roman Catholics who thought it was a sin for him to take his own life. And so they not only sinned against life, but also sinned against death itself. A free person should be able, like Lucius Seneca, David Hume, Arthur Schopenhauer, and Sidney Hook advised, to determine with courage and fortitude the time and manner of his death. This is an expression of the freedom and autonomy of the person, and it is a mark of the ultimate power of an individual.

There is no predetermined future; an individual's life is not predestined by some hidden plan of some beneficent or diabolical being. One's destiny, to some extent, is in one's own hands, limited though it is by nature, one's genetic endowment, and the world in which one lives. We make choices, and consequences flow from them; our choices are conditioned by these outcomes. Nonetheless, we are free to make our own life worlds, to create our own futures, and to leave our mark upon the world. Aristotle recognized that there are tragic aspects to life that may befall a noble person who is reduced to nothing, as in *Oedipus Rex*. But this he attributed to a defect in character, which leads to a person's demise and destruction.[12] Thus one cannot deny that there are some tragic situations in life: the sudden death of a loved one by a haphazard accident or a cruel disease, the collapse of a building, the failure of a noble enterprise, or a betrayal by a close friend in whom one has placed great confidence. Life is often impoverished not only by evil and the unexpected, but also by conflicts of goods and rights, not all of which we can fulfill or possess. There is no reason to claim, however, that life is tragic in a cosmic sense. There are little tragedies and great ones, but on the whole, the good may outweigh the bad, and life can be abundant with both. "It is a miserable state of mind to have few things to desire and many things to fear," observed Bacon.[13] It is an affirmative state of mind to find life full of opportunities, satisfactions, and excellencies, the courageous person asserts. The point is that a free person has some realistic appraisal of the human condition, and he never abandons the human prospect because of the sorrow and defeat that is endured. These are mitigated by the joys of achievement. It is the courageous person who can best bear adversity in spite of it, and who, in response to the theist and nihilist, finds life significant and worthwhile.

I should point out that courage as a virtue in and of itself is inadequate, for one may be foolish and stupidly defend a patently false doctrine or unattainable cause. It is therefore important that one's hopes be realistic in character and that they be grounded upon a cognitive appraisal of the facts of the situation. Similarly, the expression of courage may be selfish, and people may be impervious to the effect of their actions on others. Accordingly, courage should be harmonized with a caring attitude toward other people.

Many humanistic philosophers have considered reason or rationality to be more fundamental in the lexicon of humanistic virtues than courage. Indeed, I have at times defined secular humanism primarily as "a method of inquiry," meaning that we need to submit all claims to truth to a process of evidential and rational inquiry.

Courage in one sense must precede reason. One may be intelligent or perceptive but use reason only in limited contexts, and fear may so overtake a person that he submits to a fanciful transcendental myth to "save his soul." A person may lack the courage of his convictions and cave in to the compelling demands of religious authority. Many atheists and agnostics are afraid to come out of the closet, and so they submit to religious authority, even though they know it to be false. Thus the courage to face the universe in the light of reason and devoid of a supernatural creator is crucial for the humanistic outlook. One may say that inasmuch as viewing reality in naturalistic terms depends upon the use of reason, the courage to face the universe for what it is and is not is a correlative virtue. Therefore, courage and reason may be said to go hand in hand as two key humanistic virtues, though the former still has a kind of priority.

11

LIBERTARIANISM AND MORAL FREEDOM

What is the relationship between liberty and morality? Can one coherently espouse libertarianism, yet deny that it presupposes a moral philosophy? To attempt to so argue, in my judgment, is contradictory, for the defense of liberty assumes a set of underlying values. A problem of definition emerges when we attempt to ascertain the meaning of *libertarianism*. It has been taken as an economic doctrine concerned primarily with preserving economic liberty and the free market against the encroachments of government. It has also been used in political philosophy to defend human or natural rights, civil liberties, and the open democratic society. Economic and political liberty are indeed central to the libertarian philosophy, but they are, I submit, derivative from an even more fundamental libertarian ideal: the high moral value placed upon individual freedom of choice.

The classical liberal is concerned with expanding the autonomy of persons over their own lives. This means that social restraints placed upon individual choice should be reduced. These are many, for large-scale governmental power is a primary threat to individual freedom. Many twentieth-century liberals under the influence of Marx abandoned the classic libertarian emphasis on individual freedom in favor of a concern for social welfare. They sought to extend the paternalistic role of the state in regulating the private sector and fulfilling functions that they believe are not being adequately performed by other social institutions. The welfare liberal believes that it is the duty of society to ameliorate the lot of poor persons and to redistribute wealth—all in the name of a theory of "justice," "fairness," or "equity." Welfare-statist mentality has unleashed a self-righteous egalitarianism that has undermined the incentives of productive citizens in favor of the disadvantaged. The principle of equality in its extreme form has led reformists beyond "equality before the law" and "equality of opportunity" to guaranteeing equality of results. They argue that because not everyone has the same access, social policies must equalize the conditions of opportunity. They would force people to be equal against their will. Libertarians thus have rightly pointed out that doctrines of social equality have been often counterproductive, smothering individual initiative and in Marxist cultures leading to the infamous gulags of the spirit.

The libertarian agenda is incomplete, however, if it is only concerned with the evils of government. For government is not the only social institution that can unduly restrain human freedom. Powerful economic corporations can erode human freedom. They can limit an individual's freedom by defining the conditions of employment, fixing prices, driving out competition, and setting the whole tone of social life. I am not taking the Marxists' side here, for I believe that a capitalist society (with some concern for social justice) is the best guarantee of human freedom. Wherever the state has a monopoly of power, both economic and political freedom soon disappear. A free market and a strong private sector are thus necessary conditions for political freedom. One needs vigorous competition and a pluralistic economy, in which there are diverse centers of economic decision making.

Libertarians abhor governmental control of the media of communication. The libertarian seeks a free market of ideas. Yet he must likewise be apprehensive of the de facto domination of the media by powerful corporate interests. Much of the mass media—television, movies, magazines, and newspapers—have been dominated by one point of view. If conglomerate control of the publishing industry continues to grow, it tends to push out small publishers and debase the quality of publishing. Still, western capitalist societies allow more freedom than others. Thus I do not agree with Marcuse's pessimistic diagnosis outlined in *One-Dimensional Society*. Nevertheless, not all capitalists are libertarians; nor are they necessarily concerned with preserving and extending individual freedom.

What I have been saying seems also to be the case in respect to religious institutions. Powerful churches have often suppressed nonbelievers. In this regard, religious institutions may function as oppressively as the state, dictating thought and practice, regulating morality and sexuality, on a de facto if not a de jure basis. I am always surprised to discover that some conservatives will defend economic liberty yet readily condone the suppression of religious dissent. American society has had a proliferation of religious denominations and as a result has developed a truce based on the principles of ecumenism. Given the fact of opposing sects, all should have a place in the sun. In some areas—fundamentalism in the South or Roman Catholicism in the North—freedom of conscience in religion and morality is still suspect. There is hardly room left for the secular humanist, freethinker, or village atheist in a society dominated by religious tradition. The religious liberal thus defends the separation of church and state and liberty of conscience. Yet conformist pressures seek to impose sanctions on those who violate prevailing religious conventions.

Perhaps the most encouraging development in the past three decades on the freedom agenda has been the growth of moral libertarianism. The moral premise is familiar: individuals should have the right to satisfy their tastes, cultivate their values, and develop their lifestyles as they see fit as long as they do not impose their values on others or prevent others from exercising their own values.

Moral libertarianism, as is apparent, has made considerable progress in democratic societies. There has been a noticeable lessening of censorship in the arts, television, movies, the theater, and magazine and book publishing. Liberty of expression has been extended far beyond what was imagined only a generation ago—but it has led to the growth of a pornography industry. In sexual morality, there has been a loosening of traditional restrictions; divorce has been made easier and is now widespread. Laws regulating sexual practices have been repealed, as well as those concerned with adultery, anal–oral sexuality, and so on. The belief that two or more consenting adults should have the right to pursue in private their sexual proclivities without social or legal interference is now widely accepted by a significant sector of the community. This has led in part to the gay-liberation movement. Similar changes have occurred in regard to women, who demand that they be treated as persons capable of choosing their own destinies. Permissive attitudes have also developed concerning drugs. If the state permits alcohol and cigarettes, why not marijuana? Today marijuana is as common in some circles as soft drinks and beer, and so are cocaine and heroin.

In one sense some of these new freedoms—though they liberate people from stultifying customs—have gone too far. Although one may in principle agree that individuals ought to be allowed to do their own thing, in practice this may lead to a breakdown of civilized conduct, indiscriminate promiscuity, violence, drugs, and a lack of moral virtue and excellence. This is particularly the case with many young people. Many college graduates have betrayed the hope and promise placed in them. They are the products of broken homes and a narcissistic morality gone astray. Living off the generosity of relatives or friends, many have abandoned self-reliance and have become self-indulgent. How can one simply defend moral liberty and ignore the loss of virtue? This question is not simply theoretical, but has high practical import for our society. In mass consumer-oriented society, products are manufactured and sold and tastes conditioned without any regard for their moral worth. The immediacies of enjoyment are taken as ends in themselves, divorced from the hard work and effort necessary to achieve them. The quality of life has given way to banality.

This is the indictment of the libertarian society that one hears today. It is no doubt overstated. Nonetheless it has an element of truth. If a choice were to be made between a free society and a repressive one, libertarians would opt for the former over the latter, even though they recognize unfortunate by-products as the price of freedom. Moreover, perhaps the only way for some to learn to appreciate responsible freedom is to experience the consequences of their mistakes. Nevertheless, at times liberty may surely lead to license when it should be accompanied by virtue. Is the breakdown of the moral order due to the excessive moral freedom we have enjoyed? May it be attributed to the decline in religious faith and the growth of secular humanism and libertarianism? Can morality prevail only if it is guided by religion?

I do not think it is evident that religious societies are any more moral than nonreligious ones. It may be true that outward displays of sexual conduct and other "immoral" practices are often prohibited in repressive religious communities. Yet they may be masking a hypocritical double standard. Religious societies may be insensitive to other forms of injustice. They may seek to impose order, hierarchy, and the status quo on those who resist them. But more decisively, a libertarian conception of the moral life that has a secular foundation is different from a religious–theistic one. It is not obedience to a prescribed moral code that is the mark of the moral person but the flowering of the free personality.

The libertarian in ethics maintains as his first principle the autonomy of moral choice. And this means the independence of the ethical judgment: that is, values and principles are not to be deduced a priori from absolute rules, but grow out of moral inquiry. Ethical choice requires a sensitivity to moral dilemmas, a willingness to grapple with conflicts in values and principles, rights and duties, as they are confronted in actual life. Authoritarian and legalistic systems of ethics are not based on final or fixed standards. Many traditional religious systems may seek to indoctrinate a set of norms by fiat. This is supposed to guarantee stability and regularity of conduct and to inhibit sinful behavior. A religious code, such as is found in the Ten Commandments, the Koran, or the Sermon on the Mount, may be supported by the authority of clergy and tradition. It may act as a regulative force, guarding against "deviant," "anomic," or "amoral" behavior. But in what sense are these systems moral? There are traditionalist libertarians in the economic sphere who insist that liberty needs to be supported by religious strictures. And they justify religious–moral repression for channeling conduct along approved lines.

A moral libertarian by contrast rejects authoritarianism in the moral domain as much as he does political statism or economic regulation. Yet he is faced with a profound dilemma. For if individuals were suddenly released from all restrictions—political, social, moral, and traditional—what would ensue? Would they be, as the romantic anarchist hopes, noble, beneficent, and sympathetic in their relations to other individuals? Would they be temperate and rational in their inner personal lives? Would their choices be truly autonomous and issue from reflective deliberation?

Regretfully, to emancipate individuals who are unprepared for it from all social restraints may indeed result in license. Autonomous choice is not genuine unless individuals are first nurtured to appreciate and handle it. Perhaps the familiar distinction between two kinds of freedom needs to be restated: freedom from restraint is not the same as the developed freedom of a person to realize his or her potentialities. But there is still another dimension: the full autonomy of choice can only occur in a developed personality.

Some theists attempt to impose authoritarian structures from without by establishing rules of conduct and instilling them in the young, offering no rhyme or reason other than God's commandments. These homilies often do not take hold, for they do not issue from within a person's felt life. Although they may erect defenses against temptation and immorality, they can often be weakened and may collapse. Basically irrational, they do not serve the individual in a changing social world in which new challenges are constantly being presented. If they are overthrown, what can the libertarian offer in their place?

The solution to the problem seems to me to be clear: libertarianism in its full sense—that is, the development of autonomous individuals capable of free choice—is not possible unless certain antecedent conditions are fulfilled—a program of moral education and growth is necessary to instill virtue in the young, not blind obedience to rules but the ability for conscious reflective choice. The Thrasymachian man, the absolute tyrant, as Plato long ago observed, is prey to every lust and passion, every temptation of power and ambition. He is buffeted by random irrational drives within, unable to resist or control them, and by amoral power conflicts from without. The truly free individual is one whose choices in some sense emanate from a harmonious personality, one with some developed character, a set of dispositional traits, capable of a deliberate process of reasoned decision making.

This seems to me to be the message of the great philosophic tradition from Socrates and Aristotle to Spinoza, Mill, and Dewey: that rationality and virtue are the source of freedom. If this is the case, to grant freedom without preparation to a child or adolescent, a savage or despot, incapable of reflective choice or mature judgment, unrestrained by a seasoned disposition, is hardly a test of a person's freedom, for one may be at the mercy of impulses.

Accordingly, freedom makes no sense and is literally wasted unless it is first nourished in the soil of moral growth, where it can be watered and fed. It is as if democracy were suddenly imposed on a people unready for it, or for which it was alien. It can only function effectively where there are values of tolerance, respect for the views of others, a willingness to negotiate and compromise differences, and a sense of civic virtues and responsibilities. Similarly, true freedom for the individual presupposes the concomitant emergence of moral development. It presumes moral education.

What kind of education and by whom and for what ends? These are important questions. Education is a social process. It goes on constantly—in the family, the churches, the schools, business organizations, the media, and in the greater society. It is not the sole responsibility of the state, for that may convert it into a form of mere indoctrination. By education, I mean the Greek form: self-actualization. We need to educate individuals so that they can realize their intellectual, aesthetic, and physical talents. And part of moral education is the developing capacity for self-mastery and control. It also involves the maturation of the ability to appreciate the needs of other human beings. In other words, moral education is training in responsibility: first, toward one's self, one's long-range self-interest in the world, learning how to cope with and solve problems that emerge in the environment; and second, toward others, developing altruistic concern for other human beings, an ability to share life's experiences, to help and be helped, to cooperate with others.

Kohlberg and Piaget have written at length about what they consider to be the stages of moral growth. One need not accept the precise theory as presented: from anticipation of reward and punishment, or conformity to social expectations, as motives of moral behavior, to considerations of utility, or the development of a sense of justice, as higher stages of moral growth. Nevertheless, one should surely recognize that there is a process of moral development. For there is a clear difference between the narcissistically self-centered individual (although some self-interest is an important component of a realistic ethics) and the person able to relate to others under conditions of mutual respect and cooperation. One should be more willing to entrust freedom to the latter person, and may be apprehensive about entrusting it to the former. As a libertarian, Mill was disturbed by the possible abuse of the hedonic criterion and insisted that pleasures differ on a qualitative scale.

To argue, as I have, that a philosophy of liberty most appropriately should involve a theory of virtue does not imply that we should deny freedom to those who are incapable of using it in the fully developed sense. Nor should the government or any self-appointed group set itself up as the arbiter of human freedom. One may consistently believe in a free society, yet also recognize that we have a double obligation: to grant freedom to individuals and also to encourage them to acquire the taste and capacity for growth and autonomy. The best way of doing the latter is not by dictate but by means of education and persuasion. Because we tolerate diversity does not mean that we necessarily approve of every style of life, however bizarre or offensive, that has been adopted. We need constantly to keep alive the art of criticism and moral suasion. Liberty does not imply permissiveness. It needs to be accompanied by an ethic that highlights the virtues of the mature personality. This includes *wisdom* (some capacity for intelligent reflective choice), *prudence* and *moderation* (some concern for one's long-range good), and *responsibility* (a genuine interest in the needs of others). Without virtue, the person freed from restraint may indeed be transformed into a moral monster.

Philosophers of ethics have consistently maintained that in the last analysis intelligence in an ordered personality is the most reliable guide for moral choice. What we ought to do is a function of a deliberate process wherein we examine alternatives, means, and consequences and after a comparative analysis make a choice that we consider to be the most suitable in the situation. One of the tasks of moral education is to develop persons who are capable of engaging in moral inquiry.

This will not do, we are reminded by critics of moral libertarianism, particularly those of a nonsecularist bent. Merely to have an autonomous individual is no guarantee that he will behave morally toward himself or others. We cannot educate individuals to be virtuous, we are told, without the authority of divine sanction. If the only guide is utilitarian ends, whether for the individual or the social good, then anything is possible and all things may be permissible. The critics of secular humanism and libertarianism also attack the effort to develop moral education and values clarification in the schools. They believe this is a "secular religion" that will only further undermine the moral standards of society.

Now it is true that many or most libertarians have emphasized utilitarian considerations in the decision-making process. Moral principles are held to be largely instrumental in the fulfillment of ends or values. The hedonic calculus judges actions by whether they maximize pleasure or happiness in the individual and society. Most libertarians have been relativists, situationalists, and naturalists. Such ethical theories have lacked a well-grounded theory of moral duty and obligation. In my view, however, this need not be the case. Libertarianism is incomplete as a moral philosophy and remains seriously in need of repair unless it is willing to modify its ethical system so that it can introduce deontological considerations.

What I have in mind here is the recognition that there are general ethical principles that ought to prevail in human relationships. These are grounded in human experience and have been tested in the crucible of history. Moral principles, in my judgment, are not simply an expression of subjective taste or caprice, but may have some empirical foundation. They are amenable to objective criticism. The human decencies are readily recognized by most human societies. We ought to tell the truth, be sincere and honest, and deal fairly with others; we ought to be cooperative, kind, considerate, thoughtful, and helpful; we ought not to waste our patrimony needlessly; we ought not to misuse others or be arrogant and unforgiving; we ought not to inflict pain needlessly or cruelly nor to be excessively vindictive; we ought to have friends, not simply acquaintances; we ought to seek justice and be beneficent.

This list of ethical principles is embodied in the proverbial truths discovered in human affairs. Many or most—but perhaps not all—are transcultural. They are general guides to conduct, not universal or absolute, because exceptions can be made to them on occasion. Nor are they intuitive or self-evident; if they are tested, it is by their observable consequences in conduct. They have some foundation in our sense of reason, and they may be given some strength in our motivation and be enhanced by emotion and feeling. They involve both our attitudes and our beliefs. They are prima facie, for they would seem to express general rules of conduct, which people come to recognize and respect as binding. How they apply and to what extent depend on the context. Sometimes one or more ethical principles may conflict. They may conflict with our cherished values. Moral deliberation is usually difficult, and often we must choose between the lesser of two evils. Or there may be a clash between two goods or two rights, both of which we cannot have.

These ethical principles embody moral truths. We may learn from practical experience that they cannot be easily violated without unfortunate consequences. They may be certified on their own merits without being derived or deduced from questionable theological or metaphysical assumptions. Human experience lends them authenticity.

Thus one may respond to the critics of moral libertarianism in the following manner:

1. Moral conduct is possible without belief in God, or benefit of religion or clergy. Believers are not more moral than nonbelievers.
2. Reasonable moral choices can be made and moral knowledge discovered in the process of human living and experience.
3. Accordingly, there can be an intelligent basis for moral obligations and responsibility.

One can be a moral libertarian and a secularist without being a libertine or a degenerate, and one may display the marks of nobility and excellence as part of the good life (as exemplified in the philosophies of Aristotle and Spinoza). In this post–Freudian age one may also live a significant moral life, which contains passion and reason, enjoyment and happiness, creativity and responsibility.

Freedom is not simply a claim to be made against society or a demand to be left alone. Freedom is not to be experienced indiscriminately nor squandered stupidly. It is an art to be cultivated and nourished intelligently. The intemperate person is neither autonomous nor civilized in respect to himself or his relations with others. Liberty and moral development go hand in hand; one can enhance the other. There is no complete freedom until there is the developed capacity for maturity in judgment and action. There can be no fully autonomous person unless there is realized growth.

Various forms of libertarianism can be defended independently of a secular focus. One can be an economic or civil libertarian and at the same time a born-again Christian, Buddhist monk, practicing Jew, devout Hindu, or Roman Catholic. We should not insist that secular libertarianism is the only basis for the moral life. I happen to believe that it is the one most in accord with the realities of nature and the promise of individual attainment. In a pluralistic society, those who wish to believe in God or to base their morality on religious faith should be perfectly free to do so. For many moderns, however, God is dead. But to be committed to the secular city does not mean that morality is dead or without moorings. Ethics is a vital dimension of the human condition, and a recognition of the ethical life has deep roots within western philosophy, antecedent even to the Judeo-Christian tradition. The current attack on secular morality is a display of ignorance about the origins of western civilization in Hellenic culture and its historic philosophic development. It is an attack on the philosophical life itself.

The charges against moral libertarianism are thus unfounded. Those who now oppose it cannot tolerate moral freedom nor can they stand to see other individuals suffer or enjoy life as they choose. But who are they to seek to impose their values on others? The fact that they assume a mantle of divine sanction for their views does not make them authoritative. Moreover, they fail to appreciate the fact that a moral person is not one who obeys a moral code out of fear or faith but who is motivated to behave morally out of a sense of moral awareness and conviction. The exemplar for the moral libertarian is the free person, capable of choice, yet one who has achieved some measure of moral growth. Such a person is the master of his own fate, responsible for his own career and destiny.

The free person is unlike the obedient servant or slave, who follows a moral code simply because it is commanded by authority or tradition. The free individual is independent, resourceful, and has confidence in his power to lead the good life. Moreover, he can enter into dignified relationships of trust and sincerity with his fellow human beings. He can live a constructive, productive, and responsible life. The moral philosophy of libertarian humanism is thus worthy of admiration. It needs not apologize to those who seek to demean or denigrate its excellence or virtue. In a sense it is the highest expression of moral virtue: a tribute to the indomitable creative spirit of human personality and achievement.

PART III

ALTRUISM

12

LOVE AND FRIENDSHIP

OUR NEED FOR LOVE

Many critics of humanism believe that it is primarily concerned with the individual's personal satisfaction and creative fulfillment. This they charge is too self-centered and egoistic. But this is far from the case, for the autonomous human being cannot find life completely satisfying unless he can relate to other human beings. Sociality is so basic to our natures as humans that unless we can share our joys and sorrows, we are condemned to lead narrow and futile existences. The purely autistic person has limited horizons. His life lacks full body and flavor; it misses the most important ingredient of the full life, without which we can never feel complete: *les autres* (others).

We are defined as persons by the objects of our interest. If our interests are narrow, then so are we. Insofar as we can extend the range of our concerns, we are able to expand the dimensions of our being.

There are several ways in which we can broaden our horizons. On the simplest level, I have already pointed out the need for intimacy with at least one other person. The fullest expression of this need is in loving someone else. Love can be possessive, especially when we consider another human being an object and seek to monopolize him or her for our own consummatory enjoyment. Here the primary motive may be selfish: we wish to be loved, stroked, and caressed, to receive pleasurable stimulation. But there is another sense of love: the ability to *give* love without necessarily receiving it in return. Here, we derive satisfaction simply because we do something for someone else, not because that person responds fully in kind. Possessive love is infantile. It says, I want you to love me, I miss you, or I need you. The ego dominates this relationship. The possessive person becomes insanely jealous because he believes that the relationship will be threatened if another person enters the scene. Historically, husbands possessed their wives, who were considered little more than chattel. For the wife merely to look at another man would provoke jealous rage. Similarly, women had a smothering attitude toward their husbands and lovers and could not tolerate any sign of interest in another woman. But matrimony should not mean the extinction of our personalities or interests in others as friends, colleagues, or even lovers—difficult though it is for most people to overcome the consuming flames of jealousy.

Many relationships are simply contractual, that is, we agree to do someone a favor knowing that it is good policy and that the person will reciprocate. This is an important ingredient in a relationship; it involves prudential self-concern. Yet there is another kind of relationship that is based on the ability to give of oneself without any thought of direct gain. This kind of feeling especially manifests itself in the relationship of a lover to the person loved. A person who truly loves someone would, under certain conditions, virtually give his life for the other person. He is willing to do things, day in and day out, for the loved one. No one compels him or her to do so; it is not forced but is an act of genuine affection. One gladly goes out of his way for the sake of the partner and does so because one wants to, because doing so gives intense satisfaction. I am not talking about dutiful acts that are done grudgingly because one believes one ought to do them, but about freely performed deeds of merit.

I surely do not wish to argue that one should always act selflessly. Relationships are not one-way streets to be used by another for his own advantage. A person who does not recognize another's needs as a human being is destructive both to himself and to the other person. Indeed, it is the ability to share with another some loving devotion that can bolster personal strength and autonomy. An individual who has not developed this other-regarding love remains dwarfed as a human.

The sharing of a full life with another human being—as in marriage—can be a special source of profound affection. Granted that some marriages fail; yet where marriages are viable they are cherished relationships (for however long they last—one year, five, ten, or a lifetime). One person relates to another on many levels—not only through sexual passion, but also through altruistic love, the joining together of careers, the raising of children, living together and sharing a home, pursuing activities cooperatively, and so on. To be alone in life and to do things by and for oneself is, of course, common; some individuals do not wish to enter into relationships they consider confining. But to partake of life with another can be a source of deep fulfillment. If one has someone to love—and that love is returned—one can remove the mask worn in the world and can experience the joys and sorrows of life with another without the need for pretense. The ability to share intimately with at least one other human being (whether inside or outside of marriage) is a priceless adornment of the good life.

LOVE WITHIN THE FAMILY

Another form of other-regarding love is, of course, the attitude of parents toward their children—their devotion and their willingness to make sacrifices for their children, even though the children many not appreciate them. One doesn't say, *I* am more important than my children; nor does one calculate what one's children will give in return—whether they will love me and appreciate what I am doing, or even support me in my old age. Rather, one gives of oneself without thought of gain; I worry about my children's health, education, and welfare. My family is a *whole*: I am identified in everything I do with them. My bounty belongs to them. We share cooperatively our food and shelter. My deepest hopes and dreams involve them. Their prospects for success in life are mine and their trials and tribulations also are mine. If my child is sick or languishes, I am troubled; if he or she does well, I beam with pride.

There exists, of course, parental love that is selfish. All too frequently children are viewed simply as an extension of the parent's self. Many parents project all of their unrealized dreams and aspirations onto their children. All of the things they were unable to achieve themselves are wished for their children; conversely, if parents succeed in their careers, they often want their children to follow in their footsteps. Such demanding attitudes are infantile and self-indulgent; adults who have them are trying to dominate their children. They require submissiveness and acquiescence. Where children do not live up to the parent's values, or where their love is unrequited in kind, they may be rejected, disowned, or disinherited.

A genuinely loving parent will attempt to do the best for the child, if one wishes the child to be a person in his or her own terms. Let the child become whatever he or she wishes. One may provide guidance and sustenance where it is needed, but if one loves one's child, one should want the child to develop its own unique personality. One can love one's child even though one disagrees fundamentally with the choice of a mate, career, or lifestyle. One should make allowances for one's children, recognize their limitations as well as their virtues, not demand the impossible, but love them for what they are. One ought to try to do the best for one's child, nourishing his or her physical and mental growth. At some point, however, one should let him or her go out into the world alone, to discover and create his or her own destiny.

To love someone in a healthy sense (whether a husband or wife, a son or daughter) is to want that person to flourish in his or her own terms and to develop his or her own autonomy. I am not arguing for self-sacrificing devotion beyond the limits of human endurance; nor am I saying that parents should give without limits to their children and never expect anything in return. Such a relationship would be debilitating to both the child and the parent. One wants one's child to be a *mensch*; yet some children may turn out bad, become self-centered, be incapable of loving. In such cases to continue to spill one's lifeblood for a good-for-nothing is the height of folly. We should do the best we can for our children; but if after all is said and done they are mean and inconsiderate, there should be limits to what we should continue to do for them. An unremitting giving without end may be more harmful than helpful: "my child, right or wrong" cannot apply forever. If parents have obligations to their children, the children in return bear certain responsibilities to their parents. If they fail consistently in their concern for their parents, the time may come for the parents to call a halt to their unquestioned giving.

As parents we should try to develop creativity in our children, to cultivate their individuality, assertiveness, independence, freedom. But we also need to cultivate in them the ability to relate to others. If we do not succeed in teaching our children to give love as well as to receive it, then we have indeed failed. However, if children turn out bad, it is not always the parents' fault. There may be other influences at work: bad friends, poor schooling, different psychological tendencies and needs. Doting parents who are too good to their children often unknowingly ruin them. To give our children everything they desire may be more destructive of developing responsible personhood than allowing them to earn what they want. To work and save, to plan and conserve, are important qualities of character that need cultivation. To go overboard in showering children with favors, toys, and trinkets that they did not themselves earn is to spoil the children—at least it contributes to a distorted view of the world. One reason that the children of affluent parents often turn sour is that they have been reared on an immediate-gratification demand basis. The child never becomes the adult. The parents are always there to help them if they falter, to make excuses if they fail, to gratify their hedonic needs as they demand.

Such children, overwhelmed by their own need for self-gratification, are self-centered; they take everyone around them, including their parents, for granted. They believe that they can always count on their parents to help them, no matter what they do. But what they lack is the ability to give love, not for a reward or out of habit, but out of genuine and loving concern. The question of how children should relate to their parents is a perennial problem that all human societies have faced. There are societies that have emphasized complete filial piety. This is best illustrated by traditional Chinese society. The parents were venerated by their children and grandchildren. Their word was final; they controlled money, power, and privilege. They demanded obedience; if their children did not follow their advice, they would be cast out. In this authoritarian family the entire life of the child was often dictated by the parents, including the choice of a mate and a career. This family structure hardly exists in modern society.

At the other extreme there is the youth-oriented culture in which the old are abhorred and their wishes and desires ignored. The extended family was able to provide members of the family with many more bonds of security and affection; the nuclear family often has ostracized grandparents and divested them of virtually all rights and dignity.

It is clear that for healthy relationships children need to develop a loving concern for their parents, a concern that will remain even after the children have gone out on their own. The desire of parents not to interfere with the lives of their children, to avoid any suggestion of authoritarian domination, has had the reverse effect of emotionally starving the parent. And their elderly parents or grandparents, having little contact with their children and a lack of love and endearment, are gradually strangled by their need for affection. Children should—even when they are older—demonstrate their love and affection for their parents. In order to do this, they need to develop an appreciation for the fact that their parents are themselves human: like everyone else, they have their own defects and limitations, their own needs and desires. Parents should not be placed on a pedestal as either models of perfection or as unquestioned authorities. Thus it is essential for children at some point in life to come to appreciate their parents as unique persons and to love them in spite of their foibles and idiosyncrasies. To be able to assist one's parents, especially to be concerned for them as they grow older, is important not only for the parent but also for the child, whether the child is a teenager or a middle-aged adult.

Similar considerations apply to other members of the family, to sisters, brothers, aunts, uncles, and cousins. How sad that the ties of family affection have been narrowed and loosened in modern society. The nuclear family, divorce, and geographical mobility have uprooted individuals from the broader family. Belonging to the tribe or clan had provided rich soil for the development of the human species. Those who are cut off from strong kinship relationships lose a great deal: the wider bounds of joy and affection. Can the values of the extended family be recovered? That is a dilemma of our time.

The family, whether nuclear or extended, has many functions to perform: biological at first, then as a basis for the economic division of labor. It is the psychological function of the family that needs emphasis as a source of security and affection. A basic educating force, the family provides the nourishment for stable growth and for the development of the ability to relate to others.

The best family, in a sense, is the egalitarian one. By this I do not mean that each member functions with equal power and authority. Parents have a greater role to play, and they should not abdicate their responsibilities. Yet children have rights as well. Each member of the family should count for one person and have equal dignity and value. A truly just family is democratic; it is one in which there is an equality of consideration for each member. Individuals have different needs and interests, power, and resources, and each family must allow for these differences. The family should provide the basis for the self-actualization of its members; it should appreciate common needs but recognize diverse ones as well. The family can become a growth matrix for all its participants. But to do so, the family must itself become actualized as a unit. Its members need to work in harmony and do things cooperatively.

As this implies, the best family is the joyful one: a group that works together, shares defeats, celebrates important family events, exults in common pleasures. It is exuberant. How unfortunate are troubled families, full of hatred and strife, divorce and alcoholism. How damaging they are to tender minds and delicate souls. How beautiful is a joyous family, full of loving relationships, happy, zestful, overflowing with bountiful interests and affection.

A good family is active, involved, creative, interesting; it provides an environment for both individuality and sharing. It does not suppress Anne, who plays the piano; Valerie, who is into Zen; Jonathan, who loves sports; mother, who is constantly redecorating and has her career; or father, who is an active professional. It allows each latitude and quietude, while at the same time providing support and strength. It is open and flexible; the growth potential of everyone is at stake. It is a wondrous foundation for warmth, sincerity, closeness, loyalty, humor, laughter, seriousness. It is life affirming, and a vital nourishing ground for the fuller flowering of a meaningful life. People may be able to achieve a good life, even if they had a deprived childhood or a bad marriage; but not to have enjoyed a family life is to have missed so much that life has to offer.

THE MORAL DIMENSIONS OF FRIENDSHIP

Blood kinship is a powerful binding force; it gives rise to emotions that hold humans together. Kinship has its roots in biology: sexual reproduction stimulates passion and love, maternal nurturing provides the milk to sustain the young, and parental care provides the psychological warmth and physical security necessary for the survival of the offspring. Moreover, the family provides a biological and economic basis for joint survival. Out of common needs grow the bonds of love and affection.

However, if consanguinity were the only basis of human affection, the human species would be in a bad way. The problem for society is to extend the range of affection and caring. Plato thought that familial love was so important that it needed to be generalized throughout the entire polis. He deplored selfish attitudes that reserved loving concern for those within the family. Hence parents in *The Republic* did not know their children and thus would relate to all children as their own.

It is the ability to care about those outside of one's immediate family and to build ties of friendship and congeniality that are important for human fulfillment. Familial love has its roots in biology and instinct, but relating to strangers can often present a problem. Sexual attraction is usually between those who are not blood relatives. But how far can the bonds of friendship and of moral concern between individuals outside of the family be extended?

Aristotle recognized the importance of friendship as a source of immediate appreciation and of lasting significance in life. One must have *some* friends; to be unable to relate on the level of friendship with other human beings is to lead an impoverished and deficient life. We may develop many different kinds of relationships with others, and on many levels. A friend is one whose company you enjoy, one whom you help gladly without any thought of return, and one with whom you can develop trust, sincerity, honesty. A true comrade accepts you for what you are.

Since personal friendship is on the level of face-to-face encounters, we are limited in the number of true friends that we can have, though we can continue to make new friends throughout life. Childhood chums are important to one's sense of well-being. Indeed one's peer group may be more influential than one's parents and teachers in developing values. Childhood friendships give meaning and depth in life: there are things that a child will confess to a friend but not to a parent. Exploring streams and woods, playing games, going through school, reaching puberty, discovering puppy love, suffering adolescent crushes are all part of friendship; children learn about life and the world together.

In modern mobile societies it is sometimes difficult to maintain permanent relationships. We do have, however, the opportunity for meeting many new people, particularly if we move about: colleagues at work, their wives or husbands, our neighbors, members of the same clubs and associations. There are various kinds of relationships. If we are fortunate, we can find others whom we can relate to, who will become our confidants, our close and faithful friends, trustworthy and constant, whom we can rely upon in time of need and distress. They may be schoolmates, playmates, teammates, roommates, shipmates, colleagues, neighbors, or companions.

There are important moral dimensions to friendship that, if violated, can disrupt the bond. Basically, friendship is built on a spirit of mutual benevolence for each other. It is a relationship of amicability, conviviality, congeniality, cordiality, and harmony. Friendship, to be true, must be based upon a general concern for the other. This means that a number of moral virtues are present: caring, honesty, sincerity, trust.

One must not misuse a friend to one's own advantage, though one will do a friend a favor gladly. Nor may one betray a friend, or else the friendship is over. Jealousy, pride, and vindictiveness are absent among friends. Instead there is a genuine concern for the other, an acceptance of his or her faults, and a joy in his or her prosperity and achievements. A friend is one who knows your faults, yet loves you in spite of them.

Some of our social relationships are disproportionate in terms of age, power, money, influence, and prestige; but friends, as friends, are equal. They do not erect barriers but seek to break them down as they reach out to touch the other soul.

There are some persons who are so timorous and diffident that they make friends with difficulty. Their hearts ache for sympathetic companions, but they cannot relate easily to others. There is also the extreme case of the friendless person who suffers a destitute life in sorrow and tears. How sad not to be able to make friends. How essential it is if one is to enjoy life.

We can be friends with members of the same or the opposite sex. Historically, men banded together in hunting groups or as warriors, and comradeship was essential for survival. Thus friendship, no doubt, had adaptive value; today it seems necessary for our psychic health. Indeed there remains a kind of masculine bond that remains strong. Men like to get away from women at times: to work or play together on the team, to associate in business or in the army. They seek private clubs or bars to escape. Women also find intimate relationships with other women, without male intrusion, sometimes desirable.

One may have many acquaintances, but they are not one's friends. For friendship is a special moral relationship held together by empathetic concern. Like love, however, friendship is not a relationship in which one simply receives favors; one must also be willing to give them. Indeed it is the ability to give to another person without question or complaint, and to share life's blessings and sufferings, that is perhaps the highest sign of human nobility.

13

THE BELOVED CAUSE

EXTENDING OUR MORAL REACH

Human beings cannot live caring only for themselves, their own families, and close friends. At some point there should be a broader outreach and concern. Granted that our first obligation is to our immediate circle; yet we should not neglect the greater moral universe.

First and foremost we belong to a community. There is the face-to-face social network in which we function on a daily basis, the tribe, clan, village, or town in which we live. Given the growth of mass society and large-scale, impersonal organizations, small-community identities are increasingly difficult to maintain. Yet perhaps humans always need to belong to some community in which they have roots and to which they are morally loyal. The problem of morality becomes even more pronounced when we recognize that there is a need to develop a sense of responsibility even for those who are beyond one's identifiable community. How far shall we extend our moral concern: to our nation, state, race, ethnic group, religion—to the whole of humanity?

The test of morality is thus not simply how one relates to others in small group encounters—whether one is, for example, honest in one's dealings—but how one relates to strangers, rarely seen, or to the future, barely known. To claim that one has some sense of a wider moral obligation is a sign of the development of a mature moral awareness. It is similar to that point in the growth of the intellect when one becomes interested in a larger universe beyond the immediate present, or in the expansion of one's aesthetic imagination. A person's lack of concern about what happens to other human beings outside of one's range of action is a sign of distorted development and moral immaturity.

The basis of one's moral outreach may be questioned; the question "Why should I be moral?" is often asked. In my view, the universe per se has no moral structure: there is no set of absolute values enshrined in the temple of nature or human nature that needs to be discovered and fulfilled. Rather, the sea of human morality is open and unchartered. Morality goes hand in hand with creativity, for it is we who create our own moral principles in terms of which we live and act.

The touchstone of morality is always human experience as lived, and the goods, bads, rights, and wrongs of human life are tested by how well they serve and fulfill our aspirations and needs. We must grant that there are basic human needs that require fulfillment if we are to survive and function in our environment. There is a form of moral development that human beings go through in learning to appreciate and to be sensitive to the needs and interests of others. The nature of society is such that some rules must govern interpersonal transactions if chaos and disorder are not to prevail. These rules set limits and place constraints upon what we may do, and they provide some guidelines for choice and action. Yet there is an element of freedom, and there are moral options that are open to every society and individual. This is illustrated by the wide individual diversity and cultural relativity that exist in moral principles and values.

From the standpoint of the individual, one may ask: What is the source of one's obligations, duties, and responsibilities? And from the standpoint of the society: Which principles and rules ought to prevail?

In response to the first question, I would suggest that perhaps every human being ought to deliberately break some moral rule (especially one that applies to himself) at some time in his life in order to test his sense of freedom. Surely we should do this, not to increase the sum total of evil, but only to develop some sense of our own power as moral agents. It is we who should master our moral principles; they should not enslave us. And if we are to have some power over our own careers and destinies, we need some sense of our own freedom of action concerning morality. Morality has been taken as an inviolable code. It has been imposed by the sanctions of custom, the church, and the state. Morality has been used as an instrument of repression to limit impulse and eros and to protect society from alleged harm. The moral whip was used, in the infancy of the race, to tame the savage beast and break his spirit.

There is a profound difference, however, between a morality that is legalistic, absolutistic, and censorial, and one that is nourishing, encouraging, and fulfilling. Moral principles should stimulate human creativity, not seek to repress it; they should contribute to the fullness of life, not denude it of creative joy. The ultimate source of moral choice should be human experience; and its test, the consequences of the choice in action.

What is at stake here is the scope of morality. There are at least two senses: first, morality as it applies to the individual, and second, morality as it affects others in society.

Personal morality—in regard to one's career, creative work, sexual behavior, or quest for passion or pleasure—should be considered to be a private matter. Neither the state nor any other social institution should seek to impose a uniform code of values on adults. This does not mean that we may not criticize excessive immoderation nor suggest principles of prudence—only that we should not compel compliance with a uniform moral code. Tolerance is the key moral principle of a democratic society. One should allow individuals to express their tastes and proclivities as they see fit, though one need not necessarily approve and should reserve the right to criticize.

The most difficult question of morality, and one that is of proper concern to society, is how an individual's actions relate to others. We may ask: What is the basis of regulative moral rules in society? I do not believe that the traditional accounts are adequate, for I reject the notion that there is a moral order in the universe at large. The universe has no divine purpose that can be discovered; it is indifferent to the fate of humans on this planet. Whether or not we will survive as a species is of no moment to nature: it is of profound significance to humans. We alone are responsible for our destiny: "No deity will save us, we must save ourselves."[1] Efforts by theologians to read a moral purpose into nature at large or to anchor morality in some divine reality is an expression of human conceit. The religious impulse mistakenly looks beyond the facticities of human existence for a deeper meaning. But the attempt to root a moral code, commandments, and injunctions elsewhere than in the soil of human life is an expression of a vain illusion. Those who attempt to ground morality in metaphysics often undermine it, for they go beyond human experience to sanctify or prohibit deeds, which then become absolutes. To be moral simply because the moral law (or God or the church) commands it is to act without moral freedom or responsibility.

Morality, if it is anything, should be considered a product of human choice. The theist, more often than not, is a fanatic in his dedication to the strict letter of the law: absolute righteousness, he believes, should prevail. But in so insisting, he is insensitive to the deeper nuances of the moral life. He is unwilling to deal with the concrete contexts of moral choice, where one has to decide between competing goods and rights, or the lesser of evils.

There is no substitute for moral reflection. When faced with a moral dilemma one cannot simply apply a general rule to the particular case; one has to work out a decision in the light of a full consideration of the facts relevant to the situation. In our interpersonal dealings with others—whether as lover, relative, friend, or stranger—we soon learn that there are some things that we cannot do if we wish to maintain our relationship. The rules of the game become fairly common knowledge. We know that we cannot consistently lie or cheat, or use violence with those we deal with, or else trust and honesty will break down. The moral principles governing transactional living and working together become apparent. We grasp them and teach them to our young, who will in turn teach them to their young. These principles have a double root, in our intelligence and in our compassion. And if what we do is based simply on rational calculations of self-interest, without any feelings of empathy, we will in time be discovered by others, who will not wish to relate to us on this basis alone. *Both* reflection and feeling are essential in human relationships, not only for others, but for ourselves; they stoke the fires of fraternity, and they keep alive our commitment to meaningful human relationships.

What is essential in morality is some degree of flexibility. Although there are the proverbial general rules of living that apply to most human communities, these should not be taken as rigid or fixed. Many social and legal systems, and institutional and moral principles that are no longer relevant, may disappear; new ones will emerge. Different contexts and cultures provide opportunities for the creation of alternative moral principles. The ethics of the Stone Age no longer apply to the Space Age, nor those of an agricultural society to a postindustrial one. The problems we now face were not faced by our forebears. Nor will those of our children be exactly like ours. Thus morality needs to be open to modification by intelligence. Morality is connected to our sense of power and freedom, and it needs to come up with new solutions to life's future challenges.

HUMANITARIANISM—WITHOUT ILLUSIONS

Let us return to our original question: Why should one have a concern for the stranger, or for other human beings outside of one's range of action? We should have such concern because, in one sense, no one on this globe is any longer a stranger: all humans now come, directly or indirectly, into the range of one's action; I affect and am affected by them. While this is true enough, the question remains, Why should one have an interest in and concern for a broader perspective? Why not be self-centered and private? Life is brief. Why not tend to one's own garden?

I submit that to be concerned with the broader interest—even from one's own private standpoint—is to broaden the definition of oneself as a person. To be loyal to a cause that outreaches one's own parochial interests is to widen the expression of one's power and perspective as a person. Unfortunately, too many individuals are overly concerned with their day-to-day cares of making a living and fulfilling their goals; as such, they are focused on a narrow circle of friends and colleagues. To take the larger view can be a source of enlightenment and freedom; it emancipates us from bondage to trivia.

One can share with others a dedication to a greater dream. One can live, in part, for a noble cause. There are any number of causes that we can strive for. They are as multifarious and diverse as culture itself: launching a crusade; feeding the hungry; housing the homeless; working for freedom, social democracy, or world government; campaigning for a political party or candidate; working for equal rights for women or minorities; protecting the empire against barbarian invaders and extending its domain; spreading learning and enlightenment throughout the world; joining the conservationist movement or the flat-earth society; propagating the faith; believing in UFOs, world peace, miscegenation, liberation, the Kiwanis, Masons, Holy Rollers, or vivisectionists; helping to stamp out smoking, cancer, fascism, or demon rum.

Thus espousing and working for a cause—whatever it is—is important for the person so involved, for it enables one to transcend restricted values. To be interested in the cause of others and to wish to share enthusiasm with them is to contribute to one's growth as a person. One's private aims are surely worthy of one's effort and energy, but the broader aims may equally have a claim upon one's energy. To be indifferent to the needs of our time and to the broad movements of social change is to be morally insensitive. Thus we need to cultivate moral fervor for the beloved vision of a better world, and "loyalty to loyalty" is itself a moral value, as the American philosopher Josiah Royce has pointed out.

I have known many humanitarians who have been passionately involved in social issues and who have labored hard to see their ideals fulfilled. Unfortunately, some forms of humanitarianism are misplaced, illiberal, and bigoted, and they may do us more harm than good. How can we be saved from those who would save us? For as much misery in the world may be caused by the fanaticisms of so-called do-gooders as by those who would leave well-enough alone. We thus face a dilemma: those who have no sense of a greater moral vision are limited as persons; but some who do, if overwhelmed by excessive zeal, can be equally destructive. Thus, in appraising a humanitarian cause, we need to know the consequences of the proposed programs as well as the motives of the activists.

Some causes are so wicked that we ought to oppose them. We should always be cautious of movements that are absolutist or that claim to have final solutions. Life goes on, and we learn that there are few foolproof solutions to any human problems. Movements that are hateful of certain races, classes, or groups of people, that are full of rancor, that wish to destroy before they build, are suspect. Those that demand utmost sacrifices today for a future that may never come or those that would entrust supreme power to any one group (or party or elite) in society are dangerous.

If there is any lesson to be learned from the twentieth century, it is that millennial movements, especially where they are intolerant and divisive, not only fail to bring the new millennium but probably set back the cause of human progress. A genuine humanitarian movement should have a sense of compassion. It should be limited by an ethic of principles governing the means it would employ: it cannot simply be judged by its vision of a utopian end.

In diagnosing the motives of people who are deeply involved in moral movements, we often find that some of them are pathological. There are those who so love humanity in its universal form that they are unable to bear it in the particular human person, and so are all too willing to sacrifice the individual to the ideal. We must beware of individuals who worship humanity in the abstract but think nothing of exterminating it in the concrete. A good illustration of this is the terrorist syndrome: the willingness to maim and kill innocent humans in order to excoriate wickedness and achieve a better world. The paradox of moral fanaticism is the tendency to vindicate one's evils in self-contradiction. The terrorist is prepared to wage war to achieve peace, to abrogate democracy to preserve it, to use despicable means in order to realize noble ends. I surely do not deny that sometimes we may have to use force and violence in order to secure our aims—but that should be a *reluctant* choice. We should not be corrupted by using the evil means available to us; we should not be too ready to resort to force and violence.

Those who are eagerly swept up by large mass movements, leaders and followers alike, seem to have a superabundance of zeal and passion. But there may be a variety of questionable motives for their dedication: empty personal lives, banal and trivial (the fascists); sexual repression (religious crusaders); rebellion against parents or elders (revolutionaries). In each case they may be acting out their vengeances in the name of the cause. Not the least of motives are those of power or personal fame, prestige, and recognition. There are those who care less about the cause than about their own self-gain.

There are some causes that are generally limited in their ideals, especially those that set nations, races, or ethnic groups against one another. We do, or perhaps we should, have some allegiance to our own national, religious, or ethnic roots. Each culture needs to have its place in the sun. Individuals are defined by linguistic symbols and values imbibed from their ethnic group. But these should not be allowed to imprison one. A more universalistic outlook is desirable. We should be able to find many forms of cultural life enriching, to tolerate and appreciate qualitative diversity—providing, that is, that the wider cause of humanity is not overshadowed by our devotion to ethnicity.

One should also guard against the doomsday pessimists who cannot enjoy this life for worry about the next. These are the critics who so hate present society because they think it so unjust that they cannot abide any exception to their indictment, nor admit that there can be any genuine progress. Such utopists are often closet hedonic-phobics. They are unable to find pleasure in their world because it falls short of their impossible dreams. They are self-denying secular priests devoted to a vision. Though they claim to love life and humanity, they are infected by a venom against both; they fail to see the possible joys before them, because they are blinded by life's sorrows.

But a utopian tomorrow may never come, for life always has its injustices and imperfections. There are times that are bad and times that are good, but never times that are perfect. Society goes from one problem to the next, whether depression, social conflict, or war. The utopian can never enjoy life fully—not in Egypt, nor in Athens in the Golden Age, nor during the Renaissance or the Enlightenment, nor today nor even tomorrow—for ideal perfection is always yet to be achieved.

I believe, in contrast, that we need a joyful humanism, not a pessimistic one. We need to have a humanitarian concern and to work for the common good. Yet life is short, and one should not squander opportunities for exuberance. A genuine moral altruism should have a double focus: there should be concern for one's own good, but there should also be a loving concern, a sense of benevolence and sympathy, for others. We need a humanitarianism that is positive and wholesome, that believes in both humanity and the human person, that is not willing to compromise moral standards in the process, that is entranced by the ideal possibilities of a better world and is willing to work constructively for them.

I should add that even though one may dedicate one's life to a cause (or causes), this should not blot out other aspects of one's life; nor should all of one's private needs be sacrificed in the process. If Moses had lived to see the Children of Israel reach the Promised Land, there might have been other tasks in his life besides deliverance. One should be prepared to take up new interests. One's whole personality should not be bartered to the cause; one should reserve some domain for personal dreams and enjoyments. One should not abandon oneself entirely. If the cause is worthy, it should not destroy but fulfill individual personhood.

Being devoted to a cause or causes is part of living the full life, for it takes us beyond our narrow limits. It is interesting and exciting to work for a cause. We are involved, not for our own sake, but for the sake of the greater good. And in this sense there is a positive qualitative dimension that is contributed to one's life. But the cause should not itself undermine one's capacity for happiness.

At the present moment in human history, there are any number of moral causes that might well concern intelligent and compassionate people. But we must distinguish a rational humanitarian concern from mere do-goodism. Often the emotional humanitarian allows his feelings to color the facts, his compassion to overwhelm his intelligence. One should be committed to a general benevolence toward all humans and do what one can, within reason, to alleviate suffering and to improve the lot of all. But this does not imply a blind devotion to the underdog or the naïve view that if only social conditions were changed, all people would be kind, sympathetic, charitable, and industrious.

One should be willing to modify or abandon one's political or economic views if the evidence warrants it. There is nothing so vulgar as a lifelong commitment to a political party. To be a rock-ribbed Republican all of one's life is a sign of pure Babbittry, but so is being a staunch Democrat or a dedicated member of the Labor, Conservative, or Communist parties. An inflexible commitment to "libertarianism," "conservatism," "socialism," or "radicalism" can be an expression of an intransigent faith. There is a kind of insularity to persons so devoted to a cause that they think that only those who agree with them, pay dues to the same club, contribute to the same party, or go to the same church are virtuous, and that those who are on the opposite side of the fence are ignorant, wicked, or corrupt.

Moral righteousness and political wisdom are not the exclusive domains of any one faction in society. It is naïve to believe that those who share my moral principles and ideals and are involved in my causes are necessarily better than those who are not.

True, one *believes* in one's principles and strives for the success of one's causes. One has some reason to believe that the increase in knowledge and enlightenment is a good thing and that there is a progressive process in which we can shed worn-out illusions, eradicate injustices, and achieve a better world. Yet, at the same time, we need to recognize that even the so-called incorruptible may be corrupted and that even the most noble movements and institutions may, in time, become sedentary or asphyxiated. The moral impulses of the first generation of fervent activists are often transformed by the second wave of true believers; then they atrophy in the process of being codified by the third generation, who are often simply bureaucrats. Thus we should have no illusions that once we have created a revolution, stamped out a practice, passed a law, or built a new social institution, everything will be fine and dandy. Only the socially blind will refuse to see the new problems and inequities that may arise; only the stupid will choose to deny them. We should be committed to the general cause of human progress; but we should not be so swept up by it that we become unwilling to dissent from some new twist or turn in doctrine or platform. In so doing we should not feel that we are renegades or heretics, nor that we have betrayed our youthful idealism for the conservatism of old age or privilege.

Life teaches many lessons about our early dreams. Not to dream is to abandon the whole human enterprise; yet not to recognize that our ideals are rarely fully achieved, or that unforeseen complications may arise that need to be corrected by still newer policies, is to remain insensitive to the nuances of lived experience. We need to temper idealism with realism, a humanitarian concern with an intelligent appraisal of the facts. Even our most esteemed leaders may have defects; they too are only human.

One of the limitations of loyalty to sectarian causes results from their tendencies to become divisive. We tend to oppose those who disagree with us, and this may separate human beings. We loathe to pay heed to what our critics say, or we are skeptical of what they say, or we suspect their motives. It is true that they may be wrong, and we right. On the other hand, however, truth is often a product of give-and-take; the sensible course is to leave open the possibility that it is we who may be mistaken, partially or in whole, and our opponents correct. Some critical skepticism, even about our own deepest values, is a necessary antidote to foolishness. The ability to compromise in life is a moral virtue that is not sufficiently distributed. We are not necessarily "selling out" if we concede that our enemies may have a point; nor are we inconsistent if we are willing to meet them halfway. For example, in whatever age, the critics of détente on both sides want nothing to do with compromise, for they think that to modify their position is to abandon their principles. But the political life is, by definition, the life of the possible, which implies compromise. The community is best served by the spirit of tolerance, and the negotiation of differences is the most effective method of social change.

I readily concede, of course, that some factions may be so evil that any attempt to reach a compromise may be venal, for example, the Mafia, Murder Incorporated, the Stalinists, or the Nazis. Sometimes we need to act decisively, and the radical, revolutionary, or even the reactionary stance may be the only one to take. What we ought to do depends upon the needs of the times. We should be prepared for strong measures, even if they lead to conflict or violence.

Yet, in principle, particularly where there is some social consensus about moral ideals and principles, we need to meet our friends halfway and to endeavor to convert our foes into our allies. We need to recognize that our opponents may be sincere and well-meaning in their dedication to their cause, and we need to work with them cooperatively. Because we live in the same world and face similar problems, we need to work out a common basis for the resolution of our differences.

There is a tendency on the part of some humanitarians to offer oversimplified solutions: to attribute social problems to one or another causal factor and to think that to get rid of that is to solve the problem. For example, many liberals blame racism for the plight of minorities, many communists blame capitalist imperialism for the world's troubles, and many conservatives simply blame big government for domestic economic problems. But wisdom recognizes a multiplicity of causes of social problems and the need for a variety of solutions. There is a strong tendency today toward an excessive commitment to environmentalism—that is, the belief that *all* problems have an environmental origin and that if we change the social conditions, we will of necessity ameliorate the human problem. Yet some human problems may have genetic causes, or they may be due to defects in character. On the other hand, to blame all social ills on biological causes and to advise eugenic programs can be equally in error. Racial doctrines of superiority are despicable, but equally dangerous is the Lysenkoian view of social environmentalism. Both forms of faith are based upon one-factor theories—the tendency to find single solutions to social problems.

Related to all of this is the need to go on living in spite of the evils in the world. As I have said, there are some purists who cannot rest content while injustice still persists. They will never find peace of soul or happiness in this life. But, as I have also said, we need to tolerate ambiguities and uncertainties, to be able to live in spite of tragedies and failures. We need to accept the fact that we live in a world of defects as well as of virtues. A resolute personality, one in command of one's own powers, is willing to enter into and attempt to change the world but is not overwhelmed by the inequities that remain. A sensible humanitarian will work for a cause and will do the best that he can, but he does not allow the cause to get the better of him. Some skepticism should be a concomitant of even our most beloved devotions. We may never be able to get rid of all evil, yet we can enjoy life in spite of that. We should attempt to ameliorate social conditions as best we can, but we should have no illusions that we will achieve perfection.

14

AN ETHIC OF RESPONSIBILITY

Does humanist ethics have a theory of moral responsibility? Can it provide a ground for obligation? The critics of secular humanism maintain that it fails to do so. There is the familiar argument against "relativistic ethics." Without some belief in God, we are admonished, obligation collapses. This argument is as old as ethics itself. The theist believes that if religion is absent, ethical duty has no source. Many philosophers have been concerned with this challenge. Kant attempted to provide a foundation for ethics without deriving it from God—though he was confronted in the last analysis with moral antinomies.

The view that belief in God is a secure ground for ethical obligation is fallacious. Since there is insubstantial evidence and surely no proof that God exists, the problem of ethical obligation is only pushed one step back to a premise that is itself precarious. The theistic universe presents an ethical order full of inconsistencies: the problem of evil for one, the abandonment of genuine moral freedom for another. If one's ethical principles depended in the final analysis upon the existence of God and His moral commandments, then one's free moral conscience is compromised. Doing something because God commands it, not because it is right or good, is not itself morally worthy. In the Old Testament, God commanded Abraham to sacrifice his son Isaac and he was willing to obey God's command. This illustration of faith and obedience is hardly morally commendable. The fact that God then bade Abraham not to do so is insufficient reason for Abraham's desisting. It was wrong for Abraham to sacrifice Isaac and one does not need a theological system to say so. Ethical judgments should have autonomous grounding in moral experience, and we would expect people to be truthful, honest, sincere, generous, whether or not they believe in God. Moreover, individuals who believe in God derive contradictory moral commandments: Christians and Jews are for monogamy; Muslims for polygamy. Mainline Protestant denominations are for freedom of choice in abortion; Roman Catholics and fundamentalists are opposed. Christians will turn the other cheek to an offender; Muslims will cut off his hands. Theological moral codes depend as much or more on doctrines of revelation, church dogma, and a priestly class than on simple belief in divine power. From belief in the Fatherhood of God any number of opposing moral prescriptions—full of stern admonitions of duty—have been drawn.

Now one can understand the concern of the theist that humanist ethics without religious guidelines and the institutionalization of a code may not provide sufficient support for moral responsibility. There have been modern secular movements that have brutalized man: Nazism and Stalinism as quasi-theological, ideological doctrines abandoned traditional norms and ended up by creating infamous gulags and moral monsters. Surely the humanist cannot be burdened with or blamed for the totalitarian excesses of the twentieth century. Humanists generally have defended human rights and democracy, and they have been among the first to condemn such tyrannies. Theistic religious institutions, particularly where they have had a monopoly of religious power, are surely not immune to the suppression of freedom, as the Crusades, the Inquisition, and the wars between Muslims and Hindus, Protestants and Catholics, Jews and Muslims, vividly demonstrate.

Nevertheless, the humanist is faced with a crucial ethical problem: Insofar as he has defended an ethic of freedom, can he develop a basis for moral responsibility? Regretfully, merely to liberate individuals from authoritarian social institutions, whether church or state, is no guarantee that they will be aware of their moral responsibilities to others. The contrary is often the case. Any number of social institutions regulate conduct by some means of norms and rules, and sanctions are imposed for enforcing them. Moral conduct is often insured because of fear of the consequences of breaking the law or of transgressing moral conventions. Once these sanctions are ignored, we may end up with the Thrasymachian man—concerned with his own personal lust for pleasure, ambition, and power, and impervious to moral constraints. The broader question is not simply, can you have morality without religious sanctions? Rather, the question is, can you have morality without any political, legal, or economic restraints; without, that is, any of the rules of law and order that govern a civilized community?

Some utopian anarchists maintain that human nature is basically beneficent; it is restrictive societal laws that corrupt human beings, not the contrary. Their solution is to emancipate individuals from these laws; this they believe will untap a natural propensity for altruism. Regretfully, there is no guarantee that this will occur. Human motivation is highly complex, and human nature is capable of both good and evil. Love and hate, self-interest and generosity, sympathy and jealousy, cooperation and competition are so deeply ingrained that we cannot be assured that only the best will in the end prevail. Thus we have no guarantee that individual moral beneficence will reign once all institutional sanctions are removed. Moreover, even *if* the world were only full of people with good intentions, these people might still differ in their interpretations or applications of their moral convictions; this can be a further source of conflict.

Let me say at this point that I do not believe that humanists, who are devoted to a philosophy of freedom or of social progress, need be any more altruistic or responsible than the nonhumanist or theist. Humanists can be as deceitful and nasty, full of pride and as moved by the lust for fame and power—or conversely as beneficent and other-regarding—as anyone else. No one group can claim a privileged possession of the moral virtues. There is no moral exclusivity for any one philosophical, religious, or ideological party. Life would be oversimplified if all the good guys were on one side and all the bad guys on the other. Thus there is no assurance that if one is identified as a "humanist" that he will be moral, especially in regard to the common human decencies. Indeed, some modern-day humanists are prone to an exacerbated moral self-righteousness that may at times be as wicked as the wickedness they wish to extirpate. Traditional morality, often unthinking, carries with it the smug complacency of the double standard. Humanists are critical of the devout businessman (the modern-day Cephalus) who prays on the Sabbath yet uses sharp and exploitative business practices during the week, condones conventional morality as sacrosanct yet is insensitive to hypocrisies and injustices. Often pitted against him, however, is the moral reformer, who—though reform is necessary to the cause of human moral progress—may become an intolerant moral fanatic, willing to chop off the heads of those whom he judges to be unjust or with whom he disagrees. Regretfully, some egalitarians are impervious to the complexities of problems and are willing to impose simplistic moralistic solutions to them.

In raising the basic question, "Can humanist ethics provide a framework for responsible action?," I am leaving aside still another challenge, which is often presented to the secular humanist: "Can humanism adequately answer the question, 'What is the meaning of life?'" I have addressed myself to this question earlier in this book. The theist mistakenly believes that life is not meaningful if God is dead, or if there is no divine purpose to the universe. To that I answer, life has no meaning per se, but it is full of opportunities. The meanings we discover depend on what we are willing to put into life, the dreams and ideals we cherish, the plans and projects we initiate. A vital virtue for humanist ethics is the courage for a person to become what he wishes. Here one can say that the good life is possible for individuals without the need for an external support system. Such an ethic emphasizes independence and self-reliance, the development of one's potentialities, the cultivation of critical intelligence and creative self-actualization. For such autonomous persons, an exuberant and full life, overflowing with meanings, is readily available. This does not deny that our fullest happiness involves other persons and presupposes some harmonious relationships with them. But the problem of the ground of moral responsibility is a separate question. A eudaemonistic interest may indeed become self-centered and the desire for one's own self-realization egoistic. A central question of ethics thus concerns our relationship to others: What are our responsibilities and duties to our fellow human beings?

MORAL EDUCATION

I am persuaded that a humanistic ethic of freedom by itself is not sufficient without fulfilling at least two further conditions: first, it presupposes the theory and practice of moral education, and second, insofar as reason can be applied to moral choice, it presupposes a set of prima facie ethical principles that should have some claim upon our action.

As I have said, moral freedom is a central humanist value: the freeing of individuals from excessive restraints so that they may actualize their potentialities and maximize free choice. However, such a normative value is hardly sufficient unless moral growth takes place. It is not enough to release individuals from authoritarian institutions, for some individuals may degenerate into hedonistic fleshpots or amoral egoists. Thus we need also to nourish the conditions for moral development, in which an appreciation for the needs of others can emerge, and this is dependent upon moral education.

This need seems to be particularly strong in affluent postmodern societies today where narcissism is endemic: many individuals are consumers first and foremost. The entire domain of their universe is immediate self-gratification. The quest for pleasure is located in buying and consuming, using and discarding things, the gluttonous wasting of food and drink, adhering to the dictates of fashion and adornments, the amassing of trinkets and gadgets to play with and show off. Much of this consumption is not based upon rational use but upon capricious tastes that are conditioned and titillated by advertisers. The banal bipolar syndrome of narcissistic morality alternates between entertainment and boredom. The never-ending quest of the passive consumer and spectator is to be amused, but ennui always lurks in the background. The heroes of the consumer morality are celebrities—comedians, show business personalities, and sports figures—who exemplify the surface character of life: all show, no depth. If affluent societies have solved the problems of poverty and disease for large sectors of their societies—the bane of all societies heretofore—they now have the problem of enhancing the level of taste.

The need for moral education has been recognized by philosophers. This has at least a twofold dimension: first, the elevation of standards of taste and appreciation, the cultivation of qualitative pleasures and creative enjoyments, intellectual, aesthetic, and moral; and second, the development of moral virtues and moral character.

There are different pedagogical views about how to develop moral character. The traditionalist opts for training in discipline. He uses Sunday sermons, rote learning, and the threat of punishment to engender good habits. Religious indoctrination has always attempted to instill respect, fear, and love for the moral code. More recently, educational psychologists have argued that moral education in children and young adults involves a process of growth and development. Although at the most elementary level, moral education depends on some training and example, eventually the goal is the cultivation of autonomous agents, free to choose, aware of moral principles, cognizant of their responsibilities to others, capable of some reflective judgment.

The cognitive element in moral education, though, is not sufficient by itself. Morality must enlist the whole person and must address itself to the emotive and aesthetic components of the moral life: to develop attitudes in which some genuine concern for the needs of others is rooted in rational comprehension at the same time that it is fused with sentiment and feeling. Aristotle recognized this in the *Nicomachean Ethics* (book 1, chapter 3) when he observed that students would not appreciate his course in ethics and politics unless they had already developed some of the moral virtues through experience and living.

The question of moral responsibility is as much a psychological question as it is a theoretical one: How does one develop an appreciation for others, the moral point of view, a sense of altruism and giving, honesty, truthfulness, sincerity, and trust. Some individuals are autistic, self-centered, selfish, concentrating on their own private gratifications. Such individuals lead the lives of crippled moral dwarfs. How does one develop moral growth in them?

Some say by exposing such individuals to the free give-and-take of moral inquiry and by examining moral dilemmas. I agree, though regretfully at times this may lead to moral subjectivism and nihilism, rather than a developed moral sense. Whether moral sympathy is innate or acquired is difficult to say, given the complexities of human nature.

Psychologists have differed on this point: Some, such as A. H. Maslow, maintain that moral sympathy is intrinsic to human nature and that the inner self that needs to unfold is basically good. Others, such as B. F. Skinner, believe that various forms of moral behavior can be conditioned by operant reinforcement. I believe that both theories have an element of truth: the roots of morality are found in our dependence and reciprocity as social animals, but whether morality is actualized depends in part upon cultural conditions. Surely the schools alone cannot accomplish the task of nurturing moral character, even though they still remain a vital source, for all of the institutions of society have a formative role in developing character.

One issue concerns the question of the neutrality of the schools, particularly in pluralistic democratic societies, where opposing sets of values may compete. Should the teacher simply seek to clarify existing values that the student already possesses and has brought to the classroom, or should the teacher attempt to "indoctrinate" (a bad word for libertarians and democrats) new values? Some believe that the schools should remain neutral, merely placing value problems under cognitive scrutiny. This is the position of the values clarification movement. Whatever one's approach, values clarification or moral development, some values are being assumed by the teacher: intelligence, democracy, and tolerance as a minimum, the quest for fair play or a universalistic criterion as a maximum.

Secular humanist educators have suffered heavy attack, particularly in the United States, at the hands of theists who maintain that in teaching moral education in the schools, a new religion of secular humanism is being indoctrinated and that this is contrary to the constitutional prohibitions against the establishment of a religion.

I think that this latter charge is unfounded, for if it were generalized, then the schools could not teach science (some indeed refuse to allow them to teach evolution without also teaching creationism), contemporary literature, classical philosophy or ethics, or many other fields without being accused of indoctrination in the "religion of secular humanism." What the critics wish to repeal is the modern world, and they wish a return to fundamental biblicism.

Nonetheless, I believe that the schools need to engage in moral "instruction"—a better term than "indoctrination"—of some kind; they do it anyway. In one sense virtually all education is moral. Insofar as education strives to expand the horizons of the person, even the person's intellectual understanding, there is some modification, however subtle, and reconstruction of values is ongoing.

In a democracy, the schools can, and should, consciously provide this moral instruction by focusing on the most basic and commonly shared moral values as the fabric of the community and the basis of human relationships: truth, honesty, sincerity, trust, kindness, generosity, friendship, sharing, concern for others, and so on. This can be accomplished without raising ultimate ontological questions of where these values are rooted—in theology or nature. Moral education thus attempts to develop within the child and the young person both an emotive and an intellectual basis for character formation. That this should be done is the message of philosophical ethics from the Greeks to the modern world: the autonomy of the moral virtues independent of a religious or non-religious framework.

Now a good deal of the opposition to moral education in the schools concerns the attempt to offer solutions to specific moral issues that are under dispute in society. Granted, the schools cannot live in isolation from the concrete moral problems that trouble society, but courses in sexual education, abortion, euthanasia, women's rights, homosexuality, racial integration and intermarriage, and war and peace are saddled with opposing viewpoints in society. Here it is enough for the schools to discuss such moral dilemmas, examining alternative positions, without imposing the viewpoints of the teachers or of the community. But this is distinct from *the need to root within the psychological makeup of each individual a set of moral dispositions and virtues.* If they are absent, then libertarian societies may be faced with an increase in the number of morally retarded individuals, free to do what they want, insensitive to the hurt they may cause others.

A tragic illustration of the problem faced by democratic societies that do not have programs of moral education is the wanton murders many years ago of philosopher Charles Frankel, his wife, and two neighbors in Bedford Hills, New York. The Frankels and their neighbors were brutally shot and their homes rifled by thieves. Charles Frankel, an eloquent defender of humanism and democratic freedom, had faith in human intelligence. He was sacrificed by the excesses of passion and violence unleashed by those in a free society who lacked the moral virtues.

Some sociobiologists believe that moral turpitude may be in part genetic and that some individuals, particularly hardened criminals, are incorrigible. How, for example, should the penal system deal with repeat offenders? By coddling or punishing them? Should the legal system be rehabilitative or retributive in its approach? The humanist does not wish to give up in the constant effort to reform the institutions of society so that the best that human beings are capable of will emerge. Konrad Lorenz and others, however, maintain that aggression is innate in the human species. Human vices, such as selfishness, laziness, vindictiveness, hatred, sloth, pride, and jealously, are so widespread in human behavior that we are all capable of their temptations at times. Perhaps humanists have been overly optimistic about the full reaches of human nature. Perhaps "original sin"—in natural and biological terms—is present in some individuals, who are immune to our efforts at amelioration. What we need is a deeper empirical understanding of human nature, without reading in what our values demand.

The difficulty in postmodern society is that moral education no longer can be entrusted to the family or the schools, and it surely cannot be left to the churches insofar as they preach false doctrines of redemption and salvation. In the western world moral values often are a product of an economic system that prizes consumer entertainment as the highest value, and the mass media, in which violence, pornography, born-again religion, spirituality, and the paranormal are sold to gullible consumers. I am not here simply indicting capitalism nor am I approving governmental regulation of the free market in ideas. What I am pointing to rather is the critical need for some measure of moral education in the larger media of communication. Those who live in democratic societies need to influence the content of the media in an effort to raise the standards of appreciation—if we are to have any hope, that is, of developing moral character. Totalitarian societies have hardly solved the problems either, for they have imposed in their systems of education and in the mass media encapsulated moral programs. They have abandoned an ethic of freedom in favor of indoctrination. The result is that the individual is lost. Dispossessed of rights, the individual has only duties to the state, but few freedoms against it.

PRIMA FACIE ETHICAL PRINCIPLES

But this still leaves open the question for one committed intellectually to a humanist ethics: Can the question of moral responsibility be resolved? How does one reconcile self-actualization and personal freedom with the rights and needs of others? On the scale of human values, which have higher priority: *my* needs and interests or *yours*?

There is, in my judgment, no ultimate resolution of this problem, no deductive proof of the "moral point of view." It seems to me that some constructive skepticism is a necessary component of moral philosophy; although a reflective person will, in general, come to abide by the moral point of view, it is not universally binding. To some extent, one's own best interest—such as in cases of one's health or survival—ought to have one's first commitment; in others, one's responsibility to other human beings (one's children, family, friends, colleagues, or countrymen) should have a stronger claim on one's action. In still other cases, a person recognizes an obligation to consider humanity as a whole and future generations yet unborn (as in questions concerning worldwide pollution or nuclear holocaust). Our duties and obligations are always dependent upon the situation at hand and the kinds of questions being raised. We must be prepared to examine and revise our options by means of deliberative inquiry.

Yet I do not think that we need be led to a completely relativistic position in which no general principles are relevant. On the contrary, I submit that a naturalistic and humanistic ethical theory can incorporate general ethical principles that have significance in a situation.

How do we decide what to choose? I do not think that utilitarianism gives us an accurate guide for all moral choices. Surely, we need to take into account the *consequences of our action* in evaluating various alternatives, a pragmatic rather than a strictly utilitarian criterion. The greatest-happiness principle, though relevant in some contexts, is too general to be of much help. If a teleological ethics by itself is insufficient—even though it is essential for any balanced ethical theory—some naturalistic form of deontological ethics should be recognized. Problems of ethical choice for the humanist involve an individual's quest for happiness; a person will undertake those things that activate him and contribute to the fullness of his life. But maturity of judgment soon enables him to recognize that his deepest well-being is tied up with others and that *caring* is an essential nutrient in human relationships. Still it is not simply a question of the prudential calculation of a person's long-range self-interest. There are general principles of behavior that a developed moral agent will come to accept, and these will have some bearing upon his conscience and conduct.

These ethical principles are not derived from God or divinity, nor do they come simply from some moral law implanted within the womb of nature or human nature. Nor indeed are they absolute or final in the sense that they are inviolable. I prefer the term "general" rather than "universal," because they are only approximate guides for conduct and there may be exceptions to them.

W. D. Ross uses the term *prima facie* to denote the fact that some duties are conditionally obligatory, but whether it is our actual duty to fulfill them depends upon a full examination of our obligations within the situation. According to Ross, among the prima facie duties are those that rest upon our previous acts, those resting on the acts of others, the contracts and commitments entered into, and the claims made upon us. There are also middle-range duties incumbent upon us: positive duties, such as keeping our promises or paying our debts, and negative ones, such as not cheating others. But there are more general duties as well: duties such as nonmalfeasance, not injuring others; justice, attempting to distribute goods as widely as possible; and beneficence, helping to relieve distress where we are able to do so.

I prefer to use the term *principles* rather than *duties*, because we can generalize various kinds of action and recognize that these are general prescriptions, rules, and policies that we ought to observe. Most of these are part of the proverbial wisdom, such as "Honesty is the best policy," or "Do unto others as you would have them do unto you."

Now the question that can be raised is, "What is the foundation of these prima facie general ethical principles?" Many who have defended them have done so on intuitive grounds. They have said that either they cannot be proven and are true without proof, or that they are self-evident to the reflective conscience.

I deny their intuitive character. Such general principles are not mysterious or sacrosanct, but are naturalistic and empirical phenomena. They have developed in social relationships over long periods of time—in part because of common human needs and necessities, and in part because they have come to be recognized as imperative in human relationships if we are to realize social harmony. They are tested by their observable effects in human conduct. A relationship between two persons cannot long endure if there is insincerity between them, and a human community cannot long endure in peace if there is widespread duplicity. General ethical principles, however, are not simply justifiable as instrumental; in time they come to have some intrinsic merit, and we come to feel strongly about them for their own sakes: they are both means and ends. Those who consider them simply expedient may have no compunctions about breaking or compromising them at will and may be corrupted in the process.

There is an ironic legacy that dependence upon some forms of purely utilitarian or pragmatic moral systems has bequeathed us; that is, some individuals and groups have been willing on utilitarian grounds to justify the use of *any* means to achieve ends that they considered worthwhile. The conclusion that Machiavellians have drawn is that if they are to remain in power, they must be ready to employ unscrupulous means. Authoritarian defenders of the status quo have applied the full force of the state, thus violating human rights, in order to secure their ends; and despots have always employed heinous methods of torture and terror. The paradox of moral compromise—that one is prepared to use dastardly means to achieve noble ends—has also undermined Marxism-Leninism as an ethical philosophy. Marxist-Leninists were critical of the injustices of capitalism; they wished to usher in a utopian system of ideal values. But some apparently felt that this justified them to use terrorist means to defeat their opponents, even if it resulted in the slaughter of innocent bystanders. Totalitarian regimes have, on the same ground, crushed dissent and opposition of so-called enemies of the party or revolution.

Humanists are not immune to moral corruption either. They are as prone to vanity, jealousy, vindictiveness, and other foibles as are other human beings. Some so-called humanitarians and philanthropists make contributions or are devoted to a cause not for the good they will achieve, but for personal power and acclaim. And others may stand by and allow the rape of the moral dignities to occur, on the mistaken assumption that sin is always committed by nonhumanists (bishops, divines, and other such personages), not by the emancipated. The result is often that the emancipated, bereft of all conventional standards, are left without any viable principles of ethical conduct at all. All the more reason why humanist ethics needs double rooting: (1) a teleological interest in realizing worthy ends, goods, and values, *and* (2) a deontological concern for fulfilling obligations, responsibilities, and duties; an ethic of principles as well as an ethic of ideal ends.

Which of these roots ought to prevail in ethics? Which ought to have the deepest priority, the good or the right? I am unwilling to affix an a priori solution to this question. It all depends upon the situation at hand. In problems of moral choice, we need to take into account empirical and pragmatic criteria: the facts of the case, the means at our disposal, the consequences of our actions. We also need to consider the prima facie ethical principles that are relevant. Our actual duties, obligations, and responsibilities will depend upon the situation and the social milieu in which we live. These are always particular and concrete, growing out of our commitments and values, the contracts entered into, the claims made upon us. Only empirical inquiry can tell us what we ought to do in a given situation.

In moral problems there is often a conflict between values, not all of which we can attain. We may wish to travel widely, raise a family, and have a successful career all at the same time—which may be difficult or impossible (unless we become a travel agent or airplane pilot). In other cases, there may be a clash between a good to be achieved and a responsibility to be fulfilled, as in a conflict between what we may desire and what others expect of us—and in such a situation one may have to give way to the other. Similarly, an act may be justifiable, even though in itself it is evil, because of the preponderant long-range good that will ensue, as when we reluctantly decide to go to war to defend ourselves or others against aggression. In still other situations, all of the alternatives may be bad, and we may be compelled to choose the lesser of two evils, as in the case of a person suffering from an incurable disease, who is faced with death, a prolonged and horrible one, or euthanasia, but death in any case. The point is, we need to *balance* the competing claims of our values and principles, considerations of the good and the right.

Humanist philosophers have recognized that our ultimate obligation, in the final analysis, is the use of rational thought to resolve, as best we can, such moral dilemmas. What we will decide to do, as I have said, presupposes some moral education and a sensitivity to general ethical principles—an important concomitant of humanist ethics. Still, it is the autonomous person capable of reflective choice who is the best guide. We need to appreciate at the same time the limitations of absolute moral certitude and the possibilities of moral wisdom. Authoritarian and legalistic moralists will no doubt object to such a conclusion and will wish for something more. Humanist ethics can only provide something less than they desire, but this does not mean that ethical choice need be capricious or subjectivistic, nor that it is not amenable to some form of objective critical appraisal. Indeed, humanist ethics, although the least pretentious of ethical theories in what it promises, may yet be the most reliable; for it may be best able to allow both the good life to be realized and the moral decencies to prevail.

15

THE COMMON MORAL DECENCIES

C an critical ethical intelligence discover any prima facie general principles that transcend the limits of cultural relativity and apply to all human beings, no matter what their social condition? Are there any ethical principles that we can affirm to be objectively true, independent of whether there is a God who has declared them to be binding? I submit that there are and that they are so fundamental to human intercourse that they may be characterized as the "common moral decencies." Indeed, virtually all human cultures have now come to recognize their significance, for they lay down moral imperatives necessary for group cohesion and survival. Individuals who abide by them are commended and praised, and those who flout or transgress them are condemned and blamed as immoral, wicked, or evil.

To state that certain forms of conduct are decent, admirable, or proper, and that other forms are indecent and improper, even despicable, is not simply subjective caprice or an expression of cultural bias, but is, I think, a function of a level of moral development that has cross-cultural dimensions. There is still wide diversity in human conduct, there are numerous disputes about what is considered decent or indecent behavior, and there is much variation in moral judgment. Nonetheless, there is a basic core of principles that we have come to recognize as binding in human conduct. We may apply the term *common* to these "decencies" as a qualification, for we speak only of the most fundamental principles that are widely held, leaving many other layers of moral principles open to further critical examination. I use the term *moral* rather than *ethical* because I think the recognition that there are fairly basic moral principles that ought to govern conduct between civilized individuals has become deeply ingrained in long-standing social traditions. These principles are supported by habit and custom, are enacted into law, and are even considered sacred by various religions.

Far from being derived from some transcendental source, the moral decencies are taken as divinely revealed precisely *because* they are considered so basic to the human community. The fact that they have been converted into

143

the language of divinity is a further sign of how highly esteemed they are. They can, however, have an authentic cognitive and independent ground; these principles are justifiable by rational considerations and are based upon practical ethical wisdom. Indeed, they express the deepest wisdom of the human race and can be discovered by anyone who digests the fruit of the tree of knowledge of good and evil. Interestingly, theists and humanists share in their commitment to the moral decencies, for people of all persuasions inherit a common wisdom, even though they may dispute the ultimate foundations of morality.

The following catalogue of moral principles should not be taken on a scale of ascending or descending priority. The order in which they are listed is simply one of convenience, for in any particular situation, one or more may assume higher priority than another. They should be interpreted as general guides for conduct rather than absolute or universal commandments, but this does not mean that their obligatory force is weakened; for a rational moral being can recognize their significance no less than can a God-intoxicated believer. It is important that we present them explicitly, because ethical philosophy should not be a metatheoretical and abstract exercise but should have a normative relevance to conduct. It is especially important for humanism to provide a catalogue of the moral decencies, in order to counter the unfounded charge that it has no moral principles.

Moral principles concern our relationship to other human beings living in communities; they would have little meaning for a hermit living in isolation in a cave or on a desert island. Some can also be applied to other sentient species, so that it makes some sense to talk about animal rights. Although moral principles are forms of social behavior, they need to be structured within the character of the individual if they are to have any efficacy or force.

There is some overlapping of these principles, and some are subsumed under others. Nevertheless, it is important that they be separately defined and classified. The following list should not be taken as exhaustive or complete. There are no doubt other principles that might be added. But at least the following provides a basic framework for ethical conduct and choice.

I. INTEGRITY

1. *Truthfulness:* the quality of being truthful; veracity; accuracy in representing reality. This quality is basic to all human social relationships, for people cannot live and work together if there is a deliberate effort to withhold, falsify, or erase the truth. Negative: to lie; to be deceitful.

Interestingly, this principle does not appear in a forthright statement in the Ten Commandments, although one variant does appear: "Thou shalt not bear false witness against thy neighbor." Nor is it central to the Sermon on the Mount.

Nonetheless, telling the truth is a common moral decency expected in all civilized communities and probably in the majority of so-called primitive societies. When people deceive each other, it is difficult to count on them. Lying makes true communication impossible. When we do not know when to believe a person, we cannot rely on any aspect of his behavior.

People may disagree about what the truth is. They may differ as to what the facts of a particular case are, or how to interpret them, or what their causes are, but they are obligated to state the truth insofar as they know it—or believe they know it—without any deliberate intention to deceive others. The person who does not follow this principle is a liar.

The question of telling a harmless white lie is not an issue here, but there are moral dilemmas that may arise when lying to someone may be considered; for example, when not lying conflicts with other general ethical principles equally binding. There are exceptions to any general rule, but such transgressions need to be justified before the rule can be overridden. Still, this does not deny the widespread human recognition that, all things considered equal, we have a prima facie obligation to be truthful.

In social contexts, one may swear an affidavit, take an oath, certify that one is telling the truth, or even take a lie-detector test, if it is believed that such will guarantee truthfulness. Truthfulness is basic to science, philosophy, and any discipline concerned with discovering the truth. It is fundamental to an open and free society but lacking in totalitarian and authoritarian societies, in which the elite attempts to cover up inadequacies, suppress dissent, and censor any attempt to speak or publish the truth. Such lying is a violation of a basic moral principle, not only from the standpoint of the individual but also from the standpoint of the community.

2. *Promise keeping:* the quality of honoring a pledge; living up to one's agreement. In everyday life, if one makes a promise in good faith to another person, then it would be immoral to break that promise. Negative: to fail to honor one's commitments; to be derelict and unfaithful; to not be true to one's word; to exhibit bad faith.

A promise is a declaration made to another person, who then expects that it will be fulfilled in the future by either performance ("I promise I will repay you") or forbearance ("I promise not to tell anyone"). It is a commitment other people may rely upon. It may include a solemn oath, vow, or assurance. The one who makes the promise has a responsibility to the person to whom he makes the promise. Implicit in this is the recognition that in some cases circumstances may become so altered that one does not have the means to fulfill a promise made in good faith.

This may involve the fulfilling of *contracts*, where two or more parties enter into an agreement or pact, in which the parties agree to perform or avoid certain acts, and in which one party, should it fail to fulfill its contractual obligations, stands in breach of contract. We have not only a moral but a legal duty to abide by agreements entered into freely and without duress. These include covenants entered into freely between contractual parties, such as oaths of office and vows of marriage. If one party to a contract violates it substantially, then the other party may not be bound to honor the terms of the contract. Some people make some promises they cannot possibly keep. They may do so to please others, in which case their motives may be beneficent; or perhaps they do so to deceive others, in order to get them to buy a product or contract a service, in which case their motives are malevolent.

3. *Sincerity:* the quality of being candid, frank, free of hypocrisy, and sincere in one's relations with others, especially on a one-to-one, personal basis. Negative: to be insincere, hypocritical, false, deceitful.

Sincerity is essential to building trust. It is a sign of moral integrity. A sincere person is truthful in his dealings with others; he is not disingenuous or artful in concealing ulterior motives. Between lovers and friends, sincerity is essential if confidence is not to be broken. If a person cannot trust what another says, then it is difficult to cooperate on common tasks. An insincere person takes another in and misuses him for his own purposes. In extreme cases he may be cunning. On the other hand there may be some limits to the degree of sincerity possible in human relations. One may be artless and too self-effacing in dealings with others. Such a person may confide too quickly in another or confess affection or love too readily, so as to disarm or embarrass the other person, who may not share his feelings. Sincerity is a necessary bond in human relations, and we have an obligation to follow it, though we need not bare our inner soul to anyone and everyone at the first opportunity.

4. *Honesty:* the quality of integrity or fairness in dealing with others. "Honesty is the best policy" is an aphorism widely accepted in common parlance but often flouted in behavior. If no one could be trusted, all social interactions would break down. Negative: to be dishonest, deceitful, fraudulent, false, crooked.

I am using the term *honesty* here to pertain primarily to not using deceitful means to take material advantage. In human relations, it is important that we be able to trust another person's word. If someone says one thing and then turns around and does something else, such a person is without integrity. If the person conceals a hidden motive and is seeking to beguile or deceive another, then he cannot be trusted. Dishonesty is distinct from insincerity, though these vices overlap, because it is resorted to in order to gain some advantage. Dishonest people are willing to commit fraud. They may cheat or sell out for a price. Their behavior is not honorable, and they soon lose credibility and respect. The temptation to dishonesty is for the profit or prestige that a person can reap. Dishonest people are hypocritical and duplicitous; they are insincere and willing to lie and break promises. Conversely, honest people will tell the truth and fulfill their contractual obligations insofar as they are able to do so.

Probity in dealing with others is essential if we are not to lose our reputations. Once one has a reputation for false dealing, one's career may be ruined.

In the economic sphere, selling adulterated products, lying to consumers, or cheating them are pernicious forms of dishonesty. On the political and economic level, the opposite of honesty is graft and corruption.

II. TRUSTWORTHINESS

1. *Fidelity:* the quality of being loyal; showing allegiance and fealty. This principle applies to a person's attachments to friends, relatives, and the community. Negative: to exhibit infidelity, treachery, perfidy, betrayal.

In human relationships we build up bonds of common interests, we share values, and we are committed to similar goals to which we all strive together. We are expected to continue loyalty to another in a one-on-one relationship, or to a group if we have pledged allegiance and have received mutual benefits. We are not to betray the trust—particularly for personal gain or advantage—unless we have an overriding justification. Our obligation to be faithful is based on our previous commitments, which we have the responsibility to uphold.

Fidelity is an essential principle in a viable marriage, where the partners have demonstrated trust and love for each other. It also applies to brothers and sisters, parents and children, and other members of the family. Fidelity is the bond that also holds friends together through adversity or prosperity. This means that there is some constancy of commitment and steadiness of attachment, rather than capricious or infantile behavior. Fidelity not only applies to relationships between people but also to an individual's commitment to a cause, to personal principles, or to the group or nation. We are not talking about blind allegiance or fanatic loyalty, but fidelity that is responsible and devotional. Fidelity is a mature commitment, opposed to fecklessness, vacillation, and disloyalty. No matter what our relationship to others or to a group, we are expected not to betray them. The principle of fidelity needs to be extended to ever wider communities of humankind, though it has its origin in small interpersonal relationships.

Where the trusted individual or group has committed a grave moral transgression (for example, treachery, murder, and so on), then one may deem it permissible to waive fidelity in the name of a higher principle or cause, but a clear justification must be given for this.

2. *Dependability:* the quality of being reliable and responsible. The importance of reliability in human affairs is well recognized. Negative: to be untrustworthy, undependable, irresponsible.

We depend on other persons to do the things they promise to do, for which they are employed or with which they are charged. People assume different roles in society, and in the division of labor we come to expect that they will discharge their obligations and duties honorably. Parents have responsibilities to properly nurture and care for their children. Teachers are charged with the education of the young. People in public life have the duties of their offices to discharge. We expect that workers, office personnel, doctors, lawyers, administrators, and so on be trustworthy and do their jobs well. If they are undependable, lazy, indifferent—if we cannot count on them—especially when they have agreed to assume a job, then they are negligent and can rightly be criticized. In human relations we bestow confidence on certain individuals; if they betray our trust in them, then it is difficult to live or work cooperatively with them. Irresponsible behavior is blameworthy. Accordingly, once people are specifically entrusted with certain duties, they are obligated to fulfill them or to responsibly notify the appropriate person if they cannot.

III. BENEVOLENCE

1. *Goodwill:* the quality of having noble intentions, a virtuous disposition; demonstrating trust. In our dealings with others, it is important that we have a positive attitude toward those who are deserving of it and that we express good intentions toward them. Negative: to be malicious; to show ill will, hostility; to be distrustful, suspicious.

This principle means that we should have good feelings about others, wishing them well and not seeking to do them harm. It suggests that we should always think the best of others unless they are scoundrels, and even then they may have some redeeming virtues that we can discover. We should always try, if possible, to find something good to say about another person, and seek to appreciate his virtues rather than to criticize his faults. Moreover, we should be glad when that person prospers and should be pleased when he is happy. We should not exult in the misery of others. In general, it means that we show some care, concern, or thoughtful regard for the needs of others.

The antonym of this is *malice,* to wish people to make fools of themselves, to fail in their efforts, or indeed to suffer harm. The Tenth Commandment says that we should not *covet* another person's belongings. Among the most difficult of human vices to control is *envy* of what someone has, or *jealousy* of a person's achievements, talents, or possessions. This passion may be all consuming and destructive to viable relationships of trust or to effective learning, working, and functioning. If allowed to grow unimpeded, it can destroy persons and corrode nations. The principle of goodwill is the willingness to allow others to live and let live. People with goodwill do not wish to deny other persons good fortune or success because they themselves may lack them. Instead, they hope for the best for everyone. People of genuine goodwill often find that their motives are misinterpreted by people who lack goodwill; though they are sincere in their aims, others lacking in goodwill may accuse them of the same perfidy to which they themselves are prone.

The opposite of goodwill is *hatred*, which can lead to an all-consuming and seething rage between enemies, jilted lovers, former friends, or competitive rivals. Though we might compete against rivals in a sports contest or commerce or in time of war, we should strive to maintain some degree of fairness and courtesy toward our opponents. If we lose, it should be with some grace; we should not wish to get even or bear undue resentment. This means that *vindictive* conduct is patently wrong. We should not seek to retaliate, or to make others pay, for their victories or for our own misfortunes.

One form of goodwill that is more general than its expression on the personal level is *benevolence*, the love for humanity and the desire to increase the sum total of human happiness. This is expressed in a philanthropic, charitable, and humanitarian devotion to worthy projects.

2. *Nonmalfeasance as applied to persons:* the quality of refraining from harming or injuring others. This principle is related to goodwill; it denies the right to inflict harm on other persons, without necessarily requiring that we confer benefits upon them. Negative: to perform harmful or malefic actions or evil deeds against others.

Nonmalfeasance involves the following important list of prohibitions that are necessary in any civilized community. Anyone who flouts them transgresses the most basic principles of moral conduct. This applies not only to the members of our own inner circle, tribe, or nation, but to all men and women, whatever their ethnicity. It is the principle of brotherhood, which unfortunately is violated constantly in times of war, when the rules of decent behavior are usually abandoned:

Do not kill other human beings.
Do not inflict physical violence or bodily injury on them.
Do not deprive them of food, shelter, clothing, or other necessities of life.
Do not be cruel, spiteful, vengeful, or vindictive.
Do not inflict harsh or inhuman punishment on anyone, even those who have
    severely transgressed these principles.
Do not torture or inflict unnecessary psychological suffering upon them.
Do not kidnap persons, take them as hostages, or hold them against their will.
Do not terrorize innocent persons by threats to life or limb.
Do not rape (see "Sexual consent" below).
Do not libel, slander, defame, or seek to destroy the careers of others.
Do not harm others by gossip or innuendo; do not spread false rumors or
    calumny.
Do not abuse children, the helpless, the weak, or the disadvantaged, who are
    unable to fight back or defend themselves.
Do not harm by revenge or carry on a vendetta for past wrongs.

3. *Nonmalfeasance as applied to private and public property:* the quality of show-ing respect for the property of others or of the community. Persons have a right to possess property they acquire honestly, without fear of theft or plunder. Negative: to rob, steal, plunder.

The act of theft of lawful possessions is considered a crime punishable by law in all societies that sanction the holding of private property. The most ex-treme form of robbery is the use of force or intimidation to compel a person to give up property through acts that may involve threats to life or limb. Plun-der or pillage in time of war involves spoliation and extortion, often on a vast scale. In extreme cases, this involves sacking and ravaging an area. It may also occur at the hands of bandits who loot, pirates who seek booty, kidnappers who seek ransom, or even arsonists who maliciously destroy property.

Robbery may occur surreptitiously when the victim is absent, but it is ob-viously still wrong. Another form of robbery is the deliberate effort to defraud persons of what is rightfully theirs. When we say that persons ought to respect the property of others, we are referring to property that is rightfully obtained and not unlawfully gained by misbegotten means.

The principle similarly can be extended to public property. The prohibi-tion here is against the purposeful looting, defacing, misusing, or neglecting the common property of a group or association, or the public property of the state.

4. *Sexual consent:* the quality of engaging in mutually consensual, volun-tary sex. This is a form of the nonmalfeasance principle as applied to private sexual conduct between adults. Negative: to rape, require sexual submission; to abuse or harass sexually.

The act of rape is a violation of an individual's rights as a free person and is abhorred by the civilized community. This means that sexual relations de-pend upon consent given by both parties. It means that there will be no use of physical coercion to seize or force a person to have sexual intercourse. In-cluded under this is the use of intimidation or duress to force a person to sub-mit to any degree of penetration of any orifice of the body. Whether this ap-plies to marriage partners is open to dispute. Generally, it has not been applied to marriage partners, and those who force their partners to have sex have not been considered rapists; today many women think that the definition of rape should be extended to protect them from brutal husbands—and certainly from estranged ones.

Included in this principle is the recognition that sexual consent explicitly excludes children below the age of consent. The use of force or deception in order to have sexual relations with children is specifically proscribed and con-sidered even by hardened criminals to be the worst crime. It is severely pun-ished by the civilized community.

A broader form of the principle of sexual consent is its extension to private, nonmarital, and especially homosexual relations. Historically, many societies have regulated what they consider to be "deviant" forms of sexual conduct, prostitution, anal or oral intercourse (whether heterosexual or homosexual), and sadomasochism, even though it is difficult to police most forms of sexual conduct because most sex acts occur in private.

This principle would permit any type of sexual relationship between consenting adults and prohibit the state from intruding into the bedroom and prosecuting the varieties of sexual preference. Another problem that emerges is whether the state should regulate sexual relations between adult members of the same family (brothers, sisters, aunts, uncles) and all forms of sadomasochism, even where there is consensual agreement between the parties. These expressions of sexual orientation, however, are generally not recognized under the common moral decencies, and the extension of the principle of sexual consent to them is a recent development.

5. *Beneficence:* the quality of exhibiting kindness, sympathy, altruism, compassion. To perform a good deed, to be helpful or thoughtful, to be humanitarian, and to bestow gifts are acts of beneficence. This is the positive desire to help others, to improve their lives, to confer benefits, to reduce misery, to spread happiness. Negative: to be malevolent, harmful, selfish, uncharitable.

A beneficent attitude toward others is deserving of the highest praise. Some individuals may be so limited in means that they are unable to contribute very much to charity. But a beneficent person is willing to go out of his way to do a good deed. This involves empathy with the needs of others. It means that we ought to be considerate of the feelings of other human beings and seek to assist them if we can. This may not cost very much: to give up one's seat on a crowded train or bus, to help a blind person across the road, to lend a helping hand to someone injured or in need of solace are all beneficent acts. It means also that one should do what one can to reduce a person's misery or suffering, and even, if possible, to contribute to that person's care, education, nourishment, pleasure, or happiness. Many people discover that it feels better to give than to receive and that the pleasures of altruistic behavior outweigh the pleasures of self-seeking gratification.

Moralists have pointed out that the principle of beneficence, or doing good to others, is less binding than the principle of nonmalfeasance, or not harming them. Within the family unit, however, relatives have an obligation to assist family members in distress, and if possible, to afford the means for them to prosper. The more spontaneous this is, the more satisfying; the more satisfying, the easier it becomes. Altruism among friends and relatives is expected, and one condemns egocentric behavior in this context. We call upon those we love to assist us in time of need, to make sacrifices of time and money. Jesus' admonition that we should "love one another" is a noble expression of this principle. A morally decent person recognizes, for instance, that if we are all seated around a table, no one in our midst should want for food; we will willingly share our bread with others.

Beneficence has two dimensions: (1) an injunction to assist mercifully in order to alleviate pain, suffering, or deprivation for those we are able to help, and (2) a positive prescription to increase the sum of the goods a person can attain in life. The real question, again, is how far the principle of beneficence shall be extended: to humanity as a whole—including the starving in Africa and the diseased in the slums of Asia—or only toward those within our range? Hopefully the former, though only the latter may be practically feasible.

The state can enact legislation to protect individuals from harming one another; for example, force or fraud is considered a crime and can be punished. Thus, although the state can regulate negative behavior, it can hardly legislate altruism in those individuals who lack it. In some societies, it provides tax incentives for voluntary contributions to charity, thus encouraging beneficent action. The principle of nonmalfeasance is considered too important to be left to private action, and it is thus enforced by the state. The principle of beneficence, on the contrary, cannot easily be enforced.

IV. FAIRNESS

1. *Gratitude:* the quality of being grateful, of having friendly and warm feelings toward a benefactor. In human relationships, it is important that we show some appreciation for favors done for us. Negative: to be ungrateful, unappreciative.

Many individuals are pleased to bestow a gift or a favor, or to lend a helping hand to someone who needs or wants it. They may not wish recompense nor expect anything in return, but would welcome some sign of appreciation. The recipient should manifest some gratitude by thanking the person or acknowledging help. Perhaps at some future time, one may return a favor in kind or render a service. Those who are oblivious to good deeds bestowed and who act as though they believe they have favors coming to them are ingrates, insensible to what others have done for them. If a good society is to prosper with beneficent actions, the quality of beneficence is encouraged by signs of appreciative response. In some cases, the help proffered may be long overdue, niggardly, or inadequate, and may not deserve recognition. Where it is worthy, however, it merits gratitude. The recognition should be dignified, without obsequiousness or groveling; for the benefactor to demand this would itself be indecent.

2. *Accountability:* the quality of being answerable for conduct. There is a deep sense that a person who commits a foul deed that harms another, particularly an act such as murder, robbery, or rape, should not be allowed to remain unpunished. Negative: to not be answerable for conduct.

Implicit in this principle is the idea that individuals should be held responsible for injuring others and should be called to account for it. For a grave moral crime to go unanswered is considered unjust. Moreover, there is the conviction that if a criminal is allowed to go unpunished, the societal order will degenerate. The victim or his relative or the community at large may feel so aggrieved that unless some accountability to the public is rendered, moral outrage may only be compounded.

In the strong form, this includes the demand for revenge, whereby one inflicts equal suffering, pain, or loss so that the punishment fits the crime. The penalty imposed either may be invoked as an act a retribution for its own sake, or, in more developed moral communities, may be used to deter future moral transgressions and crimes. In this way society attempts to protect itself, and if possible, to reform the criminal. In civilized communities, cruel and unusual, barbarous, or degrading punishment is deemed inappropriate.

One form the principle of accountability takes is the demand for damages. Where culpability has been established, and particularly where there has been an attempt to harm another through malice, it is felt that some form of reparation ought to be made. When someone has injured another person or harmed his property, the victim can sometimes sue for damages.

The whole effort of civilized conduct is to establish procedures for determining guilt and then seeing to it that there is a just application of the laws. In extenuating circumstances or for first-time offenders, society recognizes that there are some grounds for mercy. Related to this is the need to forgive and forget at some point and to avoid vindictiveness or revenge, especially when a person has made a mistake and admits it, shows some remorse, or has learned from his errors. In such cases the better part of valor is to be forgiving, not carry a grudge, and even at some point to welcome the reformed criminal back into the community.

3. *Justice:* the quality of exhibiting fairness, equity, rectitude. That justice ought to prevail is widely held in civilized communities, even though there may be widespread disagreement about what it is. Negative: to be unjust, unfair, partial.

In its simplest sense, justice refers to meting out just deserts, that is, punishment for misdeeds and reward for merit. The principle of accountability enters here, as do notions of equity and rectitude.

Also involved in the principle of justice is the idea of equitable compensation for work performed or services rendered. This involves a normative standard for distributing the goods and services of society. People should be paid an honest wage for an honest day's work; income and wealth should be equitably divided among those who have earned or deserve what they received. The principle of fairness is present here. In democratic societies, other manifestations of justice have emerged: the rules of law, equality, and liberty. All individuals are considered equal before the law and should not seek to obtain special privileges and immunities that others in the community lack.

The modern democratic principle thus suggests equality of consideration: each person is equal to all others in dignity and value. Similar is the principle of liberty and the opportunity to pursue happiness without undue interference. New ideas of economic equality have been introduced in modern society. Implicit in the principle of justice is the belief that there ought to be penalties for discrimination based upon racial, religious, ethnic, or sexual differences. Should those who are unable to work receive some support from society? Should the basic needs of the disadvantaged be satisfied? Should society help those who through no fault of their own are unable to care for themselves? The dispute between capitalism and socialism takes us far beyond the elementary moral decencies to a more complicated doctrine of human rights and equality of opportunity and of treatment. Justice also requires an appeal to the use of peaceful methods of adjudicating differences equitably and harmoniously. It means that we should reason together in order to solve our problems and not resort to force or violence.

4. *Tolerance:* the quality of sympathetic understanding, broad-mindedness, respect. The toleration of individuals or nations who differ from us in values, manners, customs, or beliefs becomes an essential method of achieving peace and harmony in a civilized world. Negative: to exhibit prejudice, bigotry, hatred, discrimination, narrow-mindedness, mean-spiritedness.

One of the faults of human beings is the tendency to reject and deny equal access or rights to individuals or groups who do not share our beliefs and practices. This can happen within the community, where we may disapprove of the lifestyles or values of other individuals; or it can apply to other groups, cultures, races, or nations, whose customs and beliefs we find alien to ours. We may disapprove of their tastes or norms and think that their beliefs are false, bizarre, or wicked. The tendency is to seek to censor or prohibit differing values and beliefs. We may even fear them or believe that they are a great danger to our community. We may feel that if they are allowed to go unchecked, our own cherished values would be undermined. Thus our desire is to suppress them.

Tolerant people may differ with others in their communities, yet forbear any effort to suppress them. Tolerant people believe that they have a moral obligation to allow diverse styles of life to express themselves. To tolerate does not necessarily mean to approve; it merely means that we will not seek to prohibit differences by legislation, nor use force to root them out. Tolerance need not imply permissiveness. An open and pluralistic society will permit some measure of freedom as long as those to whom it is extended will not seek to prevent others from enjoying the same rights. It does not necessarily mean that "anything goes" and that no standards of criticism are possible.

Tolerance applies to a broad range of subject matter: moral and religious beliefs and practices as well as ethnic customs. It is opposed to any discrimination on racial, religious, economic, social, or sexual grounds. It also applies to philosophical, scientific, or political forms of belief.

To tolerate means that we accord other individuals or groups some respect—not that we agree with them, only that we recognize the rules of the game and allow them some degree of liberty of belief, taste, and pursuits. In biblical terms, to tolerate the alien or the stranger in our midst is to recognize that we may sometimes be an alien in another land, hoping for the same measure of sympathy. Tolerance is a basic humanistic virtue. In modern times, humanists have defended the right of dissent of nonbelievers and heretics against the demands for conformity. It is a generalized moral principle and an expression of moral decency.

5. *Cooperation:* the quality of working together for peace, harmony, tranquillity, or the social good. Maintaining a state of peace and amity between individuals within a community, between factions or states, is essential for the human social order. Negative: to be unable or unwilling to work with others to prevent or diminish war, hostility, strife, conflict, discord, and enmity.

That we should attempt to keep the peace and not resort to violent means in order to achieve our ends is a cardinal rule that all individuals and nations recognize in principle but unfortunately all too often violate in practice. We should use every effort to work out our differences peacefully. Negotiation is preferable as a mode of preventing strife or conflict, but to resort to power or force in human affairs is common. The moral principle is that we should seek to avoid this and not impose our will upon other individuals or nations. Aggression against others with whom we cannot agree is destructive to all human values. If allowed to get out of hand, it leads to the killing or maiming of individuals or the despoiling of their property. Defensive measures of self-protection are justifiable against an aggressive enemy.

Warfare, though common, is hardly the best or most effective method for resolving differences. Aggression or the fear of it leads to retaliation or encourages preemptive strikes. It engenders intense hatred against one's enemies and a seething desire for revenge. People have resorted to war for any number of reasons: for territorial expansion, financial profit or plunder; to promote a cause; to convert heathens or barbarians, ostensibly to aid mankind; and to bring down tyrants or madmen. The toll of violence often can be terrible in human suffering and misery.

We ought to beat our swords into plowshares, says the Old Testament. "Turn the other cheek," says the New Testament. But both injunctions have been violated with impunity by Judeo-Christian nations. The Koran has been used as a justification for the Jihad, or the Holy War.

The principle of cooperation beseeches us to find an appropriate resolution for our differences, to strive as mightily as we can to negotiate, and to reach compromises that all parties to a dispute can accept. We need adjudication rather than confrontation. Unfortunately, men and women often sing praises to peace as they march off to war.

Under certain conditions a war can be a just one. This is particularly the case when it is a war of self-defense. It is difficult to justify a war of aggression, undertaken in order to achieve one's political ends or to seize power or amass riches. Under certain conditions, one may not be able to reach an understanding with an invading army or a menacing individual. One should try to negotiate a compromise, and war or violence should be only a last resort. It is only in a situation of clear and present danger and in order to protect oneself that appropriate force can be justified. The general rule of moral decency is to cooperate as best we can, to tolerate the differing views of others, and to negotiate. Whether in fact it is always possible to do this remains to be seen, but it should be both the rule and goal of conduct.

Although the preceding list of common moral decencies has merit and is widely accepted, at least in principle, by most civilized communities, how they work in practice will depend upon individual circumstances or different social situations. That they are not fully realized in human conduct should be evident to everyone. No one is perfect. These general principles only establish norms of decent conduct; they do not promise that everyone will observe them. Indeed, given the conflicts that may sometimes arise in life, individuals may violate these norms and principles. But this should not weaken our obligation to recognize their binding nature, and whenever possible to seek to live in light of them.

Many new ethical principles have lately emerged in some societies, and some are still open to dispute in others. Both are products of a revisionary humanistic morality. These principles include the doctrine of human rights, the right to privacy, an ecological concern for the environment, an imperative to seek to preserve other species on this planet, our obligations to future generations, a need to transcend the limits of ethnicity, and a need to extend our ethical concerns to the wider world community.

16

CARING

CARING DEFINED

Humanists are often challenged: If we dispense with the classical religious foundations for moral behavior, what will replace them? Are there naturalistic grounds for ethical conduct? My response to these questions is twofold: first, *empathetic feeling* is the originative source of moral awareness, and second, *ethical rationality* emerges to further develop a mature sense of responsibility. In this chapter I wish to focus on the nature and source of the central moral imperative: *caring for others.*

A person may abide by the moral rules of his social group and outwardly conform to what is expected, but this may be motivated by fear of punishment from parents, teachers, the state, or God. Surely we cannot consider this motive for conduct to be fully moral. It is, of course, important that we not violate the moral rules, and it is especially important that courageous Prometheans respect the rights and needs of others within the community. Prometheus, according to the ancient myth, so loved humans that he wished to share with them the gifts of fire, science, and the arts. The key to moral conduct and a vital humanistic virtue is the presence of a genuine state of *caring*; by this is meant both the inward and outward expression of some moral regard for other persons. A caring person is not indifferent to what happens to others, to their interests and needs. In a limited sense, one may take care of another person, that is, minister to his wants—as a nurse cares for a sick patient in a hospital or a mother suckles her infant. In a broader sense, to express a caring attitude is to be interested in the well-being of some other person or persons—as, for example, a teacher helping her student to master grammar. In some cases a person may care for someone, be interested in his well-being, or be disposed favorably or be sympathetic without necessarily doing anything about it overtly. I may be interested in someone's career or marriage and hope for the best, even though I may not be directly involved. There is a moral principle that is implicit in our discussion: *a rational person recognizes that one should care about the needs and interests of others.*

There are various aspects of *caring* that may be distinguished. The first is *compassion.* Here a person has a sympathetic awareness of another human being's distress, and a desire to help reduce or alleviate suffering. Compassion may involve some degree of pity concerning the discomfort that someone is experiencing. If a person is in pain and calls for help, I may out of compassion attempt to do what I can. For example, a missing child lost in a department store may arouse my compassion, and I will do whatever I can to help the child find his parent. The compassionate regard for other people can become the be-all and end-all of life for many persons. "If I can stop one heart from breaking, I shall not live in vain; if I can ease one life the aching, or cool one pain. . . . I shall not live in vain," wrote Emily Dickinson.[1]

Compassion is rooted in empathy, a powerful stimulus to sympathetic moral awareness. The Greek root for the term is *empatheia,* which means, literally, *passion.* This term is derived from *empathés,* meaning *emotional,* which is a combination of *em* plus *pathos.* Insofar as I am able to read the inner experiences, desires, or thoughts of another human being, I can empathize with that person. If I can help, I do. Empathetic emotions enable me to recognize the plight of other persons and take on some of the burdens they face; kindness is aroused. In some cases, I may be able to accomplish very little or nothing at all because those who need assistance may not be within the compass of my activities. For example, I can feel compassion for the starving children of Ethiopia or the poor people of Bangladesh, and this sympathetic identification may be felt within my heart and mind. Thus a person can have compassion yet not do anything to help. Compassion is an attitude or belief that someone is in need and a concomitant wish that the deprivation be reduced. In one sense this is *negative*; that is, I wish to mitigate the suffering of others. This applies not only to humans, but also to animals. I may have some compassion for the deer who are starving in the winter; thus I may attempt to feed them or even attempt to thin out the herd. I may be concerned about needless pain being inflicted on animals in scientific experiments, and I may urge that experiments with animals be designed so as not to subject them to unnecessary pain. Compassion, therefore, evinces a *humane* attitude to various sentient forms of life.

There is a second sense of moral caring that is *positive*: the desire not simply to reduce the suffering but to contribute to the happiness, joy, or well-being of others. This is a form of *benevolence* whereby I wish to bestow goods on others. The recipients may not necessarily be suffering, but they would benefit from my acts of commission. I might, for example, support the building of a beautiful public park for the common good or the construction of a new library, or even take part in the distribution of gifts to children during the holidays. I am playing the role of the benefactor, and I may express benevolence by acts of generosity. The moral concern is to increase or enhance the treasury of goods available for a person or a community of persons, and this may involve feelings or thoughts of affectionate regard for their well-being. People who contribute to charitable organizations may do so with two goals in mind: they may contribute money to the orphans of Haiti because they have a compassionate concern for reducing human suffering, or they may contribute to a university because they have a benevolent interest in progress and think that education is worthwhile. Sometimes our deeds are done out of both motives: sympathetic compassion and benevolence—as when a person adopts a homeless child or provides college scholarships for disadvantaged youngsters.

Both compassion and benevolence, if concerned with the good of the recipient, may be said to express *altruism*. An altruistic act is *carried out for the benefit of another person (or persons) at some expense or sacrifice to oneself, and without any primary expectation of reward*. It is other regarding in its objective, seeking to reduce the suffering, or enhance the enjoyment, of other human beings.

What is the relationship of altruistic moral caring to Christianity? The New Testament has emphasized the importance of compassion as a moral virtue; this includes pity, mercy, sympathy, and a desire to reduce suffering. Christianity, however, is rooted in faith and feeling, and it is based on commandments from Jesus, who admonished us to love one another. This is no doubt an important contribution to the development of moral sensibility. It is a significant modification of the pagan virtues of classical Greek philosophy, by emphasizing a moral concern for other people.

Moral caring in humanistic terms, however, is not synonymous with this Christian virtue. First, because Christianity often takes suffering to have some intrinsic moral value, some Christians believe that we should suffer as Christ did on the cross. Some religious extremists will flagellate themselves in the name of the Lord. St. Bernadette allegedly suffered in silence painful canker sores, never revealing her affliction to others; this sacrifice was said to be morally worthy. For the humanist, suffering is an evil that we should in principle avoid; it can be justified on some occasions for the good that it may engender. For example, if I go to a dentist, and he reports that I have a bad cavity that needs to be drilled, I may decide to suffer short-range pain for the long-range good (though I may hope that the dentist gives me Novocain to deaden the pain). Or again, a nation may suffer great hardship in time of war in the hope of gaining victory. But this does not mean that suffering or pain has intrinsic merit.

Second, ethical compassion should not be accepted as a blind outpouring of feeling unmitigated by cognition. Not all expressions of compassion are justifiable, for some forms of compassion may be misdirected or inappropriate. For example, persons on welfare may evince my compassion and induce me to provide them with benefits, though perhaps instead I should encourage them to find jobs. A person may feel some compassion for a brutal murderer who tortures little children and may wish him to be freed from prison. I can hardly have any compassion for him, given his past behavior. Thus there are often limits to be placed on compassion, especially when it conflicts with other virtues and values.

Third, moral caring has a broader range than Christian love. It is not focused simply on the desire to reduce suffering in others; it also wishes to enhance the positive distribution of goods. Accordingly, benevolence is essential to its fulfillment, and this is focused on increasing the sum of enjoyments in this life, not suffering or deferring enjoyments to the next. Humanistic altruism is thus more full-bodied than ascetic or self-denying Christian martyrdom. An exaggerated concern for the poor and disadvantaged sometimes is a mask for resentment against the affluent and successful.

ALTRUISM

Are acts of compassion and benevolence a genuine expression of altruistic concern, done without any hope of personal gain, or are they motivated ultimately for selfish purposes? A person may contribute to a charity because he will receive a tax deduction or public acclaim. If so, the motive may be primarily self-interest. Another person, however, may do so principally for the benefit of others, without any expectation of recognition or reward; he may not even request a tax deduction and may contribute anonymously. One may ask: Are *any* acts truly altruistic, or is there an element of self-deception here?

The cynic denies that any acts are purely altruistic in intention, and he endeavors to reduce all such acts to egoism. At this point a theory of psychological motivation becomes relevant. A utilitarian might argue that the motive of an act is irrelevant to its moral quality. The important factors are the consequences to the general welfare, the increase in the sum of pleasure or happiness, and the reduction of pain or unhappiness. There may be some truth to this appraisal. It is not what you say or feel, but what you *do* that counts. This issue, however, is of vital significance to humanism and its conception of human nature. It does matter to us whether the milk of human kindness and the spirit of generosity are genuine and whether human beings are capable of other-regarding compassionate and benevolent caring.

Many theists hold a bleak view of human nature; the doctrine of original sin demeans who we are. Are humans corrupt, brutal, evil, and interested only in satisfying their own selfish desires—as the pessimistic nihilist claims? Or do we have the potentiality for real moral caring? Without being accused of naïve optimism and an unrealistic appraisal of the human condition, I submit that there are wholesome moral dimensions intrinsic to the human species—at least potentially—and that these can be nourished so that they reach fruition.

The theist denies that human beings are capable of such autonomous moral behavior. Only God can redeem us from evil; humans are impotent to save themselves. If this dismal view is mistaken and human beings are capable of empathy, compassion, and benevolence, without the sanctions and admonitions of deity or without motives of pure self-interest, then we *can* do something about enhancing the ethical dimensions of life. Whether any human being will be moved by altruistic moral caring is a complex question; it depends on the social and cultural environment in which he lives, the educational influences, and the rewards and inducements offered. No doubt we do things for a variety of motives, and these include not only self-interest and altruism, but also a whole host of other complex causes. The challenge to the humanist is whether altruistic motivation is *intrinsic* to our very natures—at least potentially—and whether we can mitigate the evils that beset us in the world and redeem ourselves. Conversely, the challenge is whether we have to barter our souls for false doctrines of salvation if we are to behave morally. To argue, as the humanist has, that moral impulses and imperatives are intrinsic to the human being requires us to examine their sources in human behavior; by doing so we have found a naturalistic ground for moral conscience.

Egoism and altruism are both partially true; they are false only if either is taken as a comprehensive theory of motivation. Extreme self-interest theories attempt to reduce all human motives to a single source: the selfish desire for pleasure, sexual gratification, power, glory, or gain. Self-interest clearly applies to patently self-motivated actions undertaken to reduce a person's needs or to satisfy his desires. But does it apply universally to any and all acts, including those that appear to be other-regarding, charitable, or self-sacrificing? An organism surely needs to engage in self-interested forms of behavior if it is to survive and function. It needs to satisfy its hunger for food, protect itself from danger, and seek sexual gratification. Thus self-interest is a necessary component of any person's life; it can be justified rationally. But the issue is whether *all* motives are self-centered. I think the error lies in the failure to ascertain whether the *primary* object of desire is one's own gratification or that of others, for there is a basic difference in the objective or goal of an act. Benevolent acts have *other* persons' interests in mind. In many acts the agent's own interest is involved, but the agent may also be interested in helping others—so there can be a double focus. Surely we should not blur all distinctions and claim that the motivation of a self-seeking hedonist or power-hungry despot is the *same as* an other-regarding parent, educator, or humanitarian who genuinely wishes to devote himself to enhancing the welfare of others.

Conversely, the egoist has a valid case to make against altruists who seek to smother creative initiative, courageous independence, or individuality, and who extol self-effacing sacrifice as the highest virtue. Antony Flew protests vehemently against the efforts by socialists and welfare liberals to use the state to impose forms of egalitarianism on society.[2] This can dampen individual initiative, he claims, which is the spark of human creativity. The egoist thus has a right to object to the effort by communitarians to condemn all self-centered behavior as evil. The common good is perhaps best fulfilled by maximizing individual freedom, not suppressing it, thus allowing incentive and enterprise to increase the sum of wealth for society. Promethean courage can likewise be destroyed by the legions of God's disciples imposing their standards of self-sacrifice in the name of compassion as the highest virtue, thereby demeaning courage, independence, and self-determination. Libertarians reject the morbid Augustinian-Christian view that anything done out of self-interest (including the satisfaction of erotic impulses) is venal and wicked.

This should not, however, deny the capacity for genuine altruistic loving, caring behavior in the human being and the need for communitarian co-operative acts. I submit that there is a need to receive love but also to give it; this is not only the desire to be at the center of affection (an infantile response in itself), but also the need to extend it to others. It is this capacity to bestow love and affection, and to be compassionate and benevolent, that is among the highest qualities of human morality. The salient point, however, is that there is no contradiction in recognizing that we are *both* self-centered, as we should be, *and* altruistic, which is necessary if we are to live and work together in communities. It is the capacity for altruistic behavior that is crucial to humanistic eupraxsophy. We need to encourage Good Samaritans to appreciate the biblical injunction, "Thou shalt love thy neighbor as thyself." We need to extend the range of our moral concern to the aliens in our midst and beyond our borders. But to what extent is this possible, given history's testimony of the capacity of human beings to be cruel and rapacious, particularly toward those outside of one's community?

Critics maintain that humanism's positive appraisal of human nature is too high; they remonstrate that mankind is incredibly selfish and vindictive. The greatest enemy to man, states the cynic, is man. Robert Burton observed that man is like Aesop's fox who, "when he had lost his tail, would have all his fellowfoxes cut off theirs."[3] William James maintained that "Man, biologically considered . . . is the most formidable of all the beasts of prey . . . and indeed, the only one that preys systematically on its own species."[4] The lessons from history about the dark side of human behavior should disabuse us of any simplistic romantic ideals about the beneficent nature of human beings. There is a recurring saga of men and women brutalizing those who are different from them. Once a person is reduced to an inferior status, by denigration of his race, gender, ethnic or national origin, or class, it is easier to violate his moral dignity.

The causes of such cruelty are complex, and they have many sources in our nature and in society. These causes are rooted no doubt in the fact that we were at one time uncivilized wild beasts, ferocious and cunning, capable of killing and destroying those who were viewed as antagonists. Our capacity to kill is demonstrated in our relationships to other animals, which we are ready and able to hunt, track, kill, and eat, and to use their skin for warmth and protection. We have domesticated some animals and used them as beasts of burden, working them to their capacity. But humans are also capable of extending the range of moral concern to animals within their own circle and to express care, love, and affection for their dogs, cats, cows, sheep, and horses. We express a complex set of attitudes and motives to animals. Some people are vegetarian and will not kill or eat animals. Many feel strongly about defending animal rights. Thus our relationship to other animal species is ambivalent: we can demonstrate hate and fear or love and affection.

The issue here concerns our relationship to other human beings. It is likewise bipolar, for we are capable of displaying either cruelty or kindness, hatred or generosity. These impulses, no doubt rooted in our evolutionary past, emerged as part of our struggle for survival. Humans are born as naked apes. The entire moral history of the race has to be instilled in every youngster from the moment of birth; each of us is only one generation away from savagery.

COGNITION AND CARING

The roots of caring behavior are biosociogenic; they develop often unconsciously, perhaps even instinctively, and surely they are emotionally charged. At some point in human conduct, however, moral awareness is enhanced by cognition. Ethical rationality is not a superfluous addition to moral caring but can become constitutive of its very form. Because our beliefs interpenetrate and mold our attitudes, empathy and compassion may be reinforced by cognitive reflection. Indeed, it is through the process of deliberative reasoning that an individual's self-interest can be reconciled with the needs of others; intellectual factors enable us to evaluate conflicting demands within situations. In some cases, compassionate actions may be undeserving or foolish; in others, fully justifiable. In some instances, intended deeds of benevolence may be unwarranted in the light of the circumstance; in others, they may be rationally justified.

Is there a rule of reason that will help us resolve complex ethical dilemmas? Yes. There is a key ethical principle that provides us with some guidance. This takes the form of the following general rule of moral caring: *a rational person ought to express some moral caring for the needs of others.*

The first part of the principle of moral caring involves compassion and empathy. Thus we may state as a general prescriptive rule: *where it is within our power, we ought to mitigate the suffering, distress, pain, and sorrow of other sentient beings.* This applies to our friends and relatives, for they are within the range of our conduct. The rule also has a wider net. But there may be little that we can do for those outside our range of conduct, except perhaps to contribute to charities or agencies that will reduce hunger, assist handicapped people, and provide aid to the victims of natural disasters.

The second aspect of the principle of moral caring is that *we ought to develop a benevolent attitude toward all persons deserving of it.* Not everyone is deserving of our benevolence; those who behave indecently may be undeserving. Again, we should act benevolently where we can to those who are within our range of day-to-day conduct. And we should try to distribute goods and services in a positive way to enhance the well-being of others. For example, we ought to help children wherever possible to attend school, to learn how to think critically, to enjoy good music and the arts, and to appreciate the diverse enrichments of culture. And we ought to help ensure a prosperous and peaceful society. Thus we also have a generalized positive moral obligation toward *all* persons. We may accomplish this by performing little deeds or large ones, by giving gifts to individuals or charities. And we may also engage in cooperative social programs for the wider good.

Why do we do so? Perhaps because it is in our self-interest to do so, but also because we wish to see the good of others enhanced and to distribute to as many people who deserve it the fruits of civilized life.

In summary, this rule of ethical rationality states that we ought to act so as to mitigate human suffering and sorrow and to increase the sum of human good and happiness, providing it is possible to do so.

This rule is still highly controversial for many conservative libertarians. They hold that it is a mistake to dole out help to others, who instead should be taught to fend for themselves. Many libertarians oppose the role of the state in providing public welfare to the disadvantaged, to the ill, needy, or elderly members of the population. They are especially opposed to the use of taxation by the state to support programs of welfare. Many would not necessarily object to other social institutions, private charities, or individuals providing assistance. Other conservatives, however, are opposed to any sustained effort at altruistic compassion and benevolence because they believe that it may undermine the virtue of self-reliance and thus foster dependency. Egalitarians, Christians, socialists, and others seek to help the weak, the poor, the homeless, and the dispossessed by distributing the goods and services of society more equitably.

Others argue that we should not simply try to divide up the existing pie but should bake more and more pies. We should seek to expand economic growth rates by providing incentives for individual achievement and entrepreneurship. All of this may be granted to some extent—though in the complex corporate world, individual enterprises have been replaced by larger economic units in which individual merit is often lost.

One might still argue on moral grounds that one ought to help those who through no fault of their own cannot help themselves. This would exclude indolent individuals who could work and prefer not to, or those who have been brought up in a culture of dependence and neither develop any independence and autonomy nor seek to pull themselves up by their own initiative.

Still another problem concerning the appropriate extent of moral caring is the fact that many conservatives today have become extremely chauvinistic or nationalistic and wish to limit the range of moral concern. They believe that their first duty is at home, not abroad. Thus a key issue concerns the following question: How far should our moral concern be extended? Should it apply to every person or community in every corner of the globe?

HUMANITY AS A WHOLE

I submit that our moral duty indeed should be extended to humanity as a whole and that this moral rule should thus be generalized. This means that we should be concerned not only with the well-being of those within our communities or nation-states, but also with the entire world community well beyond our own parochial interests.

Extreme chauvinistic partiality is divisive. Although our loyalties to the norms of our countries or ethnic groups takes us beyond selfish parochial interests to a wider concern for the good of the inhabitants of the region in which we live, extreme chauvinism between ethnic groups and nation-states can be destructive. Moral caring thus should not end at ethnic enclaves or national frontiers. Ethical rationality enjoins us to build institutions of cooperation and to attempt wherever possible to negotiate our differences peacefully. The broader injunction is that an *impartial ethical rationality should apply to all human beings who have equal dignity and value.* This implies that we should be concerned with the defense of human rights everywhere.

Accordingly, we each have a duty to help mitigate the suffering of people anywhere in the world and to contribute to the common good, thus finding some common ground with all humans. This expresses our highest sense of compassion and benevolence. This implies that people living in the affluent nations have an obligation to mitigate suffering and enhance the well-being, where they can, of people in impoverished regions of the world, and that those in the underdeveloped areas likewise have an obligation to replace resentment against the affluent with reciprocal goodwill.

PART IV

HUMANISM

17

HUMANISM AS A EUPRAXSOPHY

Many friends and foes of humanism maintain that it is a religion. I think that they are mistaken, but if humanism is not a religion, what is it? It is, I submit, a philosophical, scientific, and ethical outlook. Unfortunately, there is no word in the English language adequate to convey its meaning. Humanism combines, as I will argue, a method of inquiry, a cosmic world view, a life stance, and a set of social values.

Accordingly, I think we will have to coin a new term in order to distinguish humanistic and *nontheistic* beliefs and practices from other systems of beliefs and practices, a term that could be used in many languages. The best approach is to combine Greek roots. I have come up with the term *eupraxsophy*, which means "good practical wisdom." *Eupraxsophy* is derived from the following roots: *eu-*, *praxis-*, and *sophia*. *Eu-* is a prefix that means "good," "well," "advantageous." It is combined in words such as *eudæmonia*, which means "well-being" or "happiness"; it is also used in *euthanasia*, *eulogy*, *euphoria*, and so on. *Praxis* (or *prassein*) refers to "action, doing, or practice." *Eupraxia* means "right action" or "good conduct." The suffix *sophia* is derived from *sophos* ("wise") and means "wisdom." This suffix appears in the term *philosophy*, combining *philos* ("loving") and *sophia* ("wisdom") to mean "love of wisdom."

In its original sense, philosophy, as metaphysics or "the science of being," investigated the general principles and categories by which we can understand nature and interpret reality. The classical philosophers attempted to work out a system of nature in which certain principles were considered to be basic. Metaphysics has been in considerable disrepute in modern times, particularly in the hands of skeptical critics. At the very least, metaphysics analyzes and interprets the basic concepts of the sciences, attempts to make some sense out of them, and, if possible, to unify them. This is a very complex task today because of the continuing proliferation of new fields of learning and the enormous difficulty of any one mind being able to master the expanding corpus of knowledge.

Philosophical inquiry also focuses on epistemology, the theory of knowledge. It is concerned with questions of meaning, truth, the principles of valid inference, and inductive and deductive logic. There are many other branches of philosophy, including logic, aesthetics, ethics, the philosophy of science, political and social philosophy, and the philosophy of religion; indeed, almost any field can be approached philosophically.

Synthetic philosophy attempts to offer universal or general principles and to develop an overall view, a cosmic perspective or *Weltanshauung*. This is sometimes called synoptic or speculative philosophy, but since the development of modern science in the sixteenth and seventeenth centuries, this approach has been seriously questioned on methodological grounds, for it cannot be done independently of science but only in relation to it. Nonetheless, philosophy, in this sense, is thinking about generalities; it is concerned with root questions and cosmic coherence. Analytic philosophy and critical philosophy, on the other hand, are far more modest in scope. Analytic philosophy is concerned with understanding the nature of meaning and truth, and with defining and analyzing the key concepts within any particular field of inquiry. Critical philosophy is evaluative; it strives for clarity, but it also seeks to appraise the validity of truth claims.

These activities are primarily intellectual in purpose, and they are neutral in regard to their practical consequences. The Greeks distinguished contemplative from practical wisdom. Philosophy, as the love of wisdom, begins primarily in the theoretical or contemplative mode. There is another branch of normative philosophy, however, that strives for practical wisdom in ethics and politics. Here, classical philosophy sought to provide some guidance for the good life and the just society. Aristotle maintained in the *Nicomachean Ethics* that ethics has practical import and that we should study it in order to live well. He held that the development of character and virtue and the exercise of practical wisdom would contribute to the achievement of happiness. Many ethical philosophers, however, have focused primarily on the metanalysis of concepts such as "good," "bad," "virtue," "value," "justice," and so on. This was expanded in latter-day Kantian philosophy to the definitions of "right," "wrong," "obligation," "responsibility," and so on. Whether or not these terms can be defined has been hotly debated down to the present;[1] objectivists believe that they can be defined, but there is a skeptical tradition that denies their definability. Be that as it may, classical ethics always had a normative purpose.

A basic distinction can be made between *customary morality*, which refers to the moral conceptions that already prevail in a given cultural group, and *ethics*, which involves a reflective and critical component. Today, many philosophers concerned with ethics emphasize the need for ethical rationality—but virtually for its own sake; and many eschew making any concrete recommendations in dealing with problems that arise in customary morality. This is particularly true in universities and colleges, where philosophy is taught as an academic discipline, where philosophers do philosophical research and publish their disquisitions in scholarly journals, and where philosophy teachers have no clearly identifiable positions. They consider their primary pedagogical method to be the presentation of alternative philosophical theories and do not attempt to propose a set of beliefs or values; that is, they do not seek to persuade their students or the general public to accept their philosophical outlook. Since their task is pure inquiry, similar to that of other disciplines, such as history and the natural and social sciences, they can safely retreat into splendid isolation in an ivory tower—philosophers qua philosophers—and do not have to vindicate their personal positions.

The virtue of this form of philosophy is that the professor imparts a love of wisdom and the skills of critical thinking without imposing his or her own biases on the student. The professor does not wish to indoctrinate or propagandize for a particular cosmic outlook. He wants to be "objective"; he may even be fearful of reprisals from those who support the conventional morality of the day. Yet this kind of philosophy does not satisfy the deeper queries of students and ordinary men and women. It presents no worldview; it does not defend a theory of meaning and truth; nor does it seek to persuade others of the comparative reasonableness of the philosopher's own considered normative or social ideology. Philosophy, as the love of wisdom, aside from being committed to fair-minded and objective critical analysis, is *neutral*. It can take no position; it can draw no normative conclusions from its formal analyses. It is largely a cognitive enterprise; it involves no attitudinal or emotive component. Nor does it seek to arouse conviction or inspire commitment. Postmodernist philosophers go even further, for they deny the possibility of any objective truth.

How far philosophy has come from the Socratic vision of the good life! For Socrates, philosophy had direct relevance to how we should live. The unexamined life is not worth living, he averred, and he was even willing to die for his convictions. Spinoza's *Ethics* seems to have expressed both a philosophy and a eupraxsophy, at least implicitly. We might even say that many or most philosophical systems implicitly had a pragmatic function and that their task was to provide an alternative to religion and a guide to ethics and politics. Contemplative wisdom was often a mask for deeper utilitarian purposes. Marx clearly marked a break with the contemplative mode of philosophy, particularly when he said that the task of philosophy was not simply to interpret the world but also to *change* it! Philosophy in this sense has momentous significance—as it did for Nietzsche, Schopenhauer, Russell, Sartre, Dewey, and others. Alas, today it has become wedded to the academy and corrupted by narrow specialization. Philosophy has lost out to religion and ideology, which in competition for the souls of men and women now rule the day. That is why we need to take new directions and to carve out a new approach.

Eupraxsophy differs from antiseptically neutral philosophy in that it enters consciously and forthrightly into the marketplace where ideas contend. Unlike pure philosophy, it is not simply the *love* of wisdom, though this is surely implied by it, but also the *practice* of wisdom. By that I do not mean that ethicists should not be interested in developing the capacity for critical ethical judgment or practical wisdom. That is an eminent goal. But eupraxsophy goes further than that, for it provides a coherent, ethical life stance. Moreover, it presents a cosmic theory of reality that seems reasonable at a particular point in history in the light of the best knowledge of the day. Humanist eupraxsophy defends a set of criteria governing the testing of truth claims. It also advocates an ethical posture. And it is committed implicitly or explicitly to a set of political ideals. Eupraxsophy combines both a *Weltanshauung* and a philosophy of living. But it takes us one step further by means of commitment; based upon cognition, it is fused with passion. It involves the application of wisdom to the conduct of life.

Noneupraxsophic philosophies are unwilling to affirm this conviction. They examine all sides of a question, see the limits and pitfalls of each, but are unwilling to take a stand on any. As I have said, this has some merit; for the open mind must recognize that it may be mistaken and that views may have to be modified in the light of new arguments or evidence. Thus one needs to be skeptical—but not at the price of forfeiting all convictions. The *eupraxsopher* does make a choice—the most reasonable one in light of the available evidence—and this enables one to act. After all, theologians, politicians, generals, engineers, businessmen, lawyers, doctors, artists, poets, and plain men and women have beliefs, and they act. Why deny this right to the informed philosopher-eupraxsopher? Surely, however, one's beliefs should be based upon reason, critical intelligence, and wisdom. This is what the suffix *sophy* refers to. Wisdom in the broad sense includes not only philosophical and practical judgment, but also scientific understanding.

Let us turn to *Webster's Dictionary* for a definition of *sophia* or *wisdom*:

> 1. The quality of being wise; ability to judge soundly and deal sagaciously with facts, especially as they relate to life and conduct; knowledge, with the capacity to make due use of it; perception of the best ends and the best means; discernment and judgment; discretion; sagacity. 2. Scientific or philosophical knowledge.

Explicit in this definition is a scientific component, for wisdom includes the best scientific knowledge drawn from research and scholarship in the various fields of inquiry. Unfortunately, the various scientific specialists often feel qualified to judge only matters within their own areas of competence, leaving out the broader questions that have a direct bearing on life. There is a crisis in modern science, for the specialties are growing exponentially, with many specialists feeling that they can talk only to those within their own disciplines. Science thus has become fragmented. Who is able to cross the boundary lines and draw metainferences about nature, the human species, society, or life in general? The eupraxsopher deems it his mission to do so.

Theoretical scientific research is morally neutral. The scientist is interested in developing causal hypotheses and theories that can be verified by the evidence. Scientists describe or explain how the subject under study behaves, without evaluating it normatively. There is, of course, a pragmatic element to science, particularly the applied sciences, for we constantly seek to apply our scientific know-how to practical technology. Moreover, the scientist presupposes epistemological criteria that govern his process of inquiry. He is committed to a set of values: truth, clarity, consistency, rationality, objectivity. But the scientist qua scientist does not go beyond that, and he restricts himself in the quest for knowledge to his specialized domain of inquiry.

Humanist eupraxsophy, on the other hand, attempts to draw philosophical implications of science to the life of man. It seeks to develop a cosmic perspective, based on the most reliable findings encountered on the frontiers of science. It recognizes the gaps in knowledge and the things we do not know that still need to be investigated. It is keenly aware of the need for fallibilism and agnosticism about what we do and do not know. Yet it boldly applies practical scientific wisdom to life.

Eupraxsophy, unlike philosophy or science, does not focus on one specialized field of knowledge; it seeks to understand the total impact of scientific knowledge on a person's life. Yet the areas of philosophy, science, and eupraxsophy are not rigid. Philosophers can assist scientists in interpreting their discoveries and relating them to other fields of inquiry, and in developing a broader point of view. Still, eupraxsophy moves beyond philosophy and science in seeking to present a coherent life view as the basis on which we are willing to act. It is the ground upon which we stand, the ultimate outlook that controls our view of reality.

Accordingly, the primary task of eupraxsophy is to understand nature and life and to draw concrete normative prescriptions from this knowledge. Eupraxsophy thus draws deeply from the wells of philosophy, science, and ethics. It involves at least a double focus: a cosmic perspective and a set of normative ideals by which we may live.

THE DEFINITION OF HUMANISM

Thus humanism is a eupraxsophy. But it is not unique, for there have been other eupraxsophies historically. In the Greek and Roman world, Epicureanism, Stoicism, and skepticism were eupraxsophies. Each had a metaphysical worldview, each made concrete ethical recommendations about how to achieve the good life, and each had epistemological theories. There have been many other kinds of eupraxsophies: utilitarianism, Marxism, existentialism, pragmatism, perhaps even Confucianism and some forms of Buddhism; each contain various elements of eupraxsophy. Some of these schools, however, are concerned primarily with *eupraxia* (that is, with good practice) and they deemphasize the *sophia*, the scientific and philosophic worldview. Some, such as Marxism and utilitarianism, focused primarily on *social praxis*.

There are many variations of humanism: naturalistic, existential, Marxist, pragmatic, and liberal. We may ask, what is distinctive about the eupraxsophy of modern-day secular humanism? I wish to propose a definition of humanism that is thoroughly secular. This definition is not arbitrary, because it classifies a set of propositions held by many scientists and philosophers who consider themselves to be humanists. Nonetheless, it involves a prescriptive recommendation about how to use the term *humanism*. Humanism includes at least four main characteristics: (1) it is a method of inquiry; (2) it presents a cosmic worldview; (3) it contains a concrete set of ethical recommendations for the individual's life stance; and (4) it expresses a number of social and political ideals.

A METHOD OF INQUIRY

An essential characteristic of contemporary secular humanism is its commitment to a method of inquiry. This feature is so important that it may even be said to function as the basic principle of secular humanism. Questions concerning meaning and truth have been enduring ones in the history of philosophy, and they have come to the forefront since the growth of modern science. Epistemology is also pivotal to secular humanism.

Humanist epistemology may be defined first by what it opposes. It rejects the use of arbitrary authority to obfuscate meaning or to legislate truth. Throughout human history there have been persistent attempts by institutional authorities to do precisely that. The church and the state have been especially prone to define, codify, and enforce orthodoxy. The need for social order is such that humankind finds it useful or necessary to regulate conduct. Custom ensures some stability in social behavior and enables human beings to function with a clear understanding of expectations and of the acceptable parameters of civilized discourse and conduct. The rules of the game by which we live and work together are established—in constitutions, bylaws, contracts, laws, and regulations—and they enable us to fulfill our cooperative aims.

It is one thing, however, to lay down the rules of conduct by law and to enforce them by sanction, leaving opportunities for them to be modified and revised in democratic societies. It is quite another to uphold unchanging orthodoxies of belief in the sciences, philosophy, literature, the arts, politics, morality, or religion and to seek to legislate acceptable modes of personal behavior. Here the appeal to authority is illegitimate, for it substitutes a conformist faith for intelligently grounded knowledge. Establishing orthodoxy in belief stifles discovery and blocks inquiry. Transmitting the fixed beliefs of an early age to future ones prevents bold new departures in thought. Even the most cherished beliefs so lovingly defended in time may become archaic; blatant false-hoods persist as prejudice encrusted by habits.

History is replete with pathetic attempts by past civilizations to enshrine their belief systems in perpetuity. Efforts to censor conflicting opinions have often led to violent social conflict. In worst-case scenarios such suppression degenerates into sheer tyranny over the human mind. Dictators, ecclesiastical princes, and vested oligarchs have tried to police the thoughts of everyone under their jurisdiction, using the Holy Inquisition, the Gestapo, or the NKVD to suppress dissent. In a weaker form, conformist pressures substitute public opinion or that of the leading authorities of the day for creative and independent inquiry. Abiding by conventional wisdom thus stifles new ideas. No one group can claim to have a monopoly on wisdom or virtue, and to proclaim one's fondest convictions as obiter dicta for everyone in the society is destined to fail. Even though power is the chief criterion for the perpetuation of a belief system, that is no guarantee of social stability, for the so-called authorities often disagree about truth. The reigning beliefs of one age may become the intransigent follies of the next. Thoughtless bigots wish to prevent any questioning of their revered articles of faith; they are fearful of change and challenge. Regrettably, all of the major religious orthodoxies historically have succumbed to the temptation to enforce their beliefs—when and where they had the power to do so—and to impose their practices upon the rest of society. Orthodoxies have allowed fanatic intolerance to prevail, and they have denied the right of those who disagree to voice their contrary faiths or dissenting opinions.

The same narrow mindset appears in powerful political and economic elites, who fear any challenge to their privileged positions and thus seek to enforce by law what they consider to be the only legitimate system of belief. They strain to exclude outsiders who threaten their hegemony by declaring them political heretics or religious infidels.

In religion, orthodox belief systems are rooted in ancient dogmas held to be so sacred that they are immune to objective examination. The claims made in the name of God are shrouded in privileged revelations received from on high. The claims to divine authority are shielded from critical scrutiny by popes, cardinals, bishops, rabbis, mullahs, gurus, and other defenders of the faith. In politics and economics dissident minorities are excluded from the corridors of power. There is no forum available for them, no opportunity to participate in open inquiry. Thus the so-called Higher Truth, so protected from investigation, lies beyond contest. A similar closed syndrome can be found in philosophy or science when it is held to be immune to free inquiry. Thomism, Calvinism, and Marxist-Leninism were considered official doctrines at various times in history by those who defended them in the name of an entrenched power elite. The same is true for Lysenkoism under Stalin or racist theories under the Nazis. In the battle for civil liberties in democratic societies, political power has been wrested from repressive oligarchies. Unfortunately, the right to know has not been universally recognized as a basic human right in all societies, and there are wide areas—especially in religion and morality—that are still held to be immune to criticism.

The first principle of humanism is a commitment to free inquiry in every field of human endeavor. This means that any effort to prevent the free mind from exercising its right to pose questions and initiate inquiry is unwarranted. But which methods of inquiry should be used? How do we evaluate truth claims? Philosophers have long debated the question "What is truth?" How we appraise knowledge claims depends on the subject matter under investigation, be it science, mathematics, philosophy, ethics, politics, economics, history, or the arts. Let it suffice for now to outline a minimal set of epistemological criteria that cuts across the various disciplines, without any lengthy explication in defense. I will focus on skepticism, the scientific method, and critical intelligence.

Skepticism is a vital methodological principle of inquiry. I refer not to negative or nihilistic skepticism, which rejects the very possibility of attaining reliable knowledge, but positive, selective skepticism. This principle of skepticism implies that the reliability of a hypothesis, theory, or belief is a function of the grounds, evidence, or reasons by which it is supported. If a claim is not justified by objective validation or verification, we ought to be cautious in holding fast to it. The amount of supporting evidence will vary with the subject under scrutiny.

Probabilism points to the degree of certainty by which we are willing to ascertain truth claims. We should not attribute to any belief absolute infallibility. We should be prepared to admit that we may be mistaken. Beliefs should be taken as hypotheses: they are tentative or hypothetical depending upon the degree of evidence or the validity of the arguments used to support them.

Fallibilism is a principle which indicates that even when a claim is thought to be well supported, we should nonetheless be prepared to modify our beliefs if new arguments or evidence arise in the future that show either that we were in error or that our truths were only partial and limited. This applies in fields of formal knowledge, such as mathematics, as much as to experimental domains of inquiry. The skeptic should have an open mind about all questions and not seek to close responsible inquiry in any field. If after investigation there is insufficient evidence, the skeptic may say that the claim is unlikely, improbable, or false, or if further investigation is possible, he may wish to suspend judgment and admit that he does not know. Agnosticism, in this respect, is a meaningful option. We should be prepared to exercise doubt about a wide range of belief claims that we have little expectation at present of resolving. Fallibilism is thus an essential method used in science, technology, philosophy, religion, politics, morality, and ordinary life.

But the question may be asked: *Which* method should be used to warrant beliefs? What are the criteria of confirmation and validity? Without attempting to resolve this question fully here, let me suggest the following criteria:

First, we should appeal to *experience* in all areas in which it is pertinent to do so. By this I mean observation, evidence, facts, data—preferably involving some intersubjective grounds that can be replicated or certified. Purely subjective or private paths to truth need not be arbitrarily rejected, but, on the other hand, they are not admissible to the body of knowledge unless they can be reliably corroborated by others. This empirical test is fundamental. But if we are to draw any inferences from it then it must refer to experiential claims that are open to public scrutiny, not only in ascertaining whether they occurred but also in interpreting their likely causes.

Second, if an experience cannot be duplicated, there might be circumstantial evidence or at least *predictable* results by which we can evaluate its adequacy. In other words, our beliefs are forms of behavior, and they can be tested—at least in part—by their observed consequences. This is an experimental criterion used not only in laboratories but also in everyday life when we appraise beliefs not simply by what people say but by what they do.

Third, we use a *rational* test of deductive coherence, judging our theories or beliefs by relation to those we have already accepted as reliable. Hypotheses and theories cannot be viewed in isolation from other knowledge we believe to be true. They are logically consistent or inconsistent with it and are judged by the criterion of validity. We can see this test at work not only in mathematical, logical, and formal systems but also in science and ordinary affairs when we test beliefs by their internal consistency.

The preceding criteria are used most explicitly in the sciences, where hypothetical-deductive methods prevail and where we formulate hypotheses and test them by their experimental adequacy and logical coherence. Science is not a method of knowing available only to an esoteric coterie of experts; similar standards of reasoning are employed in common everyday life when we are faced with problems and wish to resolve practical questions.

The terms *reason, rationality*, and *reasonableness* have sometimes been used to describe the general methodology that humanists have advocated: that is, we should test truth claims objectively as far as we can, and if claims cannot pass the tests of reason (broadly conceived to include experience and rationality), we should either reject them or suspend judgment. We face an epistemological crisis today, for with the increasing specialization of knowledge, experts often restrict the use of objective methods of inquiry to their own fields of competency and are unwilling to extend reason to other areas of human knowledge. What is at issue here is whether we can apply the powers of reason so that they will have some influence on the totality of beliefs.

Perhaps the best terminology to describe objectivity in testing truth claims is *critical intelligence*. This means that we must use our powers of critical analysis and observation to evaluate carefully questions of belief. We first need to de-fine what is at stake. Here clarity in meaning is essential. We need to be clear about what we wish to know and what is at issue. We need to ask: What alter-native explanations are offered? We formulate hypotheses and develop beliefs that help solve our puzzlement. The salient point is that only objective evi-dence and reasons will suffice to evaluate alternative hypotheses.

What is distinctive about humanism as a eupraxsophy is that *it wishes to extend the methods of objective inquiry to all areas of life, including religious, philosophical, ethical, and political concerns that are often left unexamined.* There has been exten-sive research into specialized areas of scientific knowledge, particularly since technological discoveries have provided an enormous boon to human welfare; however, powerful forces have often distrusted and indeed prevented free in-quiry into the foundations of social, moral, and religious systems. The crux of the matter is whether objective methods of inquiry can be applied to these vital areas of human concern. If critical intelligence were to supplant blind appeals to authority, custom, faith, or subjectivity, it could radically transform society. Free thought can be threatening to the privileged bastions of the status quo.

No doubt a basic point of contention between humanism and theism is precisely here: the application of scientific methods, rationalism, and critical in-telligence to evaluate transcendental claims. The critics of humanism maintain that it excludes, almost by definition, claims to a transcendental realm. This, I submit, is not the case, for the humanist is willing to examine any responsible claim to truth. The burden of proof, however, rests with the believer to specify clearly the conditions under which such beliefs may be falsified. The humanist requests that whatever is under examination be carefully defined. God-talk is generally vague, ambiguous, even unintelligible. The humanist next wishes to know how the believer would justify its truth. If a meaningful claim is intro-duced, it needs to be corroborated. This means that private, mystical, or sub-jective claims to revelation or divine presence or mere declarations by ecclesi-astical authorities that something is true are inadmissible unless they can be intersubjectively confirmed. We cannot exclude on a priori grounds any in-sights derived from literature, poetry, or the arts. These express enduring hu-man interests. We only ask that they be analyzed carefully and tested objec-tively. Aesthetic experience is a rich part of human experience, and it may provide a wealth of insight and inspiration. Any knowledge about the world drawn from these sources, however, requires careful evaluation.

The humanist is open to the subtle nuances of human experience, but he insists that we use our powers of critical judgment to appraise the claims to truth. In this sense, he draws upon the tested knowledge and the best available wisdom of the day. He will accept the claims of others—even if he has not personally scrutinized each of these claims—but only if he is assured that those claims have been warranted by objective methods, and that if he or someone else had the time, energy, and training he or other persons could scrutinize the procedures used to corroborate the findings. The methods of critical intelligence apply not only to descriptive truth claims, where we seek to describe and explain natural processes, but also to normative judgments, where we formulate eupraxic recommendations in the various domains of human action.

A COSMIC WORLDVIEW

Humanist eupraxsophy does not simply assert a method of inquiry based upon the methods of science; it also seeks to use the sciences to interpret the cosmos and the place of the human species within it. The humanist thus attempts to develop some kind of generalized sense of reality. Speculative metaphysics is in disrepute today, and rightly so if it seeks to derive universal principles about reality from purely intuitive or metaphorical methods. The primary source for obtaining knowledge about nature should be human experience. It is within the various disciplines of scientific research and scholarship that reliable hypotheses and theories are elaborated and tested. If this is the case, then any comprehensive view of nature must draw heavily upon the scientific understanding of the day. Because science is a rapidly expanding body of knowledge, there are ongoing modifications of principles, hypotheses, and theories. There may at times be fundamental shifts in outlook, in which long-standing paradigms are altered, as for example, the fundamental transformation of Newtonian science by relativity theory and quantum mechanics. We note also the basic changes that have occurred in genetics, biology, psychology, the social sciences, and other fields of research in the twentieth century. There are times when we build up and elaborate a body of knowledge by a process of accumulation and addition. At other times there may be radical disruptions: novel theories may be introduced and tested, and they may fundamentally alter the prevailing outlook. One must be prepared to change a cosmic perspective in the light of new data and theories. We must be tentative in our formulations and prepared to revise theories in the light of new discoveries.

Unfortunately, scientists in specialized disciplines are often unaware of developments in other fields, and they may be unwilling or unable to relate their findings to domains of knowledge outside their competence or to develop a cosmic view. This is where philosophy enters: the philosopher should interpret the knowledge of any one discipline and relate it to other fields. Philosophy, by definition, is general, for it is concerned with finding common methods, principles, postulates, axioms, assumptions, concepts, and generalizations used in a wide range of fields. Here I refer to the philosophy of science and to the methods of analysis and generalization by which it interprets the various sciences.

The great philosophers have always attempted to do this. Aristotle's *Metaphysics* provided a critical interpretation of the key concepts and categories underlying Greek science. Similarly, Descartes, Leibniz, Hume, Kant, Russell, Dewey, Whitehead, and others reflected upon and attempted to interpret the sciences of their day. We need to do the same today, though it may be far more difficult than in previous ages because of the immense proliferation of the sciences; it is difficult for any one mind to sum up the enormous bodies of specialties in some sort of interrelated whole. If we cannot as yet succeed in this ambitious venture, at the very least we can try in a more modest way. Using physics, astronomy, and the natural sciences, we can develop some cosmologies that explain the expanding universe. Using biology and genetics we can try to interpret the evolution of life. We can use psychology and the behavioral sciences to understand human behavior, and we can draw upon anthropology, sociology, and the other social sciences to develop appropriate theories about sociocultural phenomena. This is an ongoing quest. We do not have a comprehensive theory of the universe at present. Nonetheless we do have integrated pictures of nature that are based on the sciences.[2]

What does humanist eupraxsophy tell us about the cosmos? Let us approach the question at first by negative definition, by indicating what is unlikely. There is insufficient evidence for the claim that there is a divine creator who has brought the universe into being by an act of will. The invoking of God as a cause of everything that is, is mere *postulation*, without sufficient evidence or proof. It is a leap outside nature. The concept of a transcendent supernatural being is unintelligible; the idea of a First Cause, itself uncaused, is contradictory. Even if the big bang theory in astronomy is useful in explaining the rapidly receding and expanding universe, this does not provide support for the claim that there was a Being who existed coterminous or antecedent to this explosion. The big bang may be the result of a random quantum fluctuation, not an intelligent plan.

To read into such a cosmological principle selective human qualities—intelligence, perfection, or personhood—is unwarranted. The universe does not manifest design; there is apparent regularity and order, but chance and conflict, chaos and disorder are also present. To describe the entire universe as good is an anthropomorphic rendering of nature to fit one's moral bias. If there is apparent good in the universe, there would also have to be apparent evil, at least from the standpoint of sentient beings, who at times devour one another in the struggle for survival or who encounter natural disasters that destroy them. If so, how can we reconcile evil with a provident deity? Theists are so overcome by the tragic character of human finitude that they are willing to project their deepest longings into a divine mind, and this enables them to transcend nothingness. For the theist the universe involves some teleological conception of salvation. Man, in some way, is at the center of creation, for God is endowed by man with human qualities.

Much of the anthropomorphic character of the deity is derived from ancient texts held to be sacred and to have been revealed by God to specially appointed individuals. The Bible predicates the intervention of the Holy Ghost in history. Yet scientific and scholarly biblical criticism has made it abundantly clear that the Bible is a human document, a thousand-year-old record of the experiences of primitive nomadic and agricultural tribes living on the eastern shore of the Mediterranean. There is no evidence that Yahweh spoke to Abraham, Moses, Joseph, or any of the Old Testament prophets. The biblical accounts of their experiences are the records of Hebrew national existence, seeking to sustain itself by the myth of the chosen people. These books have not been empirically validated; they express an ancient worldview and the moral conceptions of a prescientific culture that invoked deities to sanctify its ideological aspirations.

The New Testament presents the incredible tale of Jesus, a man of whom we have very little historical knowledge. Obviously this is not an objective historical account. The divinity of Jesus has never been adequately demonstrated. Yet powerful churches have sought to inculcate the mythic story and to suppress dissent. The tales of Jesus' life and ministry expressed in the four Gospels and the letters of Paul were written twenty to seventy years after his death. They are riddled with the contradictions implicit in an oral tradition. Defended by propagandists for a new mystery religion, the biblical accounts are hardly to be taken as dispassionate historical evidence for Jesus' divine origin. The tales of the so-called miracles and faith healings of Jesus are based on uncorroborated testimony by an unsophisticated people who were easily deceived. That the Jesus myth was elaborated by later generations and was eventually promulgated by powerful church institutions that dominated Europe for almost two millennia and still have inordinate influence on large sectors of the globe is evidence for the presence of a transcendental temptation within the human heart, which is ever ready to seize upon any shred of hope for an afterlife.

Similar skeptical criticism may be leveled against other supernatural religions. Islam is a religion based on the alleged revelations to Muhammad, received from on high through the archangel Gabriel, at first in caves north of Mecca and later in various other places. Careful reading of the literature about the origins of the Koran enables us to give alternative naturalistic explanations of Muhammad's ministry. He may have suffered from some form of epilepsy, which explains his trance states or swoons. He was able to convince others of his divine calling, and he used this ploy to achieve power. All of this is testimony to the gullibility of human beings and their willingness to abandon acceptable standards of rationality when they are confronted with claims to a Higher Truth. The same thing can be noted of the legions of saints, prophets, gurus, and shamans throughout history who have proclaimed divine revelations and have used their claims to delude and influence their followers.

Basic to the monotheistic approach is the belief in an afterlife. Is it possible for a soul to survive the death of the body? Jewish, Christian, and Muslim adherents fervently believe in the immortality of the soul, and Hindus, in its reincarnation from previous existences.

Unfortunately, the most resolute and objective investigations of claims of survival have shown them to be without empirical corroboration. Psychical researchers, parapsychologists, and paranormal investigators, for over a century, have produced reports of ghosts, spirits, apparitions, and poltergeists, but there is insufficient data to support the reality of discarnate existence, despite the legions of spiritualists, trance channelers, and past-life regressors who claim to be in touch with an unseen realm of spiritual reality. Although our fondest hopes and desires may *demand* life before birth or after death, the evidence points in the other direction. Even if it could be proved that something briefly survives the death of the biological body, there is no evidence of an eternal state of existence or of a blessed union with God. The evidence for survival is based on wishful thinking and is in the last analysis inconclusive. Death seems to be the natural state of all life-forms, even though modern medical science and technology are able to ward off disease and prolong life. Humanism is thus skeptical about the entire drama of the theistic universe: that God exists and that we can achieve salvation in an afterlife.

But what picture of the universe does humanism provide as a substitute? Perhaps not one that slakes the existential yearnings of the desperate soul, but one that is more in accordance with the world as uncovered by science. What we have today is an open-ended universe, perhaps ragged at the edges with many gaps in our knowledge, but it is a picture supported by the best available evidence. At the present stage of human knowledge, the following general propositions seem true:

Objects or events within the universe have material explanations. All objects or events encountered have a physical character. Matter, mass, and energy may, however, be organized on various levels, ranging from the minutest microparticles on the subatomic level in fields of energy to gigantic objects, such as planets, moons, comets, stars, quasars, and galaxies.

We encounter within the universe order and regularity on the one hand and chaos and random fluctuations on the other. Objects and events within the universe seem to be evolving. Change is an enduring trait of existing things. The cosmos as we currently understand it is something on the order of ten to twenty billion years old; it is expanding from what seems to have been a huge explosion. In any case, our planet is only one satellite of a minor star in the Milky Way, which is merely one galaxy among billions in the vast universe. What preceded the big bang, the physicists are not yet able to explain, and what will be the end of the universe—a whimper or a big crunch as matter implodes— is also difficult to say.

The universe is not, however, inanimate. There is some likelihood that organic life exists in other parts of the universe, perhaps on other planets in other star systems. The earliest known fossils uncovered on the earth are more than three billion years old. The most useful hypothesis to explain the diverse forms of life on our planet is that they evolved from common genetic material and split into diverse species. Evolution is a product of natural selection, chance mutations, differential reproduction, and adaptation. The human species most likely evolved over a period of several million years, exhibiting processes that follow similar patterns in other species. Distinctive to human primates is the large cerebral cortex and the development of highly complex social systems in which tools are manipulated and signs and symbols function to enable linguistic communication. Genetics, biology, and psychology explain the emergence of human behavior and how and why we function the way we do. The social sciences are able to account for the development of the complex social institutions that help to satisfy basic human needs.

The study of culture demonstrates that individual members of the human species are physiochemical biological systems genetically predisposed to certain forms of behavior yet are able to learn; they are influenced by environmental factors and are capable of adaptive behavior. There seems to be a creative component to all forms of organic life—this is especially true of the human species. The human organism is able to respond to stimuli not only by conditioned behavior but by expressing creative impulses and demonstrating cognitive awareness. Humans, as products of nature, are able to understand the causes and conditions of their behavior, and they are able to intervene in the processes of nature and change them by discovery and invention. Formerly, the course of human evolution was largely unconscious and blind. We can now redirect the evolution of the species to some extent by conscious effort. Human behavior may be modified by imaginative ingenuity. Human beings manifest rational choice. They are able to solve the problems encountered in living and thus, in part, to determine their futures. This is the message of the humanist outlook.

A LIFE STANCE

Men and women are capable of free choice. How much and to what extent has been hotly debated by philosophers, theologians, and scientists. Clearly, our behavior is limited or determined by the conditions under which we act. There are physiochemical, genetic, sociological, and psychological causes at work. Yet, in spite of these causal factors, we are consciously aware and we are capable of some teleonomic and preferential choice. Cognition can selectively direct our behavior.

"What ought I to choose?" and "How ought I to live?" are questions constantly raised. Are there any norms that humanism can offer to guide our conduct? Can we discover any enduring ends or goals? Is there a good which we ought to seek? Are there moral standards of right and wrong? Is there a distinct set of ethical values and principles that may be said to be humanistic?

The critics of humanism maintain that it lacks proper moral standards, that it is permissive, and that it allows subjective taste and caprice to prevail. As we have seen, such charges are unfounded. They emanate from an abysmal ignorance of philosophical ethics, for philosophers have demonstrated the possibility of an autonomous ethic in which moral obligations emerge.

By arguing that ethics is autonomous, I simply mean that it is possible to make moral judgments of good, bad, right and wrong independently of one's ultimate foundations, such as the common moral decencies or the principles of caring. Yet humanist ethics does have foundations, and these are inherent in its eupraxsophy, which in the last analysis completes it; for when questions of ultimate obligation or moral purpose arise the theist falls back on God, whereas the humanist is skeptical of that claim and places his ethics in a naturalistic evolutionary universe that is devoid of purpose. The humanist life stance thus has its grounding in nature, human nature, and human history.[3]

What are the essential ingredients of the ethics of humanism? The humanist life stance has a clearly developed conception of what "good practice" and "right conduct" are. The ethics of humanism may be said to begin when men and women eat of the "god-forbidden fruit" of the tree of knowledge of good and evil. Critical ethical inquiry enables us to transcend unquestioned customs, blind faith, or doctrinaire authority and to discover ethical values and principles. Humanists maintain that the development of moral awareness is enhanced when we go beyond unthinking habits to ethical wisdom: this includes an appreciation of the standards of excellence and an awareness of ethical principles and one's moral responsibilities to others.

Here is the humanist life stance: humanists do not look upward to a heaven for a promise of divine deliverance. They have their feet planted squarely in nature, yet they have the Promethean fortitude to employ art, science, sympathy, reason, and education to create a better world for themselves and their fellow human beings.

From the standpoint of the individual, the summum bonum is worthwhile happiness. This is not a passive quest for release from the world, but the pursuit of an active life of adventure and fulfillment. There are so many opportunities for creative enjoyment that every moment can be viewed as precious; all fit together to make up a full and exuberant life.

Humanist ethics does not rest on arbitrary caprice but on reflective choice. Ethical principles and values are rational: they are relative to human interests and needs. But this does not mean that they are subjective, nor are they beyond the domain of skeptical critical inquiry. Our principles and values can be tested by their consequences in action.

What is vital in humanist eupraxsophy is that humanists are not overwhelmed by the tragic character of the human condition; they must face death, sorrow, and suffering with courage. They have confidence in the ability of human beings to overcome alienation, solve the problems of living, and develop the capacity to share the goods of life and empathize with others. The theist has a degraded view of man, who, beset with original sin, is incapable of solving life's problems by himself and needs to look outside of the human realm for divine succor. The humanist accepts the fact that the human species has imperfections and limitations and that some things encountered in existence are beyond repair or redress. Yet even so, he believes the best posture is not to retreat into the lap of the unknown, but to exert his intelligence and courage to deal with life's problems. It is only by a resolute appraisal of the human condition, based on reason and science, that the humanist's life stance seems most appropriate. He is unwilling to fall to his knees before the forces of nature but will stand on his own feet to battle evil and build a better life for himself and his fellow human beings. In other words, he expresses the highest heroic virtues of the Promethean spirit: audacity, nobility, and developed moral sensibilities about the needs of others.

SOCIAL POLITY

Humanism is not concerned only with the life stance of the individual—however basic this is as an alternative to theism; it is also concerned with the achievement of the good society. The early Greek philosophers had discussed the nature of justice. For Plato justice can best be seen writ large in the state, but it is also seen in the life of the individual soul. Justice involves the principles of harmony, order, and reason. For Aristotle ethics and politics were related. He was concerned with the happiness of the individual, but also with political questions. Historically philosophers—Hobbes, Spinoza, Locke, Hume, Rousseau, Comte, Hegel, Dewey, and Russell—have been vitally concerned with the nature of the just society.

Does humanism today have concrete recommendations for the social polity? Surely humanist eupraxsophy must deal with the well-being of humanity on the larger scale, for if the ultimate good is life here and now, then this cannot be achieved by the solitary individual alone but only in concert with others within a larger sociocultural context. It is clear that eupraxsophy does not simply delineate a theoretical intellectual position but also has something to say about social practice.

An indelible feature of humanism is its emphasis on *freedom*. The good society must seek to maximize freedom of choice and the autonomy of the individual as a basic value, and this cannot be sacrificed at the altar of the collective. This has been the first principle of classical liberalism—as expressed by Locke, Mill, and the Utilitarians—and it cannot be compromised. The pragmatic political philosophers John Dewey and Sidney Hook have attempted to accommodate both the individualism of liberalism and the sociality of Hegelian philosophy. The individual cannot live in isolation, for he interacts with others in society and culture. But what are the appropriate dimensions of individual freedom?

For the liberal democratic humanist first and foremost is freedom of thought and conscience—philosophical, religious, intellectual, scientific, political, and moral freedom. This includes free speech, freedom of the press, the freedom to form voluntary associations and to pursue one's lifestyle as one sees fit so long as one does not harm or limit the freedom of others. In specific terms, this means that the full range of civil liberties must be recognized by the just society, including the right to dissent and the legal right to oppose the policies of the government. This entails a commitment to political democracy: the right of the people to form political parties, to elect the officials of government, to determine the policies and programs of the state, to have some means to redress grievances, to be immune from arbitrary arrest and punishment, to be entitled to a fair trial and due process. Representative democracy bases its decisions on majority rule with the full protection of minority rights. Democracy also cherishes as basic values diversity, pluralism, creativity, and the uniqueness of individual citizens and groups in society. It cherishes the right of privacy.

Humanists can disagree about many things in the political and social sphere. Humanism is not a dogmatic creed. We cannot identify humanism with specific candidates or ideological, party platforms of a particular period. Honest men and women often have differed about what ought to be done. We can dispute about policies in the economic and political sphere: "Should there be high or low interest rates or none?" "Should taxes be on consumption or income?" "How can we increase productivity and not despoil the environment?" and so on. Humanists share with orthodox Christians and Jews any number of social ideals, and they may support common programs of political reform or stability. Humanists thus may differ about concrete proposals. Such disagreement may be healthy, for there is not only one road to truth or virtue. We are all fallible.

Humanist eupraxia in regard to social polity focuses on certain *basic values and principles*. The first commitment of the humanist, I submit, is to the *method of intelligence* (as John Dewey argues in his definition of liberalism) as the most reliable way of solving social problems.[4] This means that social policies should be considered as hypotheses based on the findings of the best empirical research of the day and tested by their consequences in action. The wisest and most sensible method of political governance and social change is by *democratic methods of persuasion*. Our ultimate reliance in a democracy must be on a fully informed citizenry as the chief source of power and decision making. The broader ideal here is the need to encourage widespread participation by the people in all the institutions of society in which they live, work together, and function. How this works out depends on the specific institutions. Here we are talking about political, economic, and social democracy.

If the methods of intelligence and democratic participation are to succeed, we need a well-educated and intelligent public. Thus the *opportunity for education* must be made available to all individuals in society; the right to knowledge is not only a basic human right but is also the key instrument by which society can best solve its problems. By expanding the ranges of cultural appreciation of all citizens, we contribute to our own moral, intellectual, and aesthetic development.

A central value for humanism and democracy is *tolerance*; a just society will allow alternative points of view and a plurality of lifestyles, beliefs, and moral values, all existing side by side. The chief method of resolving differences should be wherever possible the *peaceful negotiation of differences and compromise*, not force or violence.

A democratic society is one that recognizes the obligation to provide the opportunity and means for all individuals to *satisfy their basic economic and cultural needs*. Thus an open democratic society will attempt to redress gross inequities in income and provide for the satisfaction of the basic minimal needs for those who are unable, through no fault of their own, to do so. I am referring here to policies of social welfare, unemployment and social security insurance, and aid to the handicapped and disadvantaged. This involves providing both economic and cultural opportunities so that individuals can participate in the democratic society and develop as self-reliant, autonomous, and productive citizens.

The just society will seek *to end discrimination* based on race, gender, creed, sexual orientation, physical handicap, ethnicity, or economic background and to accord all of its citizens equal rights. It will provide women with full equality under the law. It will recognize the rights of children.

The preceding is only a thumbnail sketch of some of the principles of humanist social eupraxia. Heretofore, this has been interpreted as applying only to local communities or nation-states, and efforts have been made to democratize these from within. The world has reached such a level of economic and political interdependence today that it is no longer possible to resolve many problems concerning humanity on the local or national level alone. Thus we need to develop an appreciation for universal (or general) human rights and apply them to all corners of the globe and all members of the human family. We need to build an *ethical commitment to the planetary community as our highest moral devotion*.[5]

PART V

ETHICAL TRUTH

18

SKEPTICISM AND ETHICAL INQUIRY

Is it possible to apply reason to conduct? Can we formulate objective ethical judgments? Is there such a thing as "ethical truth"?

There is a long historical tradition, from Protagoras and the Sophists down to Hume and the emotivists, and even to the postmodernists today, that denies the possibility of a rational or a scientific ethics, and that reduces ethical judgments to subjective sentiment. These skeptics deny that values are amenable to cognitive criticism, or that standards of objectivity can be discovered. I think that they are profoundly mistaken and that a modified naturalistic and situational theory can provide some basis for rationality and objectivity in ethics.

In what follows, I wish to review the key arguments brought by classical skepticism against the possibility of ethical knowledge, and my responses to them. We may distinguish three types of ethical skepticism.

ETHICAL NIHILISM

The first kind of skepticism is that of *ethical nihilism*, that is, total negative skepticism. This is the claim that it is not possible to test ethical judgments empirically or by an appeal to reason. This argument assumes various forms. Let us begin with the critique of ontological value. Ethical skeptics, I submit, correctly observe that it is impossible to discover any framework for morality in the universe at large, independent of human experience. The converse is more likely the case; namely, human beings are disposed to read into nature their fondest hopes and to attribute moral qualities to the universe, but these represent the expression of their own yearnings to find an eternal place for their values in the scheme of things.

The most common illustration of fallacious moral extrapolation is the postulation of a divine being (or beings) and the attribution to him or her (or them) of the highest good. For Aristotle, the unmoved movers were engaged in *nous*, or pure thought; they were thinking about thinking. This was considered the

191

noblest form of excellence that man could attain, and it was what Aristotle him-self prized as the highest good. The Old Testament had man created in the image of God, though in reality God is fashioned out of the human imagina-tion and assumes human form, possessed of all of the qualities that we cherish, but in extended form: power, omniscience, immortality. Yahweh is prone to anger and is vindictive and unremitting in his demands for obedience to the moral rules. He is a lawgiver, who issues commandments (through his emis-saries, the priests and prophets) that men and women are required to submit to if they are to escape punishment; but these rules in actuality reflect the social structure of the times. The New Testament continues the same kind of moral deception, for it deifies certain moral imperatives found desirable: for example, to love one another as God loves us. In the case of Jesus, this divine form of morality is embodied in human flesh at some point in history. Mohammed has given the Muslim moral code endurance and strength by claiming that it was Allah who defined and proclaimed the code.

Thus theistic creeds that attempt to ground the moral life in ultimate theo-logical truths simply mask the tendencies of humans to attribute their own moral purposes to the universe at large and to use this postulation to insist that those divine commandments ought to be obeyed. Skeptics have identified the im-plicit self-deception intrinsic to theological foundationalism. They have pointed out that mutually contradictory injunctions have been derived from the same deity. God has been used to defend both slavery and freedom, monogamy and polygamy, abortion and laws against abortion, and war and peace, depending on the religious tradition and the social context in which it was revealed or interpreted. The divine commandments are made to fulfill eminently practical purposes, and the universe is endowed with moral qualities. These ultimately have their source in existential despair, which is transferred into hope by means of religious faith. God is invoked to enable people to endure death and tragedy, to provide some consolation and resolution of the human condition and to guarantee a future existence *in saecula, saeculorum.*

Skeptics have rightly demonstrated that all human values and ethical prin-ciples are intrinsically related to the human condition. "Man is the measure of all things, of things that are that they are, and of things that are not that they are not," observed Protagoras, the great Sophist who denied the reality of moral ideas independent of human existence. Theological moral systems do not de-part from this, for their moral beliefs and Gods are drenched in human signifi-cance and relative to human concerns, although believers may deny that this is the case. Indeed, theism holds that God is a person much like a human being, which only emphasizes the anthropomorphic basis of theistic morality.

A similar indictment can be brought against any kind of Platonic moral realism, that is, the notion that eternal moral ideas are implicit in a realm of being and that the task of human reason is to discover and apply these essences to life. Socrates attempted to define "justice" and "the good," hoping that his definitions of absolute ideas would provide a beacon for both the individual soul and the polis. For Plato, nature is interpreted as the basis for "the good" over and beyond convention. Skeptics have rightly rejected this theory as pure postulate, without reasonable justification or proof. The reification of essences makes an unwarranted epistemological leap. According to Protagoras, ethics has a relativistic basis: "Whatever is seen as just to a city is just for that city so long as it seems so."

A similar critique has been brought against naturalistic theories, that is, any effort to find an ultimate ground for ethics in "human nature," "natural law," "the march of history," or "evolutionary progress." Surely these naturalistic forces are not without human content, for they are related to human institutions. Accordingly, relativism would seem to be necessary as a starting point for any conception of value.

An important distinction must be made, however, between relativism and subjectivism, for to say that morality is related to human beings does not necessarily mean that it is irreducibly subjective. Relativism and subjectivism are not the same, and the former does not imply the latter. One can be a relativist and objectivist. Total negative skeptics argue that there are no standards that can be used to appraise what the individual city deems to be just or good. They maintain that to say something is good or right means simply that we feel this to be the case, and that our sentiments are disposed to either like or dislike it. Some forms of subjectivism reduce to nihilism. For if moral beliefs in the last analysis are nothing but an expression of tastes, feelings, and sentiments—*de gustibus non disputanem est*—then we cannot really demonstrate the moral excellence of one belief over another. If, from the standpoint of the state, whatever is just is relative to convention, custom, or power, then there are no normative criteria for adjudicating differences. "Justice is the interest of the stronger," affirmed the nihilist Thrasymachus in the *Republic*; therefore "might makes right." It is the strongest faction of society that defines moral rectitude and lays down laws to adjudicate conflicting interests. Ethics is nothing more or nothing less than that.

The emotive theory, introduced in the twentieth century by the logical positivists, also expresses a strong form of ethical skepticism. The emotivists distinguish between three kinds of sentences: (1) descriptive statements, which they said could be verified directly or indirectly by factual observations or experiments; (2) analytic statements, which are tautological and established as formally true by deductive inferences; and (3) emotive utterances, which have no cognitive or literal significance but are expressive and imperative in force. To say that "rape is wrong," for the emotivists, merely means that I (or we) are repulsed by it, and that I (or we) condemn it and command others to do so as well. These sentences cannot be verified in any objective manner, for they violate the principles of verifiability and analyticity. Many college and university students today believe that one moral value is as good as the next and that there are no

objective moral standards to which we can appeal. In the name of tolerance—
a noble virtue—they enthrone individual subjectivity and extreme cultural
relativity. This skepticism is espoused by many postmodernist philosophers
who reject humanism, any rational basis for human rights, or any narrative of
emancipation.

Nihilism is a posture that we can hardly afford to adopt in practical life.
Extreme subjectivity leads us to an impasse, because we need to get on with
the business of living with others in the community. There is therefore a serious
question as to whether or not the reduction of ethics to subjectivity is true to
our ethical experiences. For to maintain that there are no rational criteria that
can be brought to bear in ethical questions, and that in the last analysis ethical
values are simply a question of subjective feeling, cultural conventions, or force,
seems to impose a tremendous strain on credulity. For example, if there are no
objective standards of ethical value, is the statement that "The policies of Hitler
and Stalin were evil" without any basis other than that I or we do not like them?
Is the ethical principle "Mothers ought not to torture their children" similarly
without any merit? If so, subjectivity reduces human morality either to the
toleration of barbarism, for there is no meaningful ground to oppose it, or utter
absurdity, in which anything is as good as anything else and right and wrong
have no signification. Under this theory, monsters may be equivalent to mar-
tyrs, sinners to saints, egoists to altruists. But if no ethical distinctions are allowed,
social life would become impossible. Why does a person not steal, murder,
torture, or rape? Is it simply a question of sentiment or the fear one will be
punished by the police (or God)? This position is contradicted by the evidence
of the ethical life: we *do* make ethical judgments, and some are considered
warranted. We criticize moral monsters and tyrants and applaud altruists and
humanitarians, and with some justification. Ethical nihilism is infantile, and those
who vehemently proclaim it in all ethical situations have not fully developed
their moral sensibilities. They are concealing their own moral ignorance, and
by their total negative skepticism reveal that they have not achieved mature
moral growth.

To argue the position of the ethical neutralist—that is, one must be "morally
neutral" about *all* moral questions—is similarly mistaken. I would agree that *some*
moral quandaries are difficult to resolve, particularly where there are conflicts
between rights and goods, both of which we cannot have, or the choice is between the lesser of two evils, one of which we must choose. To urge the *universal* suspension of ethical judgment, as the ethical nihilist advocates, however,
does not follow. If a skeptic cannot decide between two sides of *any* moral issue, and refuses to choose or to act, is he not confessing a similar blind spot
concerning the phenomenological character of moral experience and reflection? Or, if he does act, but only from feeling, or because he thinks that following conventional custom is the safest course, is he not insensitive to the

deeper nuances of the moral life? Such a position, if consistently defended, reduces one to a perverse kind of moral dogmatism.

Agnostic skepticism is not without some redeeming virtues, however. For in opposing moral absolutism or fanaticism, and in seeing through the sham of self-righteous claims that one's moral theories are the ultimate truth, skepticism may be a useful antidote for paternalistic or authoritarian claptrap. Moral absolutists assume that their views are intrinsic to reality, and they all too readily are prepared to suppress those who dissent. Many will appeal to Reason or Progress or Virtue or God to impose views that simply mask their own preferences. As such, they have substituted dogmatism for inquiry. On the other hand, the persistent denial that there are *any* moral truths at all, if it is consistently asserted, belies its own form of moral intransigence, based largely upon epistemological error, for to deny that there is any kind of moral truth or reliable knowledge is to flout the considerable body of reliable ethical knowledge that we have as a product of the collective wisdom of the race.

MITIGATED ETHICAL SKEPTICISM

A second kind of skeptical theory is less extreme than the first. This we may call *mitigated ethical skepticism.* It assumes various forms. In particular, it states that although sentiment is at the root of all human values, this still leaves some room for rational criticism and control.

One can see this position again first presented by the Sophists. Glaucon, in the *Republic*, outlines the social contract theory, which is later elaborated by modern political philosophers like Thomas Hobbes: all men seek to satisfy their own desires, and self-interest dominates their choices. But they soon see that if individuals had carte blanche to do whatever they wished, there would be "a war of all against all," in which case life would become "solitary, poor, nasty, brutish, and short." Rational persons thus are willing to limit their liberties and abide by the rule of law. Here the criterion is the social good, and this is justified because it is to the self-interest of every person to establish a framework of peace, law, and order, in which common guarantees and protections are provided by the civil society and the state. One variation of this is the utilitarian theory; namely, we agree to adhere to the moral rules of society because they provide the conditions of happiness for all. This theory does not attempt to ground justice in God, the Absolute, or Nature writ large. Ethical principles are related to human interests, and they have a conventional basis. But they also provide a consequential and experimental test. Although they are relative to the individual, it is not subjectivity alone that rules, for ethical judgments are still open to rational criticism and may be justified in terms of their instrumental effectiveness.

Hume was critical of certain assumptions implicit in classical ethical theory. He argued that a moral judgment intrinsically involves feelings: when we judge an act or trait of character as good or bad, we are saying that we approve or disapprove, and we do so because we have sentiments of pleasure or displeasure or we consider it to be useful or harmful. Hume argued that there were basic differences between judgments of fact and judgments of value. Judgments of fact can be ascertained to be true or false. Judgments of value, on the contrary, like judgments of taste, cannot. Hume inferred from this that reason by itself cannot decide moral judgments, nor can it alone make distinctions or resolve moral quandaries. It is "moral sentiment" that is the wellspring of action, not rationality. What we consider good or bad is dependent on whether moral sentiment is attached to it, and by this he meant the feeling that something is pleasant or useful. Hume was thus a skeptic in ethics, for he held that reason by itself cannot resolve moral questions. His statement that "Reason is, and ought to be, the slave of passions," is both provocative and controversial. The point that he wished to make was that moral judgments are neither like factual statements, tested by observation, nor like logical inferences, concerned with the relationships of ideas.

In his *Treatise on Human Nature*, Hume observed that in all "systems of morality" that have been enunciated, the proponent would begin with "ordinary ways of reasoning."[1] For example, he might attempt to prove that God exists, or he might describe human society; but at one point he makes a leap, going from what "is" or "is not" the case to suddenly introducing what "ought" or "ought not" to be the case. Here something not contained in the premise is suddenly introduced into the conclusion. There is an unwarranted gap in the argument. The "ought" is not deduced from the "is," but is arrived at by the surreptitious introduction of the author's sentiment or feeling. The conclusion that Hume drew from his analysis is that we cannot deduce the "ought" from the "is" and that any effort to do so is fallacious. Interestingly, given his skepticism, Hume ended up a conservative; for if there are no ultimate guides or moral truths, then we ought to abide by the customary rules of conduct.

In the twentieth century, a great deal of effort has been expended by philosophers, from G. E. Moore to the emotivists and analysts, to analyze moral language. Moore used the term *naturalistic fallacy* to describe all efforts to define "the good." The naturalistic fallacy is similar to Hume's theory of the "is-ought" dualism.[2] Moore thought that any definition of "good" was vulnerable to the open question argument and that it applied to theological as well as naturalistic systems, to John Stuart Mill as well as Thomas Aquinas. He asked, "*Why* should we accept your definition of 'good'?" and he ended up doubtful of any and all attempts to define "good." Moore's own epistemological theory assumed a form of Platonic realism. "Good" was an "indefinable, non-natural property" by definition, and that was why it could not be defined.

Other twentieth century neo-Kantians (H. A. Prichard, Henry Sidgwick, and W. D. Ross) agreed that ethical predicates could not be derived from nonethical ones.[3] They thought that the basic ethical terms were deontological ("right," "wrong, "obligation," and "duty"), not teleological ("good" and "bad," "value" and "disvalue"), and that these were indefinable because they contain an implicit *obligatoriness*. Even though they could not define ethical terms, neither Moore nor the intuitionists considered themselves to be ethical skeptics. Prichard thought that classical ethical inquiry rested on a mistake, for it attempted to prove its first principles, whereas one's moral obligations could be known intuitively and directly within moral situations.

It was the emotivists, whom we have already referred to, especially Charles L. Stevenson, who were ethical skeptics, though some were mitigated.[4] They maintained that the reason *why* we could not define ethical terms was that they were not descriptive, like "hard" or "brittle," but emotive in character. Ethical words were expressive or evocative, much like "ugh" or "whew," and imperative, like "drop dead" or "kiss me." These terms give vent to our emotional attitudes and they express our desires that people agree with us or do our bidding. Efforts to define such terms are at best "persuasive definitions," they said, for they simply express our own moral sentiments.

Of special significance is the belief of the emotivists that disagreements in the moral domain often degenerate into disputes between contending parties that could not, even in principle, be resolved. This was due to the fact that the disagreements were "disagreements in attitude," as distinct from "disagreements in belief." As mitigated ethical skeptics, they said that the latter agreements could be resolved by empirical, rational methods, where two or more parties to a dispute differed about factual claims. These controversies at least in principle could be overcome—that is, if the moral dispute was based upon the facts. In some cases the disputes may be purely analytical and concern the meaning of a term, and these could be overcome. For example, C maintains that a fetus weighs 8 ounces, and D claims that it weighs 6. Presumably they could weigh the fetus and decide the factual issue. Or again, if C and D disagree about the definition of "euthanasia" and whether or not it is voluntary or involuntary, then presumably by clearly defining what they mean, they can possibly overcome some forms of disagreement. However, if the dispute is distinctively *moral*, according to Stevenson, then it is attitudinal, and we may not be able to resolve the differences. For example, if D says that "abortion is *wrong*" because the fetus is a person, and E declares that "abortion is *right*" because it is based upon the principle of freedom of choice for women, then we may not be able to resolve the dispute, for the disagreement is not purely factual but is an attitudinal difference about which principle to accept. Hence, an impasse may be reached.

Such moral disputes may not in principle be resolvable. F may think that euthanasia is wrong, because we ought never to take the life of another, and suffering is not necessarily evil; and G may think that euthanasia is right if it is voluntary, because unnecessary pain and suffering in terminal cases are evil. Unless both parties can agree in their basic attitudes about suffering and pain,

or about voluntary and involuntary death, then they may never be able to resolve their moral controversy.

This second form of ethical skepticism is *mitigated*, because in spite of the
ultimate subjective differences in sentiment, feeling, or emotion, the moral life
is not entirely bereft of rational considerations and some moral disagreement
may be grounded in belief, not attitude. If, for example, H says that she is in
favor of capital punishment because it is a deterrent to future murders, then
that belief is contingent on the deterrence issue and presumably we can do a
factual study to resolve the disagreement. Similarly, if J is against the death penalty because she does not think it deters murder, we could again perhaps resolve this by doing a sociological study, examining murder rates in those states
or countries that have the death penalty and those that do not, to see whether
there is any statistical difference. Similarly, we can study those states or countries before and after the imposition or repeal of the death penalty to see
whether there is any significant difference. If these moral judgments pro or con
were truly a function of the facts, then if they were mistaken about the factual
truth, the persons involved might change their beliefs regarding the death
penalty.

There are other arguments that mitigated skeptics can introduce in disagreements in an effort to persuade other persons to modify their judgments.
They can appeal to the *consistency* criterion. If some persons hold a particular
moral principle and yet make exceptions to it, they are contradicting themselves. For example, they may say they believe in democracy as the best form
of government, yet they may exclude one portion of society from exercising
the franchise. Presumably, if we show them that they have disenfranchised blacks,
we would have an argument against apartheid in South Africa; if they disen-
franchise women, we could make the case for universal suffrage. And if our
moralists believe in consistency, they will change their views, for they would
want to order their values in some coherent form.

The same considerations apply to the test of *consequences*; that is, persons
who hold a principle, even with intensity, may not appreciate all of the consequences that may ensue from it. They may, for example, be committed to equal
legal rights for all adults above the age of eighteen, the age at which an individual can vote or be conscripted into the armed services. Yet they might be
willing to make an exception to this general principle and prohibit the serving of alcohol in bars to individuals under the age of twenty-one. They may
have changed their views because the dangerous consequences—in the form
of high rates of fatal automobile accidents—have been pointed out to them.
Here *consistency* may give way to considerations of consequences, and in weighing the latter they may be willing to override the former. Therefore, even
though values may at root be attitudinal, they may be restructured by rational
considerations. We have to live and function in the world and to modify our
attitudes in light of these considerations.

The subjectivistic skeptical rejoinder to this, however, is that the reason that some individuals believe in deterrence is that they find murder emotionally repulsive. The reason they find drunk driving abhorrent is that accidental death due to negligence is likewise repugnant to their feelings. Likewise, they believe that universal suffrage is right because they approve of it attitudinally. Even the mitigated skeptic agrees that rational criticisms are accepted ultimately only because they rest on nonrational grounds. These moral postulates, they insist, are without any cognitive justification beyond our sentiment.

Aware of the epistemological pitfalls inherent in morality, some skeptics have urged a return to custom, and they have adopted a conservative bias. If no sentiment is ultimately better than any other, we had best choose those that are less dangerous to society or those that do not impede individual liberty. Even this stance is mitigated in its justification. Other skeptics, in agreeing that there are no rational foundations for ethics or politics, may choose to be liberals or radicals. But this stance, in the final analysis, say the skeptics, is likewise based on taste, and no rational proof is possible.

ETHICAL INQUIRY

This leads to our third form of skepticism, that which is related to inquiry. This position involves a skeptical component that is never fully abandoned: cognition in the course of skeptical inquiry. Our search for ethical judgments is thus continuous with our quest for reliable knowledge in all fields of human endeavor. At the very least, our choices are based upon our knowledge of the world and ourselves. The relationship between knowledge and value is central to the concept of *ethical inquiry*.

If we say that ethical choices may be related to rationality, the question that is immediately raised is whether there are any *ultimate* principles that are foundational to our ethical decisions and to which we must be committed if we are to make sense of ethical rationality. I must confess an extreme reluctance to assert that there are; at least all such efforts heretofore to find such first principles a priori seem to have failed.

The salient point is that ethics is relative to life as lived by specific persons or societies, and it is rooted in historical-social conditions and concrete behavior. Ethical principles are thus in the middle range; they are proximate, not ultimate. We do not reason about the moral life *in abstracto* and hope to make sense of it; we always begin *here* and *now*, with *this* individual in *this* society faced with *these* choices. The basic subject matter of ethics is action and conduct. It is not concerned essentially with *propositions* about practice, as some analytic philosophers thought, but with *praxis* itself. The knowledge that we seek is practical: what to choose, how to act, and how to evaluate the courses of action that confront us. We are interested in formulating wise, prudential, effective judgments of practice. This does not deny that we can generalize about human practice, and indeed formulate rules of conduct applicable to similar situations or values that have a wider appeal. Still, the contents of our judgments have concrete referents.

Rarely when we engage in ethical inquiry do we begin at the beginning—except perhaps in crisis-existential situations where we are forced to examine our root values. Rather, we find ourselves in the midst of practical demands and conflicts, trying to make sense of the web of decisions and behavior in which we are entangled. And included in our nexus is the considerable fund of normative data that we bring with us: the things we cherish or esteem, or conversely detest or reject, and the principles to which we are committed. Ethical inquiry is initiated when there is some puzzle about what we should do or some conflict between competing values and norms. It is here that skeptical inquiry is vital: for it is the open mind in operation that is willing to examine our values and principles and to select those that seem appropriate. The ethical inquirer in the best sense is committed to the use of reflective intelligence in which he is able to define and clarify his values and principles and to search for alternative courses of action that seem most fitting within the context of inquiry.

The ethical inquirer, like the scientist, seeks knowledge, but he does not simply describe what is factually the case or explain events by means of causal theories. Nor is he interested in arriving at analytic or formal truths. His goal is eminently practical: to choose something that will guide behavior and affect the world. This knowledge is similar to the kinds of knowledge sought in the applied practical sciences and arts. It is similar in one sense to the use of technological know-how in such fields as medicine, pedagogy, engineering, and architecture, where we are concerned with doing something, changing events, or creating, making, or manufacturing things. These require some skill and expertise, the prudential adaptation of means to ends. The doctor, lawyer, or teacher wishes to achieve certain goals: to cure patients, protect clients' rights, or educate students. And there are reliable procedures by means of which these purposes can be achieved. An engineer wishes to build a bridge or construct a space station. There is a considerable body of technological knowledge to guide him in doing so. Ancient Greece and Rome had not developed the technological arts to the extent that they have been developed since; if they had, they would have recognized their tremendous impact, and the skeptical schools of philosophy would perhaps have made less headway. Nihilistic and neutralistic skepticism about technological knowledge makes no sense today, because technology presupposes causal theories about how nature operates, and its principles are tested experimentally. However, all such technological fields, replies the ethical skeptic, presuppose their ends—for example, the desire to improve health, to achieve rapid travel, to communicate information, and so on. Where do we get our ends from, if not sentiment? asks the ethical skeptic.

VALUATIONAL BASE

My answer is that cognition has a role in formulating our ends. But we begin again *in the middle*; there is already a body of ethical principles that we possess concerning our ends. The evaluation of ends in each case is a function of tested procedures. In any context of ethical inquiry, it is best to consider ethical beliefs—including those inherited from the past—as *hypotheses*. They should be tested each time by reference to the relevant facts, the *valuational base*. What do I mean by this?

Common Moral Decencies

First, there are, as I have shown in chapter 15, the common moral decencies, that is, the ethical wisdom that we have inherited from human civilization. I am here drawing on the abundant evidence that humans, no matter what their culture, have similar needs and face similar problems—such as the need to survive, maintain health, and find adequate food and shelter; to engage in sexual intercourse and reproduction; to nurture, protect, and educate children; and so on. In spite of cultural relativity, there are similar responses to life's problems. In order to satisfy human needs and guide human interactions, a set of common moral decencies have developed. I have listed the basic moral decencies as follows: (1) *Integrity:* truthfulness, promise keeping, sincerity, and honesty. (2) *Trustworthiness:* fidelity and dependability. (3) *Benevolence:* goodwill, nonmalfeasance, sexual consent, and beneficence. (4) *Fairness:* gratitude, accountability, justice, tolerance, and cooperation.

To illustrate: the principles that we ought to tell the truth and that we ought to keep our promises are prima facie rules that in general apply to all civilized societies, notwithstanding that in some situations there may be conflicts between them and that exceptions may be made. Our *actual* duties in practical situations are not the same as our prima facie general duties. These principles, I submit, are transcultural, and they are as meaningful to the Christian and the Hindu as to the Confucian and the Muslim, the atheist and the unbeliever. Those who violate the common moral decencies challenge the basic body of ethical truths governing moral conduct that has been transmitted to us as the collective learned wisdom of humanity. I recognize that there is still considerable cultural diversity, and that not all societies recognize all of these principles. Moreover, there are many disputes about values and principles that are virtually irreconcilable. But I submit that humankind has reached the stage where the fundamental decencies are now generally accepted by the reflective person, and they are even endowed by some with "sacred" significance or legal sanction and support. The term *civilized* is virtually identical to the recognition of the common moral decencies, and *uncivilized* or barbarous behavior means that they have been grossly violated.

Basic Human Needs

Similarly, we discover a set of basic and invariant human needs that are essential to all members of the species. These require some satisfaction if human beings are to survive and function in a meaningful way. I have discussed these needs in chapter 5.

First are the biogenic needs: (1) *Survival needs:* the need to be protected from dangers or death from natural disasters, wild animals, or threatening human beings. (2) *Homeostatic needs:* sufficient food, clothing, and shelter. The organism needs to maintain some equilibrium against threats to its health and, when it is disturbed, to restore homeostasis. (3) *Growth needs:* the normal patterns of growth and development of the infant, child, and adult, including standing, walking, talking, reading, sexual development, and maturation. These are intrinsic to the biology of the species and have some genetic basis, though they also have a sociocultural dimension. (4) *Reproduction:* this is essential to the survival of the species, though it is not necessary for each individual to reproduce. (5) *The need to discharge surplus energy*: this is also an organic requirement for healthy functioning.

Second are the *psychosociogenic needs*: (6) *Love needs*: the ability to relate to others intimately and to achieve orgasmic satisfaction. Love entails affectionate regard for other persons on many different levels: not only the ability to receive love, but also the ability to bestow it upon other persons. This implies not simply sexual love but also parenting care and other forms of tender attachment to the well-being of others. (7) *Belonging to some community*: the ability to identify on a face-to-face basis with others, both in friendship and collegiality. This involves a relationship of charity and some altruistic concern. (8) *Self-respect*: some self-confidence in one's own abilities is essential for normal growth and development. Self-love may be in part a reflection of how a society evaluates a person, but it also depends on a person's own self-validation. (9) *Creativity:* the ability to adapt to problems and to work creatively to do so, to reorganize the varieties of materials in the world, and to introduce changes in the environment.

Related to these needs are a concomitant set of excellences, or virtues, which I have outlined in chapter 6. There are comparative standards by which we may evaluate whether or not a person has achieved a good life. They are normative criteria that we may use to appraise moral excellence. They are qualitative standards of nobility that apply to moral character and behavior and they express the ethics of humanism. Thus we may ask of a person whether he (1) has developed some *autonomy* and power, the ability to control his own life, (2) has some capacity for cognitive *intelligence* and critical thinking, (3) maintains some measure of *self-discipline* and self-control, (4) has developed some *self-respect*, (5) has reached some level of *creative actualization*, (6) is sufficiently *motivated* to live and function, (7) has an *affirmative* attitude that life is worth living,

(8) has achieved some degree of *health,* (9) is able to find pleasure in living and some *joie de vivre,* and (10) has developed some *aesthetic appreciation.*

Now I realize that a skeptical challenge may be brought against elements within the valuational base as outlined above. Someone may ask the following: Why accept the common moral decencies? Why have integrity or be trustworthy, benevolent, or fair? To which I respond that some reflective inquiry can be made about the application of each of these principles to a given situation. These are only prima facie, general rules that provide us with some general guidelines, not absolute norms. Yet a nihilist may seek to deny them all. "Why not kill or rape if I want to?" he asks.

A skeptical critic may raise similar doubts about the concept of "basic human needs" I refer to above, or he may reject the ethical excellences I have enumerated. "Why actualize my potentialities, or seek to grow, or be intelligent?" he may ask. A drug addict or alcoholic may throw caution to the winds and abandon health for the sake of pleasure. "Can you prove or demonstrate *why* I cannot overthrow all of these norms?" he may plead. My response is that there are processes of growth intrinsic to the ethical person and that we are potentially moral beings, both in relation to others and to ourselves. Individuals, however, need to go through the stages of development in order to appreciate the authentic ring of ethical excellence. I am thus presupposing a level of ethical awareness, or conscience, that individuals at certain periods of life need to understand and realize. Human beings have some means of freedom, and they may choose to abandon the call of the ethical life in a mad quest for power or pleasure. Or they may wish to tempt fate by a determined effort to think the unthinkable and perform the grotesque or bestial. There are moral monsters who will lie, steal, cheat, torture, and maim others for the hell of it, or because they are self-destructive. What are we to say of them?

I submit that such individuals are grossly underdeveloped; they are moral cripples. Their ethical understanding has been thwarted or is impaired; they are impervious to ethical truths and unsuited for ethical conduct. Some individuals are unable to do mathematical computations; some lack technological know-how or musical proficiency; some are unable to change a fuse or fix a flat tire. Ethical actions likewise depend upon some degree of ethical knowledge, and some individuals may be sadly deficient in this regard. They may need ethical education in order to develop general habits of responsibility, to have an authentic regard or a loving concern for another person. They may lack self-discipline and self-restraint, temperance, moderation, prudence, or practical ethical wisdom. I am prepared, of course, to admit that some individuals may be psychopaths (such as serial killers), though this may be due to some genetic defect and some distortion in their psychosexual development. They may have lacked proper moral training as youngsters, such that they never developed a mature ethical appreciation. But this says more about their personal disorientation than it does about the existence or nonexistence of a body of ethical truths as the repository of civilized conduct.

Pluralism in Values

Now I have referred to the "common moral decencies," "basic human needs," and "ethical excellences" as data within the valuational base to which we may appeal. But this no doubt is too general to tell us what to do in specific cases. Moreover, human wants and needs, values and norms, and principles and standards are infinitely multifarious. They differ as human personalities differ, and they change as society changes. There is a wide range of tastes in food, wine, sports, art, dress, and mannerisms, and there is pluralistic diversity in cultural values. Many different kinds of idiosyncratic wants become virtual needs and are linked with our basic biogenic and psychosociogenic needs. Ethical choices are always functions of the unique, deeply private tastes and desires, wishes and preferences, of each person. The choices we make are also relative to the concrete sociocultural-historical framework in which we live, and this includes the particular laws and social customs of our society. Life in ancient Egypt, Israel, Greece, or Mesopotamia, differs from that lived in medieval China, modern Japan, the Middle East, Western Europe, or the Americas.

All of these differences must be packed into the valuational base, and they influence the choices we make. The decision whether something is good or bad, right or wrong, is accordingly a function of the actual de facto prizings and valuations, customs and mores, laws and institutional demands of the times in which we live. What was a wise choice for Pericles in ancient Athens may not be the same for the Roman statesman Seneca, or for Abelard's Heloise, or for Sir Walter Raleigh, Mary Wollstonecraft, or Admiral Peary. Hence, there is an intrinsic *relativity* and *contextuality* of all choice, for it is always related to specific individuals and cultures. Yet, although the relativity of choice is *endemic* to the ethical life, there are still ethical qualities that are generalizable to the human condition. This is why we can empathize with a Hamlet or an Othello or a Lady Macbeth as they wrestle with their moral dilemmas. They have a kind of universal message, and can speak to each and every one of us.

The point that I am making is that there is a phenomenological structure to ethical experience, and some objective considerations are relevant to choices. Our individual values and principles may be tested on a *comparative* scale, in terms of the alternatives and options facing us. They may be *evaluated* by their *effectiveness*. They may be appraised by their *consistency* with the norms that we hold. In judging, we can estimate the real consequences of our decisions in the world, the effects upon us and others within the range of interaction. Insofar as we take into account these factors, then a reflective component has intervened in the process of judgment. John Dewey has distinguished between a *prizing*, where we value something and an element of immediacy, feeling, and pleasure is involved, and an *appraisal*, where a cognitive element intervenes.[5] It is the difference, he says, between a de facto acceptance of the given and a de jure warrant that it is fitting within the situation. The difference between prizing and appraisal is that the latter involves a *transformative* aspect; that is, in the process of inquiry the reflective judgment can become constituent of the valuation and may modify the prizing.

For example, I may be in the market for a new car. The infantile approach would be to buy the automobile with the most appealing lines and color. An adolescent's response would be to purchase the sports model simply because he *likes* it. But I, as an adult, would say that I need to appraise the value of the automobile. In a process of valuation, I would weigh merit on a comparative scale: "Can I afford this car?" "How much will I receive for my trade-in?" "Does it get good mileage?" "How safe is it?" "How does it compare with other models of other manufacturers?" In the process, I may end up by purchasing a different model after having calculated the comparative costs, effectiveness, and consequences. Although my feelings are relevant in the valuing process, the final decision is also related to my cognitive beliefs. An estimate of the value of the car is a function of the objective qualities of the object. My prizings are dependent upon my appraisals. Ralph Barton Perry defined a value as "the object of any interest."[6] I would modify this definition as follows: "A value is an interest in an object in which I have both prized and appraised its worth."

A normative belief is not the same as a descriptive belief. The first entails an evaluation and prescription of a course of conduct; the second describes or explains a factual state of affairs. Formulating a normative belief is not dissimilar, however, to testing a descriptive belief. In both cases we seek to justify our belief as true or normative. In questions of valuation, we appeal to reason to justify our choices. We consider evidence, we take into account consistency and consequences, and there is a body of previously tested ethical principles upon which we draw. I know that if I have a headache and I take two aspirin tablets, I may alleviate my pain. This is a prescriptive recommendation that has been verified empirically. Similarly, I learn that, if I were to lie to another person, I would not be trusted, and that if another person were to lie to me, our relationship would be jeopardized. Thus I learn that telling the truth is the most prudential policy to adopt, and as a mature adult I come to feel *strongly* about this common moral decency on both cognitive and attitudinal grounds.

What I have been describing is the constitutive role that deliberation can have in the process of decision making. Thought becomes essential to the very fabric of the ethical life, and we thus have some role in developing our own ethical sensibilities. We are able to resolve moral questions without necessarily deriving what we ought to do from fixed or ultimate principles. The "ought" cannot be easily deduced from the "is," yet in any process of intelligent deliberation it can be a function of a process of valuational inquiry. What we decide to do is relative to the facts of the case, the circumstances before us, the various alternatives we face, a consideration of the means at our disposals, and the likely consequences of our acts. Intrinsic to the valuational base in terms of which we make our choices are value-laden data: our previous prizings and appraisals, the common moral decencies, the ethical principles of our society, considerations of human needs, comparative excellences, and our own unique wants and desires. We need not deduce our duties from absolute universal rules. Moral reasoning is not the application of simple recipes, nor is the process one of drawing inductive generalizations from the past. Ethical reasoning involves a process of what I have called *act-duction*.[7] By this I mean that we infer the actions that are most appropriate—we act-duce—given the valuation base at hand. On the basis of this, some choices may thus be said to be more reasonable in the situation than others.

Ethical Fallibilism

Ethical knowledge has a degree of probabilism and fallibilism attached to it. We need to recognize that there are alternative lifestyles and a wide variety of human values and norms. This presupposes some comprehension of the fragility of the human condition and some skepticism about our ultimate perfectibility. Thus ethical wisdom recognizes that life is full of uncertainties. In one sense, it is permeated by indeterminancies. We can very rarely, if ever, be absolutely certain of anything. There are few finalities that we can grasp. There are always new challenges, new problems and conflicts, new discoveries and opportunities that confront us. The pervasive character of human existence is the fact that we are forever confronted by ambiguities. No one knows for sure what will happen tomorrow, or next year, or during the next century. We can make predictions and forecasts, and these may or may not come true. We note regularities and trends, and we find some order in nature and society (in the sciences and ordinary life), on the basis of which we can make wise choices. Alas, life is full of surprises: An unexpected accident upsets our best-laid plans; a freak storm fells a tree and it lands on our house; the bizarre suddenly intrudes into our life world. There are sudden breaks with the past; chance contingencies occur. Anomalies beset us, like a typhoon suddenly blowing in on us, or a hailstorm in the summertime. Thus we can never rely entirely on our past experiences or achievements. There is always something new to contend with. We encounter paradoxes, dilemmas, and puzzles. And we may be faced with insuperable odds or excruciating choices. Our options may be awesome and terrible. We may suffer great financial losses and be close to bankruptcy. Or we may have an overwhelming victory in politics or war, although we cannot sustain heroic efforts indefinitely without becoming exhausted. Other persons or societies may emerge to challenge our hegemony, and this may lead to conflicts. Polarities are ever present. The virtuous may become corrupt; the corrupt may be reformed; the good may turn out to be bad; our grand successes may be followed by ignominious defeats. For every move we make there is a counter move by someone else. Life is replete with sorrow and tears, but also with laughter and joy.

Given these indelible generic factors about the human condition, we cannot escape from making choices, however painful or exciting they may be. And what we ought to do depends on the situation. Often the dilemmas we face have no solution. We sometimes have to make a choice between two unmitigated evils, or between two goods, both of which we cherish but cannot have. The skeptic or the cynic or the pessimist is wont to point out that any effort to achieve utopia, ultimate perfection, or nirvana is an illusion and bound to fail. Yet some optimism is warranted. We may be inspired by the steady progress and achievements of the human species in history. This may be attributed to the humanist virtues of courage and endurance, the will-to-become in spite of obstacles, the use of critical intelligence (mingled with compassion) to solve our problems, and the determination to lead the good life as best we can. This ethical position may be described as *melioristic*. It does not hope to attain the unattainable, whether in this life or in the next, but it does believe that we can improve the human condition and that we can achieve the better, on a comparative scale, if not attain the absolute good. But to succeed in life requires the constant use of ethical rationality. We do the best we can, given the limitations and the opportunities discovered within the situations of life. In making choices, we can draw upon our knowledge of the common moral decencies, our moral heritage, and the fund of human wisdom. But as ethical inquirers, we must be prepared to modify our beliefs in the light of altered circumstances.

There is thus a *revisionary* character endemic to morality, for new principles are constantly being discovered and introduced. It took a long time in human history to finally eliminate slavery and to begin to liberate women from male domination. It is only relatively recently that the ethical principle that "all persons are entitled to equality of consideration" has been recognized. In the field of medical ethics, the principles of "informed consent," "voluntary choice," and the "autonomy of adult patients" now provide guidelines for medical practice. A whole new constellation of "human rights" is now being recognized worldwide. Thus there is a continual revision in our ethical values and principles as we learn from experience and make new discoveries in the sciences. Yet we are constantly confronted by moral absolutists—conservatives or reactionaries on the one hand, or radical innovators on the other—who wish to substitute moral fanaticism for ethical inquiry.

Some degree of skepticism is thus a necessary antidote to all forms of moral dogmatism. We are continually surrounded by self-righteous moralists who claim that they have the Absolute Truth or Moral Virtue or Piety or know the secret path to Progress, and they wish to impose their convictions on all others. They are puffed up with an inflated sense of their own rectitude, and they rail against unbenighted immoral sinners who lack their moral faith. These moral zealots are willing to repress or sacrifice anyone who stands in their way. They have unleashed conquering armies in the name of God or the Dialectic or Racial Superiority or Posterity or Imperial Design or the Free Market. Skepticism needs to be applied not only to religious and paranormal fantasies, but to other forms of moral and political illusions. These dogmas become especially dangerous when they are appealed to in order to legislate morality and are used by powerful social institutions, such as the state or church or corporation, to enforce a particular brand of moral virtue. Hell hath no fury like the self-righteous moral fanatic scorned.

The best antidote for this is some skepticism and a willingness to engage in ethical inquiry, not only about *their* moral zeal, but about *our own*, especially if we are tempted to translate the results of our own ethical inquiries into commandments. The epistemological theory presented here, the methodological principles of skeptical inquiry, has important moral implications. For in recognizing our own fallibility we thereby can learn to *tolerate* other human beings and to appreciate their diversity and the plurality of lifestyles. If we are prepared to engage in cooperative ethical inquiry, then perhaps we are better prepared to allow other individuals and groups some measure of liberty to pursue their own preferred lifestyles. If we are able to live and let live, then this can best be achieved in a free and open democratic society. Where we differ, we should try to negotiate our divergent views and perhaps reach common ground; and if this is impractical, we should at least attempt to compromise for the sake of our common interests. The method of ethical inquiry requires some intelligent and informed examination of our own values, as well as the values of others. Here we can attempt to modify attitudes by an appeal to cognitive beliefs and to reconstruct them by an examination of the relevant evidence. Such a give-and-take of constructive criticism is essential for a harmonious society. In learning to appreciate different conceptions of the good life, we are able to expand our own dimensions of moral awareness, and this is more apt to lead to a peaceful world.

By this I do not mean to imply that anything and everything can or should be tolerated or that one thing is as good as the next. We should be prepared to criticize moral nonsense parading as virtue. We should not tolerate the intolerable. We have a right to strongly object, if need be, to those values or practices that we think are based on miscalculation or misconception, or are patently false or harmful. Nonetheless, we might live in a better world if *inquiry* were to replace faith; *deliberation*, passionate commitment; and *education and persuasion*, force and war. We should be aware of the powers of intelligent behavior, but also of the limitations of the human animal and of the need to mitigate the cold and indifferent intellect with the compassionate and empathic heart.

Thus I conclude that within the ethical life we are capable of developing a body of melioristic principles and values and a method of coping with problems intelligently. There is a form of *eupraxia*, or good practice, that we can learn to appreciate and live by, and this can be infused with *sophia*, or wisdom. When our ethical judgments are based on ethical inquiry, they are more apt to express the highest reaches of excellence and nobility, and of civilized human conduct.

AFTERTHOUGHT

SURVIVING BYPASS AND ENJOYING
THE EXUBERANT LIFE

OPEN-HEART SURGERY

In 1996, at the age of 71, I underwent open-heart surgery. Although I have since recovered, this near-brush with death has enabled me to reflect on my condition; indeed, on the power of humanism and the meaning of life.

My heart problem was precipitated by a visit to Mexico City. I had worked hard in planning a World Humanist Congress. I was especially delighted to have given a keynote address at the congress and to have been the Master of Ceremonies at the concluding gala banquet—with a string sextet and a mariachi band! However, I began to experience some difficulty in breathing, which I thought was due to the high altitude and smog.

The day after returning I suffered some chest pains (angina pectoris); these lasted only two or three minutes, but I decided that I had better go the emergency room. My wife rushed me to the hospital, and my cardiologist scheduled an angiogram the following Monday. The diagnosis was that I had one artery blocked 90%, and the doctors recommended immediate corrective bypass surgery.

A person's arteries can be clogged by a fatty, fibrous, cholesterol-laden deposit called "plaque." Over long periods of time plaque builds up, thickens, and narrows the artery channels, a condition known as arteriosclerosis. If sufficient plaque accumulates to impede the flow of blood through the arteries, restricted blood supply to the heart can cause angina or a heart attack. Medical scientists have identified several risk factors for coronary heart disease: cigarette smoking, lack of exercise, high cholesterol levels, high blood pressure, obesity, diabetes, stress, a family history of heart disease, being male, and increasing age. These risk factors are cumulative: the more an individual has, the greater the danger of having a heart attack.[1]

The diagnosis of my condition surprised me. As many of my friends know, I am an exercise addict. I have been a member of a health club for twenty-five years, where I run, bicycle, swim, and work out with weights, virtually on a daily basis. Even when traveling, I try to book a hotel with a gym so that I can work out or jog. Also, I have been watching my cholesterol for about a decade; perhaps not rigorously enough, though I managed to keep it under 200. For example, at the Mexican Congress, I had oatmeal, skimmed milk, fresh fruits, and decaffeinated coffee for breakfast. I was dismayed when I saw my colleagues wolf down bacon and eggs, cream, fried potatoes, and buttered toast.

What happened to me, I wondered? I have had borderline blood pressure, which with medication has been kept at about 120/80 for years. Moreover, I have been a type A personality, with "timeitis" and "deadlineitis." And I had also been overweight ten to fifteen pounds—until now. I am back to being slim and trim (relatively!). But more important, my chief risk factor, according to my cardiologist, perhaps has been genetic—my father died of a heart attack at age fifty-nine, and several of my uncles on my father's side died of heart attacks. My mother died at ninety-five, however, and was going strong (she bicycled twenty minutes a day) until the end; and her parents, sisters, and brothers were long-lived.

My surgery was performed, and the doctors tell me that it was successful. They also suggested that, if I had not been exercising, I might have had more arteries blocked, or perhaps suffered a heart attack, which I did not. (Some claim that running can add ten years to your life—though you have to spend ten years running!)

The heart receives its blood from the coronary arteries, which connect from the aorta (the main artery emerging from the heart) to the heart muscles. If these become clogged, normal blood flow can be restored through bypass grafts that run from the aorta to the unblocked portions of the coronary arteries. These grafts, in my case, were obtained from my mammary artery (which supplies a portion of the chest wall but is not vital to that area). They also are obtained in many patients from the saphenous vein of the legs. During the operation, the patient's heart is usually stopped so that grafts can be sewn into place while circulation is maintained by a heart-lung machine. This was not necessary in my case. My operation proceeded without complications. I came out of the anesthesia four hours later. My wife and son were at my bedside. I tried to say, "I love you," but could not pronounce a word. The next morning, in the intensive-care unit, the nurse bade me get out of bed—I couldn't believe it—wash, shave myself, and walk around, which I did! I experienced some pain in the incision that required prescription pain killers to control, but after several days the discomfort was easily controlled by Tylenol. My recovery continued, and I was discharged from the hospital.

I resumed working again and began an intensive cardiac rehabilitation program of exercise. I feel great! I have been chastened by my experience, however, and have resolved to continue to exercise and to watch my cholesterol ever more rigorously, to keep it under 160 if I can, with fat only 15 to 20% of my diet. One should avoid saturated fats. With most packaged foods now listing saturated fat and cholesterol values, this is relatively easy to do today. I also learned that I need to lower the level of low-density lipoproteins (LDL) and increase the level of high-density lipoprotein (HDL). I eat pasta, fish, lean turkey or chicken and avoid red meat, milk, eggs, and other animal products. I consume plenty of vegetables and fruit. I also take an aspirin a day and medication to control my blood pressure. And, last but not least, following the French example, I drink a glass of red wine at dinner five or six times a week.

EXISTENTIAL REFLECTIONS

May I share several general reflections about my heart surgery.

First, I was surprised to learn how many people undergo bypass operations annually (over 400,000 in the United States alone). Milton Rosenberg (Professor of Psychology, University of Chicago, and WGN Radio host) called me in the hospital to say that he had had two bypass operations. Irving Louis Horowitz (Professor of Sociology at Rutgers University and head of Transaction Publishers) called to tell me that he also had had two heart attacks and open-heart surgery twice. Len Shore in Minneapolis wrote that he had had a quintuple bypass operation in 1989 when he was seventy-four and that he was playing racquetball in thirty days. Ies Spetter (of the American Ethical Union) let me know that he had had bypass surgery at seventy-five and is now back lecturing and writing again. Steve Barrett had bypass surgery a few years ago, he is now on a strict diet of only 10% fat, maintains a rigorous exercise program, and is doing fine. Many others have similar tales. I was much encouraged to hear these stories, although I sometimes feel like a piker with only one bypass! Bypass surgery has become highly fashionable today (perhaps like orthodontic braces that so many teenagers endure). But it works in the majority of cases.

Second, I was deeply impressed by the level of scientific expertise I enjoyed at the Hospital Cardiac Care Center, where the success rate is 97%. The use of high technology (stress tests, angiogram, mugoscan, electrocardiogram, etc.), the skillful use of medication, the dedicated cardiologists and surgeons, the highly talented nursing staff, and the follow-up care with home visits by nurses, physical therapists, and nutritionists and subsequent cardiac rehabilitation (all paid for by Medicare) are a testament to the excellent health-care system that is now in place in the United States for those covered.

I found the cardiac rehab program a special joy, and I now exercise vigorously for an hour, five times a week and take a brisk walk the other two days. Indeed, I feel stronger than ever. I realize that there are many people who are offended by my advising exercise. They tell me that they have great revulsion to exercising, and every time the desire to do so arises, they lie down until it passes. Not true in my case. Recognizing the fallibility of all human endeavors, the fact is that medical science has progressed because its hypotheses are tested by clinical trials, replications, and peer review, and this is the chief advantage of its methodology.

Third, undergoing a fairly radical invasive surgical operation, and facing the possibility of my own demise, forced me to confront my life-world. I have been so preoccupied with realizing my many projects that I often did not take the time to stop and enjoy the fragrance of flowers. (I should add that this latter insight was brought home to me by the dozens of plants, flowers, and fruit baskets that well-wishers sent me—"It smells like a flower shop in here!" exclaimed a nurse upon entering my room.) I realized as never before the intrinsic worth of each moment of experience.

Although I did not have a typical "near death" experience, my bypass surgery has jolted me into the realization that I am not superman, nor am I eternal. I can defy the universe only so long, but at some time my Promethean stance—to challenge the fates while I can and to audaciously explore new directions—will be defeated, if not by others then by my own demise. This existential reality brought home my own fragile mortality. What bottomless depths to contemplate. So no doubt there are limits to what a person can achieve. If we are all finite, which we undoubtedly are, then perhaps I had better get off the roller coaster, a modern-day metaphor for the Sisyphus myth, enjoy the immediacies of the present, and not focus only on what can be attained in the future by strenuous effort. A person needs to put things into some proper perspective, to reduce the frenetic pace. Have I been oblivious to the call of death? Does my encounter with it mean that my remaining years need to be made whole? Is not the fullness of life the chief good that we sometimes forget in an effort to achieve our plans and ideals? Perhaps only such an unexpected encounter with death can focus one on the precariousness of life. As a freethinker, I have no illusion about the immortality or the afterlife. It is only this life that counts. Therefore, every minute is meaningful, on its own terms, in and for itself.

One question that I pondered is whether or not I should retire from my many activities. I have passed the proverbial three score and ten. I did retire from my university teaching job five years ago, so that I could devote more time to building the secular humanist and skeptical movements. Indeed, I had been working harder than ever in that heroic endeavor—writing, lecturing, editing, publishing, helping build the Center for Inquiry, and developing new projects.

I think that Bismarck did a great disservice in setting the retirement age at sixty-five; for in my view some form of creative work is essential for one's continued vitality. This may not apply to everyone. (My brother-in-law told me that he enjoyed retirement in Florida because he did not have to do anything.) In any case, I feel that there is still so much that has to be done; and I hope that I can go on as long as I can—perhaps die in the saddle with my boots on, not with them off sitting by the fireplace. Thus, I hope that I can continue to devote my time remaining to help achieve the causes I have devoted my life to—as long as I can; though, of course, at a slower measured pace, and taking more time to really smell the flowers.

THE VIRTUES OF HUMANISM

What is unique about secular humanism? Why should we care? I believe that the world would be a better place if the religious, transcendental, and paranormal myths that have dominated human history could be overcome, or at least moderated and liberalized. I think that humankind would benefit if reason were allowed to play a greater role in human affairs. And above all, I think humankind would be enriched if humanist virtues could flourish. I am not a utopian, and I surely do not think that it will be easy to build genuine humanist institutions, in which free and autonomous individuals can live creative lives, sharing experience with others in more just and human societies. But at least we should try to create a genuine humanist world community.

The key virtue in human life is courage, the courage not simply to be, to persist in spite of adversity, but to become, to go on and forge new frontiers and to achieve our highest aspirations and goals. This, I believe, is essential for exuberance and the fullness of life. Courage, however, needs to be guided by cognition and reason, and to be nourished by caring, an empathetic concern for the need of others.

Perhaps I am naïve, but I still believe in the potentialities for goodness in the human species. I am decidedly skeptical of the doctrine of "original sin." Humanists are constantly asked whether this view of human nature is overly optimistic, and whether evil lurks in the hearts of human beings. They point to the evils of Nazism and communism in the twentieth century. I maintain that human beings are capable of both good and evil; which tendency develops depends on biogenetic factors, but especially on the environment and education, and on the kind of society and culture in which individuals live. Any group of people can become corrupted, but they can also learn to pursue authentic humanistic virtues.

The recent intense debate about Daniel Goldhagen's book, *Hitler's Willing Executioner: Ordinary Germans and the Holocaust*,[2] which describes conditions in Germany during the war, focuses on this controversy. Goldhagen portrays ordinary German soldiers at the Eastern front who were involved in the massacre of innocent victims. He argues that the entire German nation was responsible for the Holocaust, and this he attributes to Germany's long-standing anti-Semitism.

I was fascinated by his thesis, and the bleak picture that he paints of the human condition—especially because of my own experiences in the United States Army that liberated France and invaded Germany during the Second

World War. I remained in Germany for eighteen months after the war in the army of occupation. I met hundreds of concentration camp survivors, as well as ordinary Germans and even SS troops. Countless numbers of Germans told me that they had rejected Hitler and the Nazis, but felt impotent to actively oppose them. Remember, Hitler received only one-third of the popular vote in 1933. Thus, I do not agree with Goldhagen's pessimistic appraisal. I think that the idea of collective guilt is mistaken. I do not minimize the utter barbarity of those who carried out the Holocaust.[3] Most Germans were not involved in these infamous acts, did not know what was happening in the camps until perhaps the last years of the war, and many of those who heard about it could not believe it. Moreover, all too many soldiers were simply following orders. As Stanley Milgram's chilling experiments at Yale on the authoritarian and conformist personality revealed, under closely supervised and structured conditions, otherwise decent human beings are able to tolerate cruelty, much as they may be opposed to it.[4]

If one indicts ordinary Germans because of Hitler's barbarism, what are we to say about the millions of Russians who lived in the Soviet Union during Stalin's ruthless extermination of the kulaks, Tartars, and the millions in the Gulag. Were they equally complicit? What are we to say about those who lived in the southern United States during the period of slavery or took part in the bloody Civil War, or of the Turks during the Armenian massacre? And what about those who have suffered in Rwanda, Kosovo, and Bosnia?

Clearly, under brutal conditions and repressive régimes, heinous crimes are sometimes possible, and racial, religious, ethnic, and ideological hatred can reduce victims to nonpersonhood and enable people to torture and murder them. This is especially the case in totalitarian societies where dissent is prohibited.

Yet, I submit that the common moral decencies are still widespread in human civilization, and there are deep moral tendencies within the human species. Humanists at least believe that we must nourish and cultivate the highest ethical potentialities. Humanists need to emphasize the affirmative dimensions of humanist ethics, especially tolerance and caring, and we should do what we can to help realize the humanist virtues. Moreover, we need to seek common ground above the racial, religious, and ethnic differences that divide humanity.

It is often not easy to be a secular humanist in American society today, where freethought, atheism, and agnosticism are a minority position, outspoken nonbelievers are shunned, and where spirituality and religiosity dominate the public forum. Nevertheless, I believe that humanist ethics in this age of science and technology can be a source of human enrichment and happiness. It is the positive reach of the humanist outlook that needs to be highlighted, not its rejection of the ancient otherworldly creeds. The humanistic virtues of reason, courage, and moral empathy have deep roots within human experience; by untapping them we can achieve a more bountiful life. Humanism can transform life for those who are bold enough to embrace it. And it can invest it with excellence and nobility and provide a new ground for responsible moral conduct.

ACKNOWLEDGMENTS

"What Is Happiness?" "Bursting at the Seams," "Power," "Love and Friendship," and "The Beloved Cause" are excerpted from *Exuberance: A Philosophy of Happiness* (Buffalo, N.Y.: Prometheus Books, 1977), 9–13, 17–32, 119–48, 171–78. Reprinted by permission.

"The Bountiful Joys," "The Ethics of Excellence," and "The Common Moral Decencies" are excerpted from *Forbidden Fruit: The Ethics of Humanism* (Buffalo, N.Y.: Prometheus Books, 1988), 80–96, 106–25, 244–47. Reprinted by permission.

"The Meaning of Life" and "The Fullness of Life" are excerpted from *The Fullness of Life* (New York: Horizon Press, 1974) 85–106. Reprinted by permission.

"Meaning and Transcendence" is excerpted from *The Transcendental Temptation: A Critique of Religion and the Paranormal* (Buffalo, N.Y.: Prometheus Books, 1985), 17–26. Reprinted by permission.

"The Human Condition" is excerpted from *Decision and the Condition of Man* (Seattle: University of Washington Press, 1965), 270–88. Reprinted by permission.

"Libertarianism: The Philosophy of Moral Freedom" originally appeared as "Libertarianism as the Philosophy of Moral Freedom," in *Modern Age: A Quarterly Review* 26, no. 2 (Spring 1982): 153–59. Reprinted by permission.

"Courage" and "Caring" are excerpted from *The Courage to Become: The Virtues of Humanism* (Westport, Conn.: Praeger, 1997) 19–37, 81–107. Reprinted by permission.

"An Ethic of Responsibility" originally appeared as "Does Humanism Have an Ethic of Responsibility?" in *Humanist Ethics: Dialogue on Basics*, ed. Morris Storer (Buffalo, N.Y.: Prometheus Books, 1980), 13–25. Reprinted by permission.

"Humanism as a Eupraxsophy" is excerpted from *Eupraxophy: Living without Religion* (Buffalo, N.Y.: Prometheus Books, 1989), 13–48. Reprinted by permission.

"Skepticism and Ethical Inquiry" is excerpted from *The New Skepticism: Inquiry and Reliable Knowledge* (Amherst, N.Y.: Prometheus Books, 1992), 277–301. Reprinted by permission.

NOTES

CHAPTER 1

Excerpted from "What Is Happiness," in *Exuberance: A Philosophy of Happiness* (Buffalo, N.Y.: Prometheus Books, 1977), 171–78.

CHAPTER 2

Excerpted from "Bursting at the Seams," in *Exuberance: A Philosophy of Happiness* (Buffalo, N.Y.: Prometheus Books, 1977), 9–13.

CHAPTER 3

Excerpted from *Forbidden Fruit: The Ethics of Humanism* (Buffalo, N.Y.: Prometheus Books, 1988), 244–48.

CHAPTER 4

Excerpted from *The Fullness of Life* (New York: Horizon Press, 1974), 85–94.

CHAPTER 5

Excerpted from *The Fullness of Life* (New York: Horizon Press, 1974), 94–106.

CHAPTER 6

Excerpted from *Forbidden Fruit: The Ethics of Humanism* (Buffalo, N.Y.: Prometheus Books, 1988), 106–25.

CHAPTER 7

Excerpted from *The Transcendental Temptation: A Critique of Religion and the Paranormal* (Buffalo, N.Y.: Prometheus Books, 1985), 17–26.

CHAPTER 8

Excerpted from *Decision and the Condition of Man* (Seattle: University of Washington Press, 1965), 270–88.
1. "Coduction" refers to comparative knowledge drawn from many levels of inquiry.
2. William Shakespeare, *Macbeth*.

CHAPTER 9

Excerpted from "Power," in *Exuberance: A Philosophy of Happiness* (Buffalo, N.Y.: Prometheus Books, 1977), 17–32.
1. Epictetus, *Enchiridion,* trans. Thomas W. Higginson (New York: Liberal Arts Press, 1948), 17–18.

CHAPTER 10

Excerpted from *The Courage to Become: The Virtues of Humanism* (Westport, Conn.: Praeger, 1997), 19–37.
1. Emily Jane Brontë, "No Coward Soul Is Mine," in *Emily Jane Brontë: The Complete Poems*, ed. Janet Gezari (London: Penguin, 1992).
2. Paul Tillich, *The Courage to Be* (New Haven, Conn.: Yale University Press, 1952).
3. John Gay, "The Sick Man and the Angel," in *Fables* XXVII (Menston: The Scolar Press, 1969).
4. Alexander Pope, *Essay on Man* (London: L. Gilliver, 1734), 1.
5. Dante Aligheri, *Inferno* (Boston: D. C. Heath, 1909), ii.
6. Gene Landrum, *Profiles of Genius* (Amherst, N.Y.: Prometheus Books, 1993); Landrum, *Profiles of Female Genius* (Amherst, N.Y.: Prometheus Books, 1994).
7. William James, *The Will to Believe and Other Essays in Popular Philosophy* (New York: Longmans, 1896).
8. Ralph Waldo Emerson, "Self-Reliance," in *Emerson's Complete Works* (Boston: Houghton, Mifflin, n.d.).

9. The religious author and priest Richard John Neuhaus has criticized me, remarking that I was a friendly fellow but "relentless" in the defense of humanism. I was cheerful after reading that because there is an important value in relentlessly seeking to achieve your goals. Neuhaus is surely relentless in defending Christianity. Richard John Neuhaus, "The Public Square: A Continuing Survey of Religion and Public Life," *First Things: A Monthly Journal of Religion and Public Life*, no. 42 (April 1994): 67.

10. I have changed his name to protect the privacy of his family.

11. William Shakespeare, *Julius Caesar*, in *The Works of Shakespeare*, vol. 3 (New York: Macmillan, 1905).

12. Aristotle, *Poetica*, in *The Works of Aristotle*, ed. W. D. Ross (Oxford: Oxford University Press, 1950–1952).

13. Francis Bacon, *Novum Organum*, in *English Philosophers from Bacon to Mill*, ed. E. A. Burtt (New York: Modern Library, 1939).

CHAPTER 11

Originally appeared as "Libertarianism as the Philosophy of Moral Freedom," in *Modern Age: A Quarterly Review* 26, no. 2 (Spring 1982): 153–59.

CHAPTER 12

Excerpted from "Love and Friendship," in *Exuberance: A Philosophy of Happiness* (Buffalo, N.Y.: Prometheus Books, 1977), 119–31.

CHAPTER 13

Excerpted from "The Beloved Cause," in *Exuberance: A Philosophy of Happiness* (Buffalo, N.Y.: Prometheus Books, 1977), 133–48.

1. From "Humanist Manifesto II," drafted by Paul Kurtz, *The Humanist* 33, no. 5 (September/October 1973).

CHAPTER 14

Originally appeared as "Does Humanism Have an Ethic of Responsibility," in *Humanist Ethics: Dialogue on Basics*, ed. Morris Storer (Buffalo, N.Y.: Prometheus Books, 1980), 13–25.

CHAPTER 15

Excerpted from *Forbidden Fruit: The Ethics of Humanism* (Buffalo, N.Y.: Prometheus Books, 1988), 80–96.

CHAPTER 16

Excerpted from *The Courage to Become: The Virtues of Humanism* (Westport, Conn.: Praeger, 1997), 79–107.

1. Emily Dickinson, *Poems*, I, in *The Complete Poems* (Boston: Little, Brown, 1924).

2. Antony Flew, *The Politics of Procrustes* (Amherst, N.Y.: Prometheus Books, 1981).

3. Robert Burton, *Anatomy of Melancholy: What It Is, with All the Kinds, Causes, Symptoms, Prognostics, and Several Cures of It* (Boston: William Veazie, 1859).

4. William James, *Memories and Studies* (New York: Longmans, 1911).

CHAPTER 17

Excerpted from *Eupraxophy: Living without Religion* (Buffalo, N.Y.: Prometheus Books, 1989), 13–48. I have since added the letter *s* to the term: *eupraxsophy*.

1. This is especially true in twentieth-century ethics, among such philosophers as G. E. Moore, the deontologists W. D. Ross and H. A. Prichard, and the emotivists A. J. Ayer and C. L. Stevenson. Later philosophers such as R. M. Hare and Richard Brandt sought to apply rational standards to ethical truth claims. John Dewey and the pragmatists maintained that cognition can help us appraise and modify emotive attitudes.

2. E. O. Wilson defends the idea of "consilience," the effort to unify the sciences across disciplines. Edward O. Wilson, *Consilience: The Unity of Knowledge* (New York: Knopf, 1998).

3. The term *life stance* was first introduced by Harry Stopes-Roe, "Humanism as a Life Stance," *Free Inquiry* 8, no. 1 (Winter 1987/1988).

4. John Dewey, *Liberalism and Social Action* (New York: Capricorn Books, 1955); *The Public and Its Problems* (New York: Henry Holt, 1927); *Freedom and Culture* (New York: Capricorn Books, 1939).

5. For the most recent statement of planetary humanism, see Paul Kurtz, *Humanist Manifesto 2000: A Call for a New Planetary Humanism* (Amherst, N.Y.: Prometheus Books, 1999).

CHAPTER 18

Excerpted from *The New Skepticism: Inquiry and Reliable Knowledge* (Amherst, N.Y.: Prometheus Books, 1992), 277–301.

1. David Hume, *Treatise on Human Nature* (1739), bk. 3, pt. 1, sec. 1.

2. G. E. Moore, *Principia Ethica* (Cambridge: Cambridge University Press, 1903).

3. H. A. Prichard, "Does Moral Philosophy Rest on a Mistake?" *Mind* 21 (1921); Henry Sidgwick, *The Methods of Ethics*, 6th ed. (New York: Macmillan, 1901); W. D. Ross, *The Right and the Good* (Oxford: Oxford University Press, 1930).

4. A. J. Ayer, *Language, Truth and Logic* (Oxford: Oxford University Press, 1936); Charles L. Stevenson, *Ethics and Language* (New Haven, Conn.: Yale University Press, 1943).

5. John Dewey, *The Theory of Valuation* (Chicago: University of Chicago Press, 1939); Dewey, *The Quest for Certainty* (New York: Minton, Balch, 1929), ch. 10.

6. Ralph Barton Perry, *General Theory of Value* (Cambridge, Mass.: Harvard University Press, 1926, 1954).

7. For a discussion of "act–duction," see Paul Kurtz, *Philosophical Essays in Pragmatic Naturalism* (Buffalo, N.Y.: Prometheus Books, 1990), pt. 2.

AFTERTHOUGHT

Originally published in *Free Inquiry* 17, no. 2 (Spring 1997), pp. 10–13.

1. My thanks to Dr. Stephen Barrett (*Nutritional Forum* 9, no. 1) for supplying me with these and other technical details in this article.

2. New York: Alfred A. Knopf, 1996.

3. A more balanced treatment of how a unit of ordinary German soldiers were transformed into cold-blooded murderers is found in Christopher R. Browning's book, *Ordinary Men: Reserve Police Battalion 101 and the Final Solution in Poland* (New York: HarperCollins, 1992). Although many at first protested and refused to take part in the shooting of innocent men, women and children (perhaps 10 to 20%), in time they became inured to the brutal slaughter.

4. Stanley Milgram, *Obedience to Authority: An Experimental View* (New York: Harper, 1969).

ABOUT THE AUTHOR

Paul Kurtz is considered to be the leading secular humanist spokesman in the world. He is editor-in-chief of *Free Inquiry* magazine and chairman of the Committee for the Scientific Investigation of Claims of the Paranormal, which he founded. Kurtz is a former copresident of the International Humanist and Ethical Union, a coalition of one hundred humanist organizations in thirty-five countries. Among his more than thirty books are *The Transcendental Temptation, Living without Religion, Forbidden Fruit, The Courage to Become,* and *Humanist Manifesto 2000.* He is professor emeritus of philosophy at the State University of New York at Buffalo.